PRINCIPLES OF MANAGEMENT

PRINCIPLES OF MANAGEMENT

Amar Jyoti

genNEXT Publication

Principles of Management

Rs. 890

ISBN: 978-93-80222-12-7

Published in 2009 in India by
Gennext Publication
23 Main Ansari Road, Darya Ganj,
New Delhi-110002
E-Mail:GenNextpublication@hotmail.com
Phone: 23282060

Printed at : Young Art Press, Delhi - 92

Contents

Preface

Management calls for achieving goals in an efficient and competent manner through planning, organizing, leading and controlling an organization's resources. This volume brings these management models to life through innovational instructions. The volume allows students to easily comprehend, contemplate and understand management theory. It takes a logical and student-centred approach to management from point of view of business. It first provides a broad foundation in the fundamental concepts of management, and then examines contemporary fields, promoting student knowledge and learning.

The Volume offers delivery of text material through the effective application of diagrams, charts and tables. It provides a strong emphasis on applications and continuing to show students how management is for everyone. Emphasis is given on strategic management, ethics, decision making, organizational planning, team management and future.

This book balances theory and application in a way that makes material more relevant for student learning. Written for those studying management or who are interested in this field, it provides hundreds of real-world business examples. In the course, it links the theory of management with contemporary best practice in successful companies, large and small, and shows what influences and guides managerial action in today's organizations.

At the same time that the information in the area of management is increasing, less time is available in curriculum to cover it. Students experience difficulty reading all the material available in the market. So we here put our efforts and experience to capsule the whole syllabus in this book including all the topics in a precise but comprehensible manner. Undersigned is confident enough that this book will be a handy tool for the students of management. Your sincere feedback always encourages me to improve my way of presentation. Reader's suggestions and comments are always welcome.

Introduction

Generally, the term "management" refers to the activities (and frequently the group of individuals) involved in the four common functions: planning, organizing, leading and co-ordinating of resources. Note that the four functions repeat all through the establishment and are highly incorporated. Rising trends in management constitute assertions that leading is unlike than managing, and that the nature of how the four functions are achieved must change to accommodate a "new paradigm" in management.

Management in business and human establishment activity is simply the procedure of getting individuals mutually to attain required aims. Management comprises planning, organizing, resourcing, leading or directing, and operating an establishment (a group of one or more individuals or entities) or effort for the purpose of accomplishing an aim. Resourcing covers the deployment and handling of human resources, fiscal resources, technological resources, and natural resources.

Management can also refer to the person or individuals who execute the act(s) of management. Mary Parker Follett, who wrote on the topic in the early twentieth century, defined management as "the art of getting things done through individuals". One can also think of management functionally, as the action of measurement a quantity regularly and of adjusting some early plan; or as the actions taken to reach one's intended aim. This enforces even in situations where planning doesn't take place. From this view, Frenchman Henri Fayol regards management as having six functions:

- Planning
- Organizing
- Leading
- Coordinating
- Controlling
- Staffing

A few individuals, however, find this definition, while useful, far too constricted. The phrase "management is what managers do" takes place widely, suggesting the difficulty of defining management, the shifting nature of definitions, and the connectedness of managerial practices with the existence of a managerial cadre or class. One habit of thought considers management as equal to "business administration" and therefore excludes management in places outside commerce, as for example in charities and in the public sector. More realistically, notwithstanding, every establishment must manage its work, individuals, processes, technology, etc. in order to maximize its potency.

A few individuals may also use the term "management" or "the management" as a collective word drawing the managers of an establishment, for instance of a corporation. Historically this use of the term was frequently counter pointed with the term "Labour" referring to those being managed.

In for-profit work, management has as its main function- the gratification of a range of stakeholders. This normally necessitates making a profit (for the shareholders), producing valued products at a fair cost (for customers), and providing rewarding employment opportunities (for employees). In non-profit management, add the importance of keeping the faith of donors. In most models of management/governance, shareholders vote for the board of directors, and the board then hires senior management. Some organizations have tried out with other methods (such as employee-voting models) of picking out or reviewing managers; but this occurs only very rarely.

Public, private, and voluntary sectors place different demands on managers, but all must retain the faith of those who take them (if they wish to retain their jobs), retain the faith of those individuals that fund the establishment, and retain the faith of those who work for the establishment. If they fail to convert employees of the advantages of staying rather than leaving, they may tip the establishment into a downward spiral of employing, training, firing, and recruiting. Management also has the job of introducing and of improving the functioning of organizations.

Difficulties arise in tracing the history of management. Some see it (by definition) as a late modern (in the sense of late modernity) formulation. On those terms it cannot have a pre-modern history, only predecessors (such as stewards). Others, nevertheless, detect management-like -thought back to Sumerian traders and to the builders of the pyramids of ancient Egypt. Slave-owners through the centuries faced the troubles of exploiting/

motivating a dependent but occasionally unenthusiastic or fractious manpower, but many pre-industrial enterprises, given their small scale, didn't feel obligated to face the matters of management systematically. However, innovations such as the spread of Arabic numerals (5th to 15th centuries) and the codification of double-entry book-keeping (1494) facilitated instruments for management assessment, planning and control.

Given the scale of most commercial processes and the want of mechanized record-keeping and recording earlier than the industrial revolution, it made sense for most owners of enterprises in those times to carry out management purposes and activities by and for themselves. But with growing size and complexity of organizations, the divide between owners and day-to-day managers (independent specialists in planning and control) step by step became more common.

It could be suggested that advanced management as a discipline commenced as an off-shoot of economics in the 19th century. Classical economists such as Adam Smith and John Stuart Mill gave a theoretical background to resource-allocation, production, and pricing issues. About the same time, innovators like Eli Whitney, James Watt, and Matthew Boulton developed factors of technical production such as standardization, quality-control processes, cost-accounting, exchangeability of parts, and work-planning.

But afterward by the late nineteenth century, marginal economists Alfred Marshall Leon Walras, and others introduced a new layer of complexness to the theoretical underpinnings of management.

By about the year 1900, one can see that managers were trying to place their theories on what they looked upon a thoroughly scientific basis. Some of the more current developings include the Theory of Constraints, management by objectives, reengineering, Six Sigma and many information-technology-driven theories such as agile software development, as well as group management theories such as Cog's Ladder.

As the full global recognition of managers as a class solidified during the twentieth century and gave perceived practitioners of the art/science of management a certain amount of position, therefore the way opened for generalised systems of management ideas to peddle their wares. In this perspective of use many management rages may have had more to do with pop psychology than with scientific theories of management.

Towards the conclusion of the twentieth century, business management came to include of six streams, which are as follows:

- Human resource management
- Operations management or production management
- Strategic management
- Marketing management
- Financial management
- Information technology management accountable for management information systems

In the twenty-first century observers find it more and more complicated to separate management into operational categories in this way. More and more processes concurrently involve several categories. Alternatively, one tends to think in terms of the numerous processes, jobs, and objects subject to management.

Branches of management theory also subsist concerning non-profits and to government: for example public administration, public management, and educational management. Further, management programs related to civil-society organizations have also engendered programs in non-profit management and social entrepreneurship. It ought to be noted here that many of the assumptions made by management have come under attack from business ethics points of opinion, critical management studies, and anti-corporate policy.

As one consequence, workplace democracy has become both more vernacular, and more advocated, in some places distributing all management affairs among the workers, each of whom takes on a portion of the work. Nevertheless, these models precede any current political issue, and may occur more naturally than does a command power structure. All management to some degree covers democratic principles in that in the long term workers must give mainstream support to management; otherwise they leave to find other work, or go on strike. Hence management has bugged out to become less based on the conceptualisation of classical military command-and-control, and more about facilitation and support of collaborative activity; employing principles for example those of human interaction management to deal with the complexities of human fundamental interaction.

1

Basic Principles of Management

BASIC CONCEPT OF MANAGEMENT

No one can deny the fact that the world has changed, is changing, and continues to change. The dynamic nature of today's organizations means both honours and challenges for those people who will be managing those organizations. Management is an active discipline and a course pack on the subject must undergo significant changes to prepare you to manage under these conditions.

Management is the organizational process that helps us in producing a service or product from the raw materials we have at hand. It's the total of the input processes that allow us to mould something useful from what otherwise is a disarray of human resources and raw components. The output of this controlled processing produces a valuable product or service, which someone (a customer) generally is willing to pay for. Simply stated, the manager's task is to assist all these processes run smoothly, and to address the roadblocks to productive output.

Management is global proposition in the modern industrial world and there is no alternate for good management. It makes human efforts more productive and brings better technology, products and services to our society. It's a decisive economic resource and a life-giving element in business. Without correct management, the resources of production (men, machines and materials) cannot be converted into production. Therefore management is an important function concerned with all aspects of the working of an organization. Management is a must to attain required aims through group action. It's essential to convert the disorganized resources of men, machines, materials, and methods into a functional and useful enterprise. Therefore management is the function of getting things done through individuals and directing the efforts of individuals towards a common target.

MEANING AND NATURE OF MANAGEMENT

Management is comparatively a new discipline. Being a new discipline, it has drawn concepts and principles from economics, sociology, philosophy, psychology, statistics, and so forth. The result is that each group has defined management in several ways. For example, economists see management as a factor of production; sociologists see it as a class or group of persons; practitioners of management treat it as a process. In spite of no clear agreement, it isn't hard to identify the following meanings of the term management.

a. Management is an art or skill of getting things done.

b. Management is a process of planning, organizing, staffing, directing and controlling.

c. Management is a distinct activity of any organization.

d. Management is a discipline, which represents a body of knowledge.

Let's start with the basic definition of management

Management is the process of designing and maintaining an environment in which people working together in groups expeditiously carry out the selected aim.

"Management is an art of getting things done through others". This definition underlines the achievement of jobs through the efforts of individuals. It makes a distinction between managers and non - managers. Whereas managers guide and co-ordinate the efforts of others towards certain specified aims, the non-managers actually perform the job. A manager, whatever may be his level in the organization, has to get things done through his subordinates. At higher levels, the subordinates are themselves mostly managers. It means 'management of managers'. At supervisor levels, the assistants are non-managerial white-collar or blue-collar workers.

'Getting things done' means to get jobs and activities executed. Management gets things done through individuals both as individuals and as members of the work group. Getting things done through individuals is actually an art. It constitutes a range of skills gained and refined in the course of practice. The skills which are needed to get things done through people include of conceptual skills, technical skills, administration skills, social skills, and so forth.

With a view to getting things done through others, management has to first plan the things which are to be done. The plans to be performed to attain the objectives are determined and assigned to individuals and work units. Besides planning and organizing jobs, management has to devise the techniques and methods of getting things done. These are effectual leadership, team spirit, peoples' participation, appropriate system of cash and non-cash incentives, and so forth. Further, the hindrances, the problems and the distortions in the work environment have to be removed or minimised. This art of management is more and more based on the Science of management. Professor Harold Koontz agrees with this concept of management. In the words of Harold Koontz

"Management is the art of getting things done through and with individuals in formally organized groups. It's the art of producing the environment in which individuals can perform as individuals and yet cooperate towards attainment of group's aims. It's the art of removing blocks to such performance, a way of optimising efficiency in reaching aims." However, there is danger in defining management in terms of getting things done through others. This definition is subject to the following criticism.

- The workers are simply handled as means of getting results. It entirely ignores the needs of the workers and doesn't offer them human discussion.
- The definition is quite vague. It fails to define the roles which a manager has to carry through to get results from others.
- This gives the impression of the manipulative character of the practice of management.
- Management is treated as an art. But today, it has met the fundamental characteristics of science, too. Therefore, it can be aptly said that management is both an art and a science.

To sum up, let us point out that the techniques of getting things done through and by the individuals may work for sometime but individuals cannot be oppressed or befooled all the time. Hence, management may be viewed as a skill of getting things done through others by meeting their needs. It isn't merely getting things done through individuals.

Nature of Management

The following are the important features or characteristics of management.

1. Management is getting things done: A manager doesn't do any operating work himself but gets it done through others. He must motivate the subordinates for the accomplishment of the job assigned to them.

2: Management is an action: Management is a process of organized activity. It's concerned with the efficient use of resources like men, money and materials in the organization.
3. Management is a group action: Management cannot exist independent of the group or organization it manages. It's a cardinal part of any group activity and inspires workers to put forth their best efforts.
4. Management is a general activity: Management is a global phenomenon. Nevertheless, management principles aren't globally applicable but are modified to suit the given situation and the type of organization.
5. Management is meaningful: Management is an aim- oriented activity. It's concerned with the attainment of aims through its several functions like planning, co-ordinating, staffing, directing, and checking.
6. Management is a process: Management is a process which calls for planning, organizing, directing and controlling the efforts of human resources in the use of material resources. These are the fundamental functions which every manager performs for the accomplishment of certain aims.
7. Management is an incorporating process: Management integrates men, machines and materials for performing several operations and fulfilling the stated aims. Therefore, management acts as a catalytic agent in getting maximum productivity from all the resources.
8. Management is intangible: Management is nonfigurative and cannot be seen with the eyes. It's proved by the quality of the organization and the results. Therefore, feeling of management is result-oriented.
9. Management is a vocation: Management is a vocation because some of its recognized principles are being applied in practice.
10. Management is a science and art: Management has formulated certain principles and laws which have wide applications. Therefore it's treated as a science. It's also an art, because it is concerned with the application of knowledge for the solution of organizational problems.
11. Management is dynamic: Management is dynamic because it adapts itself to the social changes and introduces innovation in methodology.

12. Management involves deciding: Management process involves decision-making at several levels for getting things done by others. It involves selecting the most appropriate alternative out of the numerous.
13. Management applies economical precepts. Management is the art of applying the economic principles that underline the control of men and materials in the organization.
14. Management is related with direction and control: Management is concerned with the direction and control of the several activities. It deals particularly with the active direction of the human effort.

MANAGEMENT AND ORGANIZATIONS

Management separates establishment and the management duties to use dissimilar structures laid over the business. Management doesn't organize or manage the business. The enterprise is organized by an establishment structure. Strategic planning lays a corporate plan over the business. Other plans and budgets from several parts of the enterprise are laid over the business. Management direction can use a variety of structures, for example, business processes or administrative structures. Other structures, for example performance management, are used for management reporting. A separate chart of accounts is laid over the business for management control.

Capital development is separated from enterprise processes and uses its own investment analysis and project management structures. Each of these structures commonly is supported by an information system using its own set of definitions and entities to describe the enterprise. But no information system catches real business data and reports real business management information. Management is overloaded with data. Much of the information is wrong and conflicting. The enterprise ends up with gigantic data system overheads, and only incidental data on the real business. The establishment structure is the fatal error of twentieth century management. Once an establishment structure is laid over the business, the business can never be managed. The business establishment isn't a management exclusive right; it is capital in a professionally-managed business establishment solution. Management decides on results to be produced and result responsibilities and ends.

Business establishment and management reposes on an organized business structure. The business establishment must organize the output results to be produced by the business and the performance solutions that are to be utilized to create results. The business structure must be maintained to record all results produced, all performance solutions utilized, and to relate results in the same set or value-quality chain. Once the business is organized, the same business construction is applied for business management.

Management planning must plan the literal future business in the results to be produced to produce future value and the performance solutions that must be utilized, improved, or developed to create future results. Strategic planning must define the strategic business outcomes to be produced at future strategic horizon date to produce strategic value. The performance solutions needed to create strategic results must be planned. This produces the strategic business structure. Once the strategic business structure is sanctioned, good corporate governance manages the progress in operations and development of the current business structure by period of time to meet on the strategic business structure. Other plans for business change, capital development, result unit processes etc. show the new or improved results at a future point and the performance results to add, improve, and apply to create the results.

Business results are supported by time period by period result aims that must be attained. Performance solutions are substantiated by performance expectation that must be met by solutions each period. The business is managed by managing the results produced and business concern solutions utilized. Management decides on new results needed by the business, and assigns an accountable manager. New results and aims are added and performance solutions are deployed to create results. Attained results are closed and deactivated and performance solutions are deployed to other results. Once the business structure is in place and professionally managed, this becomes second nature. The focus of the business result managers is on creating the results they are accountable for and exceeding result aims. Result managers are supported by performance managers for the performance solutions they need. Management ensures that results are produced and aims are reached period by period.

For management Henry Fayol gave following fourteen principles:

1. Division of Work - The differentiation of the manpower, producing specific personal and professional growth within the labour force and therefore increasing productivity; leads to specialization which increases the efficiency of labour. By

breaking a small part of work, the workers speed and accuracy in its performance increases. This principle is applicable to both technical as well as managerial work.

2. Authority and Responsibility- The issue of controls followed by responsibleness for their consequences. Authority means the right of a superior to give order to his subordinates; responsibility means responsibility for performance. This principle suggests that there must be parity between authority and responsibility. They are co-existent and go together, and are two sides of the same coin.

3. Discipline- Discipline denotes the obedience, proper conduct in relation to others, respect of authority, etc. It is necessity for the smooth functioning of all organizations.

4. Unity of Command - This principle says that every subordinate ought to get orders and be accountable to one and only one higher-up. If an employee receives orders from more than one superior, it is likely to produce confusion and conflict. Unity of Command also makes it easier to fix responsibility for errors.

5. Unity of Direction - All those working in the same line of activity must understand and engage in the same objectives. All related activities ought to be put under one group, there ought to be one plan of action for them, and they ought to be under the control of one manager. It seeks to ensure unity of action, focusing of efforts and co-ordination of strength.

6. Subordination of Individual Interest - The management must put away personal circumstances and put company objectives first. Hence the interests of aims of the establishment must prevail over the personal interests of people.

7. Remuneration - Workers must be paid sufficient amount as this is a main motive of employees and hence greatly influences productivity. The quantum and methods of remuneration payable ought to be fair, reasonable and rewarding of effort.

8. The Degree of Centralization - The quantity of power exerted with the central management depends on company size. Centralization implies the concentration of decision making authority at the top management. Sharing of authority with lower levels is called decentralization. The establishment ought to strive to attain a proper equilibrium.

9. Scalar Chain - Scalar Chain denotes to the chain of higher-ups starting from top management to the lowest rank and file. The principle suggests that there ought to be a clear line of authority from top to bottom linking all managers at all levels. It is considered a chain of command. It requires a concept called a "gang plank" using which a subordinate may contact a superior or his superior in case of an emergency, defying the hierarchy of control. Nevertheless the immediate superiors must be informed about the matter.
10. Order - Social order guarantees the smooth operation of a company through authoritative process. Material order ensures safety and efficiency in the workplace.
11. Equity - Employees must be handled kindly, and justice must be acted out to ensure a just workplace. Managers ought to be fair and unprejudiced when dealing with employees.
12. Stability of Tenure of Personnel - The period of time of service ought to not be too short and employees ought to not be moved from positionings frequently. An employee cannot render utilitarian service if he is removed before he becomes accustomed to the work assigned to him.
13. Initiative - Using the initiative of employees can add durability and new thoughts to an establishment. Initiative on the part of employees is a source of strength for the establishment because it provides new and better ideas. Employees are likely to take greater interest in the functioning of the establishment.
14. Esprit de Corps - This pertains to the need of managers to assure and formulate morale in the workplace; individually and communally. Team spirit helps develop an atmosphere of mutual trust and understanding.

These principles can be used to start and aid the processes of change, arrangement, decision making, skill management and the overall view of the management function.

Fayol also separated the management functions into five fundamental roles:

- To organize
- To plan and forecast
- To command
- To control
- To co-ordinate

FUNCTIONS OF MANAGEMENT

The four key functions of management are utilized all through an establishment irrespective of whether it is a business, a government agency, or a church group. In a business, which will be the focus here, a number of activities take place. For instance, in a retail store there are individuals who buy merchandise to sell, individuals to sell the merchandise, individuals who prepare the merchandise for exhibit, individuals who are accountable for advertising and promotion, individuals who do the accounting work, individuals who hire and train employees, and several other types of workers. There might be one manager for the entire store, but there are other managers at several levels who are more directly accountable for the individuals who perform all the other jobs. At each level of management, the four key roles of planning, organizing, directing, and controlling are comprised. The emphasis changes with each different level of manager, as will be explained as follows.

Planning

Planning in any establishment happens in several ways and at all levels. A top-level manager, let us say, the manager of a factory, plans for different events than does a manager who monitors, say, a group of workers who are in charge for assembling modular homes on an assembly line. The plant manager must be concerned with the overall operations of the plant, while the assembly-line manager or supervisor is only accountable to the line that he or she oversees.

Planning comprises setting organizational aims. This is typically done by higher-level managers in an establishment. As a part of the planning process, the manager then develops strategies for achieving the aims of the establishment. In order to implement the strategies, resources will be needed and must be acquired. The planners must also then determine the standards, or levels of quality, that need to be met in finishing the jobs.

In general, planning can be strategic planning, tactical planning, or contingency planning. Strategic planning is long-range planning that is typically finished by top-level managers in an establishment. Examples of strategic decisions managers make are what types of customers or clientele ought to be, what products or services ought to be sold, and where the products and services ought to be sold. Short-range or tactical planning is done for the benefit of lower-level managers, since it is the process of developing very detailed strategies about what needs to be done, who ought to do it, and how it ought to be done. To return to the previous example of gathering modular homes, as the home is nearing construction on the floor of the plant, plans must be made for the best way to move it by the plant in order that each worker can complete assigned jobs in the most efficient manner. These plans can best be developed and implemented by the line managers who oversee the production process rather than managers who sit in an office and plan for the overall operation of the company. The tactical plans fit into the strategic plans and are essential to implement the strategic plans.

Contingency planning provides optional courses of action when the basic plans that have been formulated do not attain the aims of the establishment. In today's economic environment, plans may need to be changed very rapidly. Continuing with the example of building modular homes in the plant, what if the plant is applying a nearby supplier for all the lumber used in the framing of the homes and the supplier has a major warehouse fire and loses its total inventory of framing lumber. Contingency plans would make it possible for the modular home builder to go on construction by going to another supplier for the same lumber that it can no more get from its previous supplier.

Organizing

Organizing refers to the way the establishment apportions resources, assigns jobs, and goes about carrying out its aims. In the process of organizing, managers arrange a framework that links all workers, jobs, and resources together so that the organizational aims can be attained; the framework is called organizational structure. The organizational chart that describes the structure of the establishment shows positions in the establishment, in general beginning with the top-level manager (typically the president) at the top of the chart. Other managers are shown below the president.

There are numerous ways to structure an establishment, which are discussed extensively all through the book with other relevant examples and management tools. It is important to note that the choice of structure is important for the type of establishment, its clientele, and the products or services it provides-all which determine the aims of the establishment.

Directing

Directing is the process that assorted individuals would most likely relate to managing. It is supervising, or leading workers to carry out the aims of the establishment. In many organizations, directing necessitates making assignments, assisting workers to carry out assignments, interpreting organizational policies, and making workers know of how well they are performing. To efficaciously carry out this function, managers must have leadership skills in order to get workers to execute effectively.

Some managers conduct by authorizing workers. This means that the manager does not stand like a supervisor over the workers giving out orders and correcting errors. Empowered workers ordinarily work in teams and are given the authority to make conclusions about what plans will be carried out and how. Empowered workers have the support of managers who will assist them to make sure the aims of the establishment are being met. It is in general thought that workers who are involved with the decision-making process feel more of a sense of ownership in their work, take more pride in their work, and are better performers on the task.

By the very process of directing, it ought to be clear that the manager must discover a way to get workers to do their jobs. There are several ways managers can do this in addition to empowerment, and there are many theories about the best way to get workers to perform effectively and efficiently. Management theories and motivation are important topics.

Controlling

The controlling process includes the evaluation of actions that managers must execute. It is the process of determining if the company's aims and objectives are being met. This process also admits correcting situations in which the aims and objectives aren't being met. There are several activities that are a part of the controlling function.

It is necessary that managers must first set standards of performance for workers. These standards are levels of performance that ought to be met. For instance, in the modular home assembly process, the standard might be to have a home completed in eight working days as it moves through the construction line. This is a standard that must then be communicated to managers who are supervising workers, and to the workers so that they experience what is expected of them.

After the standards have been set and communicated, it is the manager's responsibility to monitor carrying into action to see that the standards are being met. If the manager watches the homes move through the construction process and sees that it takes ten days, something must be done about it. The standards that have been set aren't being met. In this example, it ought to be relatively easy for managers to determine where the delays are taking place. Once the problems are examined and compared to expectations, then something must be done to correct the results. Typically, the managers would take corrective action by working with the employees who were causing the delays. There could be many reasons for the delays. Perhaps it is not the fault of the workers but instead is due to poor equipment or an insufficient number of workers. Whatever the problem, disciplinary action ought to be taken.

MANAGEMENT CHALLENGES

As business becomes more universally integrated and competitive all over the world, a focus on innovation will play a significant role in sustained growth for all organizations in the future. This is particularly true for almost all business establishments since they will play an even greater role in the economic picture for most countries as we move into the next phase of globalization. Organizations must respond to universal challenges through innovative thinking in order to grow their business and create profit. Efficient and effectual innovation through product development, process integration, and individuals empowerment will provide organizations with creative business models that allow for a foundation for sustained success.

Globalization is no more limited to large multinational corporations; it has become a business necessity for organizations of all sizes and shapes. Internet and current information technology has brought the entire world close together through outsourcing of services, development of products and software, sharing of intellectual capitals and many more. One of the key challenges in modern day business is the pressing need to integrate their wide and varied software systems and applications. Moreover, large organizations - for example banks and insurance organizations have vast amount of data that is embedded in their legacy systems. They have a need to expose those data and the corresponding applications in a 'unified' view to the customer on the Internet, resulting in what is known as 'business integration'. Nevertheless, as a result of this integration, and technical power of applications to transact over the Internet, businesses are now readily able to offer and consume 'services' across the Internet. Presently, there is a lacuna of literature on modelling and managing the challenges emanating from collaboration between varied businesses and applications. Here we will address the latest approaches in modelling collaborative business processes that transcend the boundaries of an establishment, and deal with multiple other organizations through 'services'. This will consider the affect of Service Oriented Architecture on business partnership and the significant management issues of business processes, customer expectations, trust between businesses and the unavoidable changes to the organizational structures.

Note: An in-depth exploration of basic principles of management for the purpose of gaining depth of understanding into the subject, we can take the example of Nokia Company. In 2007, Nokia was listed as number one company in Europe and number three in the world in a "Top Companies for Leaders" study carried on by Human Resources Company "Hewitt Associates" in partnership with "Fortune magazine". For detailed information, reader can visit Nokia Website http://www.nokia.com/NOKIA_COM_1/Corporate_Responsibility/CR_Report_2007/Nokia_CR_Report_2007_Printable.pdf.

2

Development of Management Process

EVOLUTION OF MANAGEMENT THOUGHT

It is a well known fact that through the practice of management and the continued growth of commerce and wealth we are transforming our lives. When appreciating the past success of 'management', we would also make out that today's accelerating pace of change is putting pressure on our organizations to be at the forefront of management thinking. If we want to preserve our standard of living, our rate of change has to be comparative to the rest of the world. But our today's management thinking has evolved from a whole range of influences over an extraordinary long period of time. Daniel A Wren in his book 'The Evolution of Management Thought' writes:

"Within the practices of the past there are lessons of history for tomorrow in a continuous stream. We occupy but one point in this stream. The purpose is to present...the past as a prologue to the future."

So with the objective of speeding up the development of our management practice for the future, let us examine that current of developing management thought of the past. In the growing of industrial society comes Scot Daniel McCallum as President of the New York to Eire Railroad. In 1854, he was facing specific problems related to the size of his organization and manpower that was generally uneducated. His workers were immigrant and with an agricultural background and not used to a factory discipline imposed by management. In that surroundings he determines sound management as being based on:

- Clearly defined hierarchy of superiors and subordinates
- Enforcement of personal responsibility and accountability.
- Frequent and exact reporting of performance

- Good discipline
- Pay and promotion based on merit
- Specific and detailed task descriptions
- The search for and correction of errors

From this viewpoint, he follows the classic hierarchical organization chart. Charles Darwin's work on 'The Origin of the Species' is published in 1859. Herbert Spencer (1820-1903) afterwards develops the theme of survival of the fittest in his 'Social Darwinism.' Our society takes over the essential nature of competition, survival of the fittest and adulation of winners. Ivan Pavlov does experiments with dogs to develop classical conditioning. He matches an artificial stimulus with a natural one. He gives the dog a piece of meat while at the same time ringing a bell. In time he can make the dog salivate purely by only ringing the bell. B F Skinner develops this train of thought into operant conditioning or convinced re-enforcement, 'Do this and you will get that.' This work gives legitimacy to the belief that you can motivate a worker by offering honours. From this grows the widespread use of bonus and commission systems.

Scientific Method would be depicted as the practice of postulating a theory and then carrying on disciplined experiments to confirm or disprove the theory. It is the method by which science has developed over the centuries. By the early 1900s, Frederick Taylor (1856-1915) was credited with bringing scientific disciplines into the ethos of management. He is known as the father of Scientific Management. He paid particular care to the study and subsequent planning of jobs. Time and motion study evolved which would lead into the setting of standards and performance measurement. Unluckily, the majority of Taylor's excellent work is clouded by his thought that workers restrict output from 'the natural instinct and tendency of men to take it easy.' He mentioned to it as 'soldering'. Henri Fayol (1841-1925) writes about leadership and the 'theory of management' and Max Weber (1864-1920) develops organizational structures - Weber would be the mastermind of the term 'bureaucracy' - management by the office. From these writings evolve the corporate structures of Alfred Sloan, CEO of General Motors during 1918-57. The motive of these practitioners was to develop principles whereby large corporations could be kept in line and developed.

Along with this need to handle and control individuals, a social dimension emerges. Robert Owen in his New Lanark experiments (1795), recognises the importance of the human element in an enterprise. Karl Marx, within a society that comprised extremes of poverty and wealth, challenged the basis of the capitalist system. He wondered the control of society's 'means of production' by the few, while it had the many trapped in burdensome and non-meaningful work. The social sciences come forth through the work of Mary Parker Folett where he recognises the interdependencies among the people, the work and the environment. There are the human behaviour studies of the Hawthorne experiments of the late 1920s, and the subsequent research into motivation by Mayo, Maslow, Hetzberg, McClelland etc.

In 1960, Douglas McGregor writes, "The answer to the question managers frequently ask - how do you motivate individuals? - is - you do not. We all come to work already inspired; the organization either captures or destroys that motivation." David McClelland (1970s) of Harvard University researches motivation for 10 years over 19 unlike cultures. He identifies 'Basic Social Motives (PSM),' the three main ones of which are Achievement, Affiliation and Power. The people or society tends to be energised by one or other of these 'Basic Social Motives.' With 'Achievement' the focus is on achieving jobs. 'Affiliation' considers relationships and friendship. 'Power' is concerned with position and influence over others. He considers, discovered behaviour is a function of the position and the Basic Social Motive of the people. Meredith Belbin (1980s) describes the 'team roles' we enact, when taking part in teamwork situations.

Peter Senge, to produce the 'Learning Organization,' argues for a holistic approach comprising:

- Mental Models - challenging deeply ingrained assumptions
- Personal Mastery - commitment to life-long learning
- Shared Vision - producing a goal with which employees can identify
- Systems Thinking - seeing cyclical processes
- Team Learning - it is the organization that learns - through individuals

Edwards Deming advocates his System of Fundamental Knowledge in his book, 'The New Economics'. He has four elements that must work together as a system, they are:

- Psychology - of people, society and change
- Systems Thinking - seeing cyclical processes
- Theory of Knowledge - The need to test our theories or assumptions.

- Variation - the need to appreciate variation and statistical process control

We are also witnessing significant developments in our interpreting of how the brain acts and how we learn. Tony Buzan on the one hand is highlighting the patterning nature of the mind. Thomas Kuhn (1962) and Noel Baker (1992) talk about paradigms and the difficulty we experience in seeing new concepts because of our past conditioning. Steven Pinker (1997) writes that mental activity is a form of computation. Further more writers, for example Edward de Bono are challenging the analytical and confrontation styles of Aristotle and Plato in their search for the truth. He talks about heuristic rule and formulating answers by building on individuals's 'half baked' ideas (parallel thinking).

We are now beginning to talk about democracy amongst organizations. While we have been committed to democracy relative to government for hundreds of years, our commercial organizations aren't conducted by elected members nor are they held accountable to the employees within the company. Nevertheless, Ricardo Semler of Semco in his book 'Maverick' (1993) explains, how he was able to translate a conventional hierarchical organization into one in which the employees constitute their respective leaders. And finally, we come to the electronic age. Information and knowledge is going to be readily available to us all. The future is going to be dominated by our need to understand systems.

CLASSICAL SCHOOLS OF MANAGEMENT

Gradually as the industrialisation increased, the several schools of management thought also came up. One of the first schools of management thought, the classical management theory, developed all through the Industrial Revolution when new problems related to the factory system started out to appear. Managers were uncertain of how to train employees (many of them non-English speaking immigrants) or deal with increased labour dissatisfaction, so they started out to test solutions. As an outcome, the classical management theory developed from efforts to find the "one best way" to perform and manage jobs. This school of thought is constructed up of two branches: classical scientific and classical administrative, reported in the coming sections.

Classical Scientific School

The classical scientific branch arose due to the need to increase productivity and efficiency. The stress was on trying to find the best way to get the most work done by examining how the work process was really attained and by scrutinizing the skills of the manpower. The classical scientific school owes its roots to several major contributors, comprising Frederick Taylor, Henry Gantt, and Frank and Lillian Gilbreth.

Frederick Taylor is often acknowledged as the "father of scientific management." Taylor believed that organizations ought to examine jobs and formulate precise processes. As an example, in 1898, Taylor calculated how much iron from rail cars Bethlehem Steel plant workers could be unloading if they were using the correct movements, instruments, and steps. The result was an amazing 47.5 tons per day instead of the mere 12.5 tons, each worker had been averaging. Additionally, by redesigning the shovels the workers used, Taylor was able to increase the length of work time and therefore decrease the number of individuals digging from 500 to 140. Lastly, he developed an incentive system that paid workers more money for meeting the new standard. Productivity at Bethlehem Steel shot up overnight. As a result, numerous theorists followed Taylor's philosophy when developing their own principles of management.

Henry Gantt, an associate of Taylor's, developed the Gantt chart, a bar graph that measures planned and completed work along each level of production. Based on time or else of quantity, volume, or weight, this optical exhibit chart has been a widely used planning and control instrument since its growth in 1910.

Frank and Lillian Gilbreth, a husband-and-wife team, studied task motions. In Frank's early career as an apprentice bricklayer, he was concerned in standardization and method study. He watched bricklayers and saw that some workers were slow and inefficient, while others were very productive. He discovered that each bricklayer employed a different set of motions to lay bricks. From his observations, Frank isolated the fundamental movements necessary to do the task and extinguished unnecessary motions. Workers using these movements raised their output from 1,000 to 2,700 bricks per day. This was the first motion study designed to isolate the best potential method of performing a given task. Afterwards, Frank and his wife Lillian studied task motions using a motion-picture camera and a split-second clock. When his husband died at the age of 56, Lillian extended their work.

Thanks to these contributors and others, the fundamental ideas concerning scientific management developed. They admit the following:

- Developing a spirit of cooperation amongst workers and management to check that work is carried out in accordance with devised processes.

- Developing new standard methods for doing each task.
- Dividing work between workers and management in almost equal shares, with each group taking over the work for which it is best fitted.
- Selecting, training, and developing workers rather than allowing them to choose their own jobs and train themselves.

Classical Administrative School

Whereas scientific management centred on the productivity of people, the classical administrative approach focuses on the total establishment. The emphasis is on the development of managerial principles rather than work methods. Contributors to this school of thought include Max Weber, Henri Fayol, Mary Parker Follett, and Chester I. Barnard. These theorists studied the flow of information within an establishment and emphasized the importance of understanding how an establishment is operated.

In the late 1800s, Max Weber didn't like that many European organizations were handled on a personal family-like basis and that employees were faithful to single supervisors rather than to the organization. He believed that organizations ought to be managed impersonally and that a formal organizational structure, where specific rules were followed, was important. In other words, he did not believe that authority ought to be based on a person's personality. He thought authority ought to be something that was part of a person's task and passed from people to people as one person left and another took over. This non-personal, objective form of establishment was known as bureaucracy.

Weber considered that all bureaucracies have the following characteristics:

- A clear power structure: All views within a bureaucracy are structured in a way that permits the higher positions to supervise and control the lower positions. This clear chain of command helps control and order during the establishment.
- Competency: Competence, not "who you know," ought to be the basis for all decisions made in employing, task assignments, and promotions in order to foster power and merit as the basic characteristics of a bureaucratic establishment.
- Division of task and differentiation: All responsibilities in an establishment are specialized in order that each employee has the essential expertise to do a particular job.

- Neutral relationships between managers and employees: Managers ought to maintain an impersonal relationship with employees in order that favouritism and personal prejudice don't determine decisions.
- Records: A bureaucracy involves maintaining complete files regarding all its activities.
- Rules: Standard operating processes govern all organizational activities to furnish certainty and facilitate co-ordination.

Chester Barnard, who was president of New Jersey Bell Telephone Company, brought in the idea of the informal establishment - in-groups (exclusive groups of individuals) that by nature form within a company. He felt that these informal organizations provided necessary and vital communication purposes for the overall establishment and that they could help the establishment carry out its aims.

Barnard felt that it was especially important for managers to develop a sense of common purpose where a willingness to cooperate is strongly encouraged. He is credited with developing the acceptance theory of management, which emphasizes the willingness of employees to agree that managers have legitimate authority to act. Barnard felt that four components affected the willingness of employees to assume authority:

- The employees must understand the communication.
- The employees agree the communication as being coherent with the establishment's purposes.
- The employees feel that their actions will be consistent with the needs and desires of the other employees.
- The employees feel that they are mentally and physically able to attain the order.

Barnard's sympathy for and understanding of employees inevitably positioned him as a bridge to the behavioural school of management, the next school of thought to emerge.

BEHAVIOURAL MANAGEMENT THEORY

As management research proceeded in the twentieth century, questions started out to come up regarding the interactions and motivations of the people within organizations. Management principles developed all through the classical period were simply not useful in dealing with many management situations and couldn't explain the behaviour of individual employees. In short, classical theory ignored employee motivation and behaviour. As a result, the behavioural school was a natural appendage of this revolutionary management experiment.

The behavioural management theory is frequently described as the human relations movement because it deals with the human attribute of work. Behavioural theorists believed that a better understanding of human behaviour at work, for example motivation, conflict, expectations, and group dynamics, improved productivity. The theorists who contributed to this school viewed employees as people, resources, and assets to be developed and worked with, not as machines, as in the past. Several individuals and experiments added to this theory.

Elton Mayo's shares came in as component of the Hawthorne studies, a series of experimentations that strictly applied classical management theory only to reveal its defects. The Hawthorne experiments consisted of two studies conducted at the Hawthorne Works of the Western Electric Company in Chicago from 1924 to 1932. The first study was conducted by a group of engineers seeking to determine the relationship of lighting levels to worker productivity. Astoundingly enough, they discovered that worker productivity altered as the lighting levels decreased - that is, until the employees were unable to see what they were doing, after which performance by nature declined.

A few years afterwards, a second group of experiments started out. Harvard researchers Mayo and F. J. Roethlisberger supervised a group of five women in a bank wiring room. They gave the women special privileges, for example, the right to leave their workstations without permission, take rest periods, enjoy free lunches, and have discrimination in pay levels and work days. This experiment also resulted in importantly altered rates of productivity.

In this case, Mayo and Roethlisberger concluded that the gain in productivity resulted from the supervisory placement rather than the changes in lighting or other associated worker benefits. Because the experimenters became the basic supervisors of the employees, the intense interest they displayed for the workers was the basis for the altered motivation and resulting productivity. Fundamentally, the experimenters became a part of the study and determined its result. This is the origin of the term Hawthorne effect, which describes the special attention researchers give to a study's subjects and the impact that attention has on the study's determinations.

The general decision from the Hawthorne studies was that human relations and the social needs of workers are essential aspects of business management. This principle of human motivation helped revolutionize possibilities and practices of management.

Abraham Maslow, an exercising scientist, developed one of the most widely acknowledged need theories, a theory of motivation based upon a thoughtfulness of human needs. His theory of human needs had three suppositions:

- Human needs are never completely satisfied.
- Human behaviour is purposeful and is inspired by the need for satisfaction.
- Needs can be classified as per a hierarchical structure of importance, from the lowest to highest.

Maslow classified the needs hierarchy into five different specific areas:

- Physiological needs: Maslow grouped all physical needs essential for keeping fundamental human well-being, for example food and drink, into this category. After the need is satisfied, nevertheless, it is no more is a motivator.
- Safety needs: These necessarily let in the need for fundamental security, stability, protection, and freedom from fear. A normal state exists for an individual to have all these needs generally satisfied. Otherwise, they become basic motivators.
- Belonging and love needs: After the physical and safety needs are satisfied and are no more motivators, the need for belonging and love emerges as a basic motivator. The individual strives to establish meaningful relationships with important others.
- Esteem needs: An individual must develop self-confidence and wants to attain position, reputation, fame, and glory.
- Self-actualization needs:L Assuming that all the previous demands in the hierarchy are satisfied, a person feels a need to find himself.

Maslow's hierarchy of needs theory assisted managers to visualize employee motive.

Douglas McGregor was intemperately influenced by both the Hawthorne studies and Maslow. He believed that two fundamental types of managers exist. One type, the Theory X manager, has a negative view of employees and assumes that they are lazy, untrustworthy, and incapable of assuming responsibility. Alternatively, the Theory Y manager assumes that employees aren't only trustworthy and capable of assuming responsibility, but also have high levels of motivation.

An important aspect of McGregor's thought was his notion that managers who hold either set of assumptions can produce self-fulfilling prophecies, that through their behaviour, these managers produce positions where subordinates act in ways that affirm the manager's original expectations. As a group, these theorists discovered that individuals worked for inner satisfaction and not materialistic rewards, changing the focus to the role of individuals in an establishment's performance.

QUANTITATIVE SCHOOL OF MANAGEMENT

All through World War II, mathematicians, physicists, and other scientists joined together to solve military troubles. The quantitative school of management is a result of the research conducted during World War II. The quantitative approach to management involves the use of quantitative techniques, for example statistics, information models, and computer simulations, to ameliorate decision making. This school consists of several branches, depicted in the following sections.

Management Science School

The management science school came forth to treat the problems related with universal warfare. Today, this view promotes managers to use mathematics, statistics, and other quantitative techniques to make management decisions.

Managers may use computer prototypes to figure out the best way to do some job, saving both money and time. Managers use several applications, for example:

- Inventory modelling helps control inventories by mathematically establishing how and when to order a product.
- Mathematical forecasting helps make projections that are useful in the planning process.
- Queuing theory helps allocate service personnel or workstations to minimize customer waiting and service cost.

Operations Management

Operations management is a small subdivision of the quantitative approach to management. It centres on managing the process of transforming materials, labour, and capital into useful goods and/or services. The product outputs can be either goods or services; effectual operations management is a business concern for both manufacturing and service organizations. The resource inputs, or factors of production, let in the wide form of raw materials, technologies, capital information, and individuals needed to produce finished products. The transformation process, in turn, is the genuine set of operations or activities through which several resources are utilized to give rise to finished goods or services of value to customers or clients.

Operations management now-a-days pays very close attention to the requirements of quality, client service, and competitors. The process starts out with attention to the demands of customers: What do they want? Where do they want it? When do they want it? Based on the answers to these questions, managers line up resources and take any action requirement to meet customer anticipations.

Management Information Systems

Management information systems (MIS) is the latest subfield of the quantitative school. A management information system co-ordinates past, present, and designed data from both inner and outside sources and processes it into usable information, which it then makes available to managers at all organizational levels. The information systems are also able to organize data into usable and approachable formats. As a result, managers can name alternatives quickly, evaluate alternatives by using a spreadsheet program, pose a series of "what-if" questions, and finally, select the best options based on the answers to these questions.

SYSTEMS MANAGEMENT THEORY

The systems management theory has had a significant impression on management science. A system is an interrelated set of elements operating as a whole. An establishment as a system is composed of four elements:

- Inputs: material or human resources.
- Transformation processes: technological and managerial processes.
- Outputs: products or services.
- Feedback: reactions from the environment.

In relationship to an establishment, inputs comprise resources for example raw materials, money, technologies, and individuals. These inputs go through a transformation process where they're planned, organized, inspired, and checked to ultimately meet the establishment's aims. The outputs are the products or services designed to raise the quality of life or productivity for customers/clients. Feedback comprises comments from customers or clients using the products. This overall systems model applies to any department or program in the overall establishment.

Systems theory may seem quite fundamental. Yet decades of management training and practices in the workplace have not complied this theory. Only recently, with enormous changes confronting organizations and how they operate, have educators and managers come to face this new way of looking at things. This interpretation has gave rise an important change in the way management studies and accesses organizations.

The systems theory encourages managers to look at the establishment from a broader view. Managers are beginning to recognize the several parts of the establishment, and, in particular, the interrelations of the parts.

Present-day system theorists find it helpful to analyze the effectiveness of organizations as per the degree that they are open or closed. The following terminology is significant to your understanding of the systems approach:

- An establishment that interacts little with its outside environment (outside environment) and therefore gets little feedback from it is called a closed system.
- An open system, in contrast, interacts continually with its environment. Therefore, it is well informed about changes within its surroundings and its position relative to these changes.
- A subsystem is any system that is part of a larger one.
- Entropy is the tendency of systems to deteriorate or break down over time.
- Synergy is the power of the whole system to equal more than the sum of its parts.

CONTINGENCY SCHOOL OF MANAGEMENT

The contingency school of management can be summed up as an "it all depends" approach. The appropriate management actions and approaches depend upon the situation. Managers with a contingency view use a flexible approach, draw on a variety of theories and experiences, and evaluate numerous options as they solve problems. Contingency management recognizes that there is no one best way to manage. In the contingency view, managers are faced with the task of determining which managerial approach is likely to be most effectual in an apt situation. For example, the approach used to manage a group of teenagers working in a fast-food restaurant would be very different from the approach used to manage a medical research team trying to find a cure for a disease.

Contingency conceiving avoids the classical "one best way" arguments and recognizes the need to understand situational differences and respond properly to them. It doesn't apply certain management principles to any situation. Contingency theory is recognition of the extreme importance of individual manager performance in any given situation. The contingency approach is highly dependent on the experience and judgment of the manager in a given organizational surroundings.

QUALITY SCHOOL OF MANAGEMENT

The quality school of management is a comprehensive concept for conducting and operating an establishment, directed at continually bettering performance by focusing on customers while addressing the demands of all stakeholders. In other words, this concept focuses on managing the total establishment to rescue high quality to customers.

The quality school of management conceives the following in its theory:

- Establishment makeup: Organizations are constructed up of complicated systems of customers and suppliers. Every person, executive, manager, and worker functions as both a supplier and a customer.
- Quality of goods and services: Meeting the customers' demands is a priority aim and presumed to be a key to organizational survival and development.
- Continuous improvement in goods and services: Recognizing the need to pinpoint internal and external requirements and continuously strive to improve. It is an idea that says, "The company is good, but it can always become better."
- Employees working in teams: These groups are main vehicles for planning and problem solving.
- Developing openness and trust: Confidence among members of the establishment at all degrees is an important condition for success.

Quality management necessitates employees in decision making as a way to prevent quality problems. The Kaizen approach uses incremental, uninterrupted improvement for individuals, products, and processes. The reengineering approach focuses on sensing the need to change, seeing change coming, and reacting effectively to it when it comes. Both approaches are reported in the following sections.

Kaizen Approach

The very notion of continuous improvement proposes that managers, teams, and individuals learn from both their achievements and their faults. Quality managers help their employees gain insights from personal work experiences, and they promote everyone to share with others what they have learnt.

In this way, everyone reflects upon his or his own work experiences, comprising failures, and passes their newfound knowledge to others. Sharing experiences in this manner helps to produce an establishment that is ceaselessly detecting new ways to ameliorate.

Reengineering Approach

The reengineering path of management focuses on producing change, big change and fast. It centres on sensing the need to change, seeing change coming, and responding effectively to change when it comes.

Reengineering, the radical redesign of business processes to attain dramatic advances in cost, quality, service, and speed, necessitates that every employee and manager look at all aspects of the company's operation and find means to reconstruct the organizational systems to better efficiency, identify superfluousnesses, and eliminate waste in every possible way. Reengineering is neither easy nor cheap, but organizations that adopt this plan have reaped remarkable results.

Reengineering attempts look at how jobs are designed, and raise critical questions about how much work and work processes can be optimally configured.

Though many individuals believe that reengineering is a euphemism for downsizing or outsourcing, this isn't true. Yes, downsizing or outsourcing may be a by-product of reengineering. Nevertheless, the aim of reengineering is to bring about a tight fit between market opportunities and corporate abilities. After organizations are capable to find this fit, new jobs ought to be made.

FUTURE MANAGEMENT

In our above discussion we discussed about the several relevant schools of management thought. Modern management approaches respect the classical, human resource, and quantitative approaches to management. Nevertheless, successful managers distinguish that though each theoretical school has limitations in its diligences; each approach also offers valuable insights that can broaden a manager's options in solving problems and accomplishing organizational aims. Successful managers work to extend these approaches to meet the calls for/of a dynamic environment.

Modernistic management approaches recognize that individuals are complicated and variable. Employee needs shift time; individuals possess a range of talents and capabilities that can be developed. Organizations and managers, hence, ought to react to individuals with a wide variety of managerial schemes and task opportunities.

Fundamental themes to be considered, as the twenty-first century progresses, admit the following:

- The commitment to meet customer needs 100 percent of the time guides organizations towards quality management and uninterrupted advance of operations.
- Today's universal economy is a dramatic effect on organizations, and opportunities abound to learn new ways of managing from practices in other countries.
- Organizations must reinvest in their most important asset, their individuals. If organizations cannot make the commitment to life-long employment, they must commit to applying attrition to reduce head count. They will not experience cooperation unless they make it clear that their individuals will not be working themselves out of a task.
- Managers must excel in their leadership responsibilities to perform a number of varied roles.

Therefore, now we can aptly conclude that from the starting of industrial age, organizational system has developed to a greater degree, but here it doesn't end rather it is a continuous and on-going process. The theories and the managerial tools for the improvement are always employed in this system of development.

Note: A sterling example in Development of Management Process is the company "General Motors". Today, General Motors Corporation is the world's largest automaker; it has been the annual global industry sales leader for 77 years. Founded in 1908, GM today employs about 270,000people around the world. For detailed information, reader can visit their site http://www.gm.com/corporate/responsibility/reports/06/

3

Managerial Functions

With the development of technology and mechanism,, the functioning of organizations is also becoming complicated and cumbersome. Now-a-days as we all know, we are living in a tough and uncertain economy, in such a situation the big organizations and organizations calls for strong managers to lead its staff toward accomplishing business aims.

But managers are more than just leaders - they're problem solvers, cheerleaders, and planners as well. And managers do not come in one-size-fits-all shapes or forms. Managers fulfil numerous roles and have many different responsibilities at each degree of management inside an establishment.

Organizations abound in today's society. Groups of individuals invariably join forces to attain common aims. Many a times the aims and objectives of these organizations are for profit, for example franchise restaurant chains or clothing retailers. Other times, the aims are more altruistic, for example non-profit churches or public schools. But no matter what their aims, all these organizations share two things generally: they're made up of individuals, and certain individuals are in charge of these individuals.

FUNCTIONS OF MANAGERS

Managers come along in every establishment, at least in organizations that want to succeed. These individuals have the occasionally-unenviable task of making decisions, solving difficult problems, setting aims, planning schemes, and rallying people. And those are just a few of their responsibilities! To be exact, managers administer and co-ordinate resources effectively and efficiently to attain the aims of an establishment. In essence, managers get the task exercised through other individuals.

The Intricacies of Management

It does not matter what type of establishment managers work in, they are generally accountable for a group of people's performance. As leaders, managers must encourage this group to reach common business aims, for example contributing a new product to market in a timely manner. To carry out these aims, managers not only use their human resources, but they also take advantage of several material resources as well, for example technology.

Think of a team, for instance. A manager may be in charge of a certain department whose task it is to develop a new product. The manager calls for to co-ordinate the efforts of his department's team members, as well as gives them the material tools they need to attain the task well. If the team fails, eventually it is the manager who shoulders the responsibility.

MANAGERIAL SKILLS

To be an effectual manager, it is essentiai to possess numerous skills. Not all managers have all the skills that would make them the most effectual manager. As technology advances and grows, the skills that are demanded by managers are invariably changing. Different levels of management in the organizational structure also demand different types of management skills. Generally, nevertheless, managers need to have communication skills, human skills, computer skills, time-management skills, and technical skills.

Communication Skills

Communication skills fall into the broad classes of oral and written skills, both of which managers use in numerous ways. It is essential for a manager to orally explain processes and give direction to workers. It is also necessary for managers to give verbal praise to workers. Managers are also expected to conduct meetings and give talks to groups of individuals. An important part of the oral communication process is listening. Managers are required to listen to their supervisors and to their workers. A manager must hear commendations and complaints regularly and must be willing to follow through on what is heard. A manager who does not listen can't be a good communicator.

Managers are also required to write reports, letters, memos, and policy statements. All of these must be written in such a way that the recipient can interpret and realize what is being said. This means that managers must write clearly and concisely. Good writing requires good grammar and composition skills. This is something that can be found out by those aspiring to a management view.

Human Skills

Relating to other individuals is very much important in order to be a good manager. Workers are available in about every disposition that can be imagined. It takes a manager with the right human skills to manage this form of workers effectively. Diversity in the workplace is commonplace. The manager must understand different personality types and cultures to be able to supervise these workers. Human skills cannot be learned in a classroom; they are best learned by working with individuals. Gaining an understanding of personality types can be learned from books, but practice in carrying on with diverse groups is the most meaningful formulations.

Computer Skills

Technology alters so rapidly it is frequently difficult to keep up with the changes. It is requisite for managers to have computer skills in order to keep up with these rapid changes. Many of the processes that occur in offices, manufacturing plants, warehouses, and other work environments depend on computers and therefore necessitate managers and workers who can skilfully use the technology. Though computers can cause headaches, at the same time they have changed numerous of the jobs that are executed in the workplace.

Time-Management Skills

Because the typical manager is a very busy person, it is important that time be managed effectively. This necessitates an understanding of how to allocate time to several projects and activities. A manager's time is frequently interrupted by telephone calls, problems with workers, meetings, others who just want to visit, and other seemingly uncontrollable factors. It is up to the manager to learn how to manage time in order that work can be finished most expeditiously. Good time-management skills can be learned, but managers must be willing to prioritize activities, delegate, deal with interruptions, organize work, and execute other acts that will make them better and efficient managers.

Technical Skills

Different from computer skills, technical skills are more intimately related to the jobs that are executed by workers. A manager must know what the workers who are being supervised are doing on their jobs or assistance cannot be rendered to them. For example, a manager who is supervising accountants, needs to know the accounting processes; a manager who is supervising a machinist must know how to operate the equipment; and a manager who supervises the construction of a home must know the sequence of operations and how to execute them.

Conceptual Skills

This technique calls for the power to think analytically. Analytical skills enable managers to break down problems into smaller parts, to see the relations among the parts, and to recognize the implications of any one problem for others. As managers assume ever-higher responsibilities in organizations, they must deal with more ambiguous problems that have long-term consequences. Again, managers may acquire these skills initially through formal education and then further develop them by training and task experience. The higher the management level, the more significant conceptual skills become.

Business and management educators are more and more interested in helping individuals assume technical, human, and conceptual skills, and develop specific competencies, or specialized skills, that contribute to high performance in a management task. Following are some of the skills and personal characteristics that the American Assembly of Collegiate Schools of Business (AACSB) is urging business schools to facilitate their learners develop.

- Leadership: Power to influence others to perform jobs
- Self-objectivity: Power to evaluate yourself realistically
- Analytic thinking: Power to interpret and explain patterns in information
- Behavioural flexibility: Power to modify personal behaviour to react objectively rather than subjectively to attain organizational aims
- Oral communication: Power to express ideas clearly in words
- Written communication: Power to express ideas clearly in writing
- Personal impact: Power to produce a good impression and instil confidence
- Resistance to stress: Power to perform under stressful conditions
- Tolerance for uncertainty: Power to perform in ambiguous situations

TYPES OF MANAGERS

Two leaders may serve as managers inside the same company but have very varied titles and purposes. Large organizations, in particular, may break down management into varied stages because so many more individuals need to be managed. Typical management levels fall into the following categories:

- Top level: Managers at this level ensure that major performance objectives are recognized and attained. Common task titles for top managers include chief executive officer (CEO), chief operating officer (COO), president, and vice president. These senior managers are considered executives, accountable for the performance of an establishment as a whole or for one of its important parts.
- Middle level: Middle managers report to top managers and are in charge of relatively large departments or divisions consisting of several smaller units. Examples of middle managers include clinic directors in hospitals; deans in universities; and division managers, plant managers, and branch sales managers in businesses. Middle managers develop and implement action plans consistent with company objectives, for example increasing market presence.
- Low level: The initial management task that most individuals attain is normally a first-line management position, for example a team leader or supervisor - a person in charge of smaller work units composed of hands-on workers. Task titles for these first-line managers vary greatly, but admit such designations as department head, group leader, and unit leader. First-line managers ensure that their work teams or units meet performance objectives, for example creating a set number of items at a given quality, that are coherent with the plans of middle and top management.

ROLES OF MANAGERS

Managers just do not go out and haphazardly execute their responsibilities. Good managers discover how to master five fundamental roles: planning, organizing, staffing, leading, and controlling.

- Planning: This step necessitates mapping out exactly how to attain a particular aim. Say, for instance, that the establishment's aim is to improve company sales. The manager first needs to decide which steps are essential to attain that aim.

These steps may include increasing advertising, inventory, and sales staff. These necessary steps are developed into a plan. When the plan is in place, the manager can follow it to attain the aim of bettering company sales.

- Organizing: After a plan has been formed, a manager needs to organize his team and materials as per his plan. Assigning job and granting authority are two important elements of organizing.
- Staffing: After a manager discerns his area's needs, he may decide to beef up his staffing by recruiting, selecting, training, and developing employees. A manager in a large establishment frequently works with the company's human resources department to carry out this aim.
- Leading: A manager task calls for to do more than just design, organize, and form his team to attain an aim. He must also lead. Leading involves motivating, communicating, guiding, and encouraging. It requires the manager to coach, assist, and problem solve with employees.
- Controlling: After the other factors are in place, a manager's task isn't ended. He needs to continuously check results against aims and take any corrective actions essential to make sure that his area's plans stay on track.

Additionally, managers' schedules are typically jam-packed. Whether they're busy with employee meetings, unexpected problems, or strategy sessions, managers frequently find little free time on their calendars.

Henry Mintzberg in his book, The Nature of Managerial Work, distinguishes a set of ten roles that a manager must fulfil. These roles are categorized into three categories:

- Interpersonal: This role involves human interaction.
- Informational: This role involves the sharing and analyzing of information.
- Decisional: This role involves decision making.

The table below contains a more in-depth look at each category of roles that help managers carry out all five functions.

Mintzberg's Set of Ten Roles

Category	Role	Activity
Informational	Monitor	Seek and receive information; scan periodicals and reports; maintain personal contact with stakeholders.
	Disseminator	Forward information to establishment members via memos, reports, and phone calls.
	Spokesperson	Transmit information to outsiders via reports, memos, and speeches.
Interpersonal	Figurehead	Perform ceremonial and symbolic duties, for example greeting visitors and signing legal documents.
	Leader	Direct and motivate subordinates; counsel and communicate with subordinates.
	Liaison	Maintain information links both inside and outside establishment via mail, phone calls, and meetings.
Decisional	Entrepreneur	Initiate improvement projects; identify new ideas and delegate idea responsibility to others.
	Disturbance handler	Take corrective action during disputes or crises; resolve conflicts among subordinates; adapt to environments.
	Resource allocator	Decide who gets resources; prepare budgets; set schedules and determine priorities.
	Negotiator	Represent department during negotiations of union contracts, sales, purchases, and budgets.

All managers at all levels of every establishment execute these roles, but the amount of time a manager spends on each one depends on both the level of management and the specific establishment.

The list does not end here in perspective of modern organizations and their managers as the managers now-a-days are accountable to supervise and take charge of the activities and productivity of their workers. They play an important role in managing the functioning of their staff.

They also take part in employee selection, career growth, succession planning and working out reimbursement and rewards. They are accountable for the growth and addition in the organizations' finances and earnings.

Apart from the above mentioned roles a few below are also anticipated from the present day managers:

Decision Making

A manager makes organizational decisions and deals a variety of problems that arise on a daily basis. You have to identify the problems, produce choices and alternative courses of actions. The daily routine of making decisions include determining how to approach an employee who isn't doing or lacking progress and how to bring about change to the establishment and its team. It involves thinking and planning out strategies on how to better quality and also being cost conscious and effectual.

Aim Setting

In order for a manager to attain long term aims and commit to strategies for significant earnings, they have to communicate the vision of the company to your subordinates. They break down and clarify the aims that each team or people have to perform and assign work schedules and strategies.

Having aims and planning out the directions allow for effectual time management and saves cost and resources.

Empowering Others

The performance of the team depends on the abilities of the manager to empower them. How well a person performs depends on his motivation. Manager's job is to encourage and coach others to improve themselves and the quality of their work. He needs to instil in them the wish to excel and agree responsibility and self-management.

Communication and Individuals Skills

As the head of the establishment, the manager's power to develop trust and confidence, resolve problems and issues will result in a productive, aim oriented work group. He ought to encourage his team to ask for help, get involved and participate. Practice empathy and respect their personal values, opinions and ideas. Listen and respond and offer praises and encouragements when they make progress. By doing that the managers will enhance their self-esteem and they will offer their workers the cooperation.

A manager is in the middle position between the top management and the team that reports to him. He has to assure that communication is smooth and conveyed clearly to avoid misinterpretations and dissatisfaction.

Evaluating and Analyzing

The manager needs to have the capability to assess and analyse a process or process and determine on the best choice to create an outcome. Manager ought to look at the implication, quality and values and then taking the best approach. He is also expected to track the progress of each individual's activities and effectiveness, review them and offer feedback and guidance.

Provide Satisfaction among the Staff and the Customers

The manager's workers are happy when they know that their seniors furnish them with the essential tools and resource. They feel safe if the management puts priority on health, safety and cleanliness issues. He satisfies customers by giving good quality of service or product and takes care of their needs.

Note: Wipro Company is exemplary role model for studying Managerial Functions. Wipro was ranked "4th on the 'Top Companies for Leaders' in India, 5th in Asia Pacific region and 20th globally" in a study conducted by Hewitt Associates in collaboration with Fortune and the RBL Group. Reader can visit their site: http://www.wipro.com/manufacturing/focus_areas/demand_mgmt.htm

4

Decision Making Process

In our previous discussion we have read about the managerial functions, skills, and roles. Now here in our further discussion we will discuss about the decision making process in the organizations. Quite literally, organizations operate by individuals making decisions. A manager plans, organizes, staffs, leads, and controls his team by performing decisions. The effectiveness and quality of those decisions decide how successful a manager will be.

DECISION MAKING PROCESS

Managers are invariably called upon to make decisions for solving the problems. Decision making and problem solving are continuous processes of evaluating situations or problems, considering alternatives, making choices, and following them up with the necessary actions. Occasionally the decision-making process is highly short, and mental reflection is essentially instantaneous. In other situations, the process can drag on for weeks or even months. The entire decision-making process is dependent upon the right information being available to the right individuals at the right times.

The decision-making process involves the following steps:

1. Define the problem.
2. Identify limiting factors.
3. Develop potential alternatives.
4. Analyze the alternatives.
5. Select the best alternative.
6. Implement the decision.
7. Establish a control and evaluation system.

Defining Problem

The decision-making process starts out when a manager keys out the real problem. The accurate definition of the problem affects all the steps that follow; if the problem is inaccurately defined, every step in the decision-making process will be based on an incorrect terminus a quo (starting point). One way that a manager can help decides the true problem in a situation is by identifying the problem separately from its symptoms.

The most obviously troubling situations found in an establishment can in general be identified as symptoms of inherent problems. These symptoms all show that something is wrong with an establishment, but they do not key out root causes. A successful manager does not just attack symptoms; he works to uncover the factors that cause these symptoms.

Table: Symptoms and Their Real Causes

Symptoms	Underlying Problem
Low profits and/or declining sales	Poor market research
High costs	Poor design process; poorly trained employees
Low morale	Want of communication between management and subordinates
High employee turnover	Rate of pay too low; task design not suitable
High rate of absenteeism	Employees believe that they aren't valued

Identifying Limiting Factors

All managers are required to make the best decisions. To do so, managers call for to have the ideal resources, information, time, personnel, equipment, and supplies; and identify any limiting factors. Realistically, managers operate in an environment that typically does not provide ideal resources. For example, they may lack the proper budget or may not have the most exact information or any extra time. Therefore, they must choose to satisfy - to make the best decision possible with the information, resources, and time available.

Developing Potential Alternatives

Time pressures frequently cause a manager to move forward after considering only the first or most apparent answers. Nevertheless, successful problem solving demands thorough examination of the challenge, and a quick answer may not result in a permanent solution. Therefore, a manager ought to think through and investigate several alternative solutions to a single problem before making a quick conclusion.

One of the best known method acting for formulating options is through brainstorming, where a group works together to give ideas and alternative solutions. The assumption behind brainstorming is that the group dynamic induces thinking - one person's ideas, no matter how outrageous, can give ideas from the others in the group. Ideally, this spawning of ideas is contagious, and before long, lots of suggestions and ideas flow. Brainstorming typically requires 30 minutes to an hour. The following specific rules ought to be adopted all through brainstorming sessions:

- Concentrate on the problem at hand: This rule continues the discussion very specific and avoids the group's tendency to address the events leading up to the present problem.
- Entertain all ideas: In fact, the more ideas that comes up, the better. In other words, there are no bad ideas. Encouragement of the group to freely offer all thoughts on the subject is important. Participants ought to be encouraged to deliver ideas no matter how absurd they seem, because such ideas may spark a creative thought on the part of someone else.
- Refrain from allowing members to evaluate others' ideas on the spot: All judgments ought to be deferred until all thoughts are presented, and the group concurs on the best ideas.

Though brainstorming is the most general method to develop alternative solutions, managers can use several other ways to help develop solutions. Here are some examples:

- Nominal group technique: This method necessitates the use of a extremely structured meeting, complete with an agenda, and restricts discussion or interpersonal communication during the decision-making process. This skill is utile because it ensures that every group member has equal input in the decision-making process. It also avoids some of the pitfalls, for example pressure to conform, group dominance, hostility, and conflict, that can plague a more interactive, spontaneous, unstructured forum like the brainstorming.
- Delphi technique: With this skill, participants never meet, but a group leader uses written questionnaires to carry on the decision making.

No matter what method is used, group decision making has clear merits and demerits when equated with individual decision making. The following are among the merits:

- Groups provide a broader view.
- Employees are more likely to be satisfied and to support the final decision.
- Opportunities for discussion help to answer questions and reduce uncertainties for the decision makers.

These points are among the demerits:

- This process can be more time-taking than one individual making the decision on his own.
- The decision reached could be a compromise rather than the optimum solution.
- People become guilty of groupthink, the tendency of members of a group to conform to the established notions of the group.
- Groups may have difficulty performing jobs because the group, rather than a single individual, makes the decision, resulting in confusion when it comes time to implement and evaluate the decision.

The results of dozens of individual versus group functioning studies show that groups not only tend to make better decisions than a person acting alone, but align order, that groups tend to inspire star performers to even higher levels of productivity. Therefore, are two (or more) heads better than one? The answer depends on several factors, for example the nature of the job, the abilities of the group members, and the form of interaction. Because a manager frequently has a choice between making a decision independently or comprising others in the decision making, he needs to understand the merits and demerits of group decision making.

Analyzing the Alternatives

The main objective of this step is to decide the relative merits of each idea. Managers must identify the merits and demerits of each alternative solution before making a final decision.

Evaluating the alternatives can be done in several ways. Here are a few possibilities:

- Determine the pros and cons of each alternative.
- Perform a cost-benefit analysis for each alternative.

- Weigh each factor important in the decision, ranking each alternative relative to its power to meet each factor, and then multiply by a probability factor to provide a final value for each alternative.

Irrespective of the method used, a manager needs to evaluate each alternative in terms of its

- Feasibility: Can it be done?
- Effectiveness: How well does it resolve the problem situation?
- Consequences: What will be its costs (financial and non-financial) to the establishment?

Selecting the Best Alternative

After a manager has examined all the options, he must determine on the best one. The best substitute is the one that produces the most merits and the fewest serious demerits. Occasionally, the selection process can be fairly straightforward, for example the alternative with the most pros and fewest cons. Other times, the optimal solution is a combination of several alternatives. Occasionally, the best alternative may not be obvious. That's when a manager must decide which alternative is the most feasible and effectual, coupled with which carries the lowest costs to the establishment. Probability estimates, where analysis of each alternative's chances of success takes place, frequently come into play at this point in the decision-making process. In those cases, a manager simply selects the substitutes with the highest probability of success.

Implementing the Decision

Managers are paid to make decisions, but they are also paid to get results from these decisions. Positive results must follow decisions. Everyone involved with the decision must know his or his role in ensuring a successful outcome. To make certain that employees understand their roles, managers must thoughtfully devise programs, processes, rules, or policies to help aid them in the problem-solving process.

Establishing a Control and Evaluation System

Ongoing actions demand to be monitored. An evaluation system ought to provide feedback on how well the decision is being implemented, what the results are, and what adjustments are necessary to get the results that were intended when the solution was chosen. In order for a manager to evaluate his decision, he needs to gather information to determine its effectiveness. Was the original problem resolved? If not, is he closer to the required situation than he was at the setting out of the decision-making process?

If a manager's plan hasn't resolved the problem, he needs to figure out what went wrong. A manager may attain this by asking the following questions:

- Was the wrong alternative selected? If so, one of the other alternatives generated in the decision-making process may be a wiser choice.
- Was the correct alternative selected, but implemented improperly? If so, a manager ought to focus attention solely on the implementation step to ensure that the chosen alternative is implemented successfully.
- Was the original problem identified incorrectly? If so, the decision-making process needs to begin again, starting with a revised identification step.
- Has the implemented alternative been given enough time to be successful? If not, a manager ought to give the process more time and re-evaluate at a later date.

PRINCIPLES OF DECISION MAKING

Each decision we make has risks involved with it. Because of these risks, making decisions is much difficult. As you make decisions, keep in mind four fundamental principles:

- Never risk more than you can afford to give.
- Never risk more than you have.
- Never risk more than you can get in return.
- Follow you intuition.

Principle 1

Never risk more than you can afford to give denotes to more than just financial adventures. Never take any chance that demands more of yourself or your resources than you are willing and able to give. You alone know what you can afford -- in terms of time, energy, emotions, and so forth. Think about the decisions you make when you choose your courses at registration. You ought to not enrol in courses that demand a lot of outside class work if you aren't willing to put the time and effort into them outside school.

Principle 2

The second principle connotes that you are limited in resources. You don't have an unlimited supply of energy, time, space, or money, and you cannot risk more of these resources than you possess. Any decision uses one or more of these resources, but no action ought to deplete all your resources in any given area.

Principle 3

This principle suggests that you view each decision in terms of what it will create for you. Take a risk only when you can gain from it.

Principle 4

This principle simply intends that you ought to feel good about your decision. No one can make decisions for you. As a teenager, you may feel that your parents have forced you to make certain decisions. This is almost never true. Even when you allow another person to decide for you, you are still making a decision -- the decision to make the choices that another person wants you to make.

And finally, a decision is a commitment and it ought to be one you are willing to trust and abide by. Good decisions are those that open up more possibilities for future choices.

CONDITIONS THAT INFLUENCE DECISION MAKING

Managers make problem-solving decisions under three varied conditions: certainty, risk, and uncertainty. All managers make decisions under each condition, but risk and uncertainty are common to the more complicated and unstructured problems faced by top managers.

Certainty

Decisions are made under the circumstance of certainty when the manager has perfect knowledge of all the information necessitated to make a decision. This condition is ideal for problem solving. The challenge is simply to study the alternatives and choose the best solution. When problems tend to arise regularly, a manager may address them through standard or prepared responses called programmed decisions. These solutions are already available from past experiences and are appropriate for the problem at hand. A good example is the decision to reorder inventory automatically when stock falls below a determined level. Today, an increasing number of programmed decisions are being aided or handled by computers using decision-support software.

Integrated problems are recognizable, straight, and obvious with respect to the data required to solve them. A manager can frequently anticipate these problems and plan to prevent or solve them. For instance, personnel problems are common in regard to pay raises, promotions, vacation requests, and committee assignments, as examples. Proactive managers can plan processes for handling these charges effectively before they even occur.

Risk

In a risk environment, the manager lacks whole information. This condition is more difficult. A manager may understand the problem and the alternatives, but has no guarantee how each solution will work. Risk is a fairly common decision consideration for managers.

When new and unacquainted problems arise, non-programmed decisions are specifically tailored to the situations at hand. The information demands for defining and resolving non-routine problems are normally high. Though computer support may assist in information processing, the decision will most likely involve human judgment. Most problems faced by higher-level managers demand non-programmed decisions. This fact explains why the demands on a manager's conceptual skills increase as he or he moves into higher levels of managerial responsibility.

A crisis problem is an unexpected problem that can lead to disaster if it is not resolved quickly and properly. No establishment can avoid crises, and the public is well aware of the immensity of corporate crises in the modern world. The Chernobyl nuclear plant explosion in the former Soviet Union and the Exxon Valdez spill of years past are a couple of sensational examples. Managers in more progressive organizations now anticipate that crises, regrettably, will occur. These managers are installing early-warning crisis information systems and developing crisis management plans to deal with these states of affairs in the best possible ways.

Uncertainty

When information is so poor that managers can not even assign probabilities to the likely outcomes of alternatives, the manager is making a decision in an uncertain environment. This condition is the most difficult for a manager. Decision making under conditions of uncertainty is like being a pioneer entering unexplored territory. Uncertainty forces managers to rely heavily on creativity in solving problems. It requires exclusive and frequently totally pioneering alternatives to existing processes. Groups are often used for problem solving in such situations. In all cases, the responses to uncertainty depend significantly on hunch, educated guesses, and hunches - all of which leave significant room for error.

These unstructured problems involve ambiguities and information inadequacies and frequently occur as new or unanticipated situations. These problems are most frequently unanticipated and are addressed reactively as they occur. Unstructured problems require novel solutions. Proactive managers are occasionally able to get a jump on unstructured problems by realizing that a situation is susceptible to problems and then making contingency plans. For instance, at the Vanguard Group, executives are tireless in their preparations for a variety of events that could disrupt their mutual fund business. Their biggest fear is an investor panic that overloads their customer service system during a main plunge in the bond or stock markets. In anticipation of this occurrence, the firm has trained accountants, lawyers, and fund managers to staff the telephones if required.

PERSONAL DECISION MAKING STYLES

Managerial decision making depends on numerous factors, comprising the power to set priorities and time decisions correctly. Nevertheless, the most important influence on managerial decision making is a manager's personal attributes or his or his own decision-making approach. The three most common decision models are as follows:

- Rational/logical
- Intuitive
- Predisposed

Irrespective of the model favoured by a manager, understanding personal tendencies and moving toward a more rational model ought to be the manager's aim. The best decisions are in general a result of a blend of the decision maker's intuition and the rational step-by-step approach.

Logical Decision Model

This approach employs a bit-by-bit process, like the seven-step decision-making process. The realistic decision model focuses on facts and reasoning. Reliance is on the steps and decision tools, for example payback analysis, decision tree, and research. Through the use of quantitative techniques, rationality, and logic, the manager evaluates the alternatives and selects the best answer to the problem.

Intuitive Decision Model

The managers who use this scheme stay away from statistical analysis and coherent procedures. These managers are "instinctive" decision makers who rely on their feelings about a situation. This definition could easily lead one to believe that intuitive decision making is irrational or arbitrary. Though intuition refers to decision making without formal analysis or conscious reasoning, it is based on years of managerial practice and experience. These qualified managers identify alternatives speedily without conducting systematic analyses of alternatives and their consequences. When making a decision using intuition, the manager recognizes cues in the situation that are the same as or similar to those in former situations that he or he has experienced; the cues help the manager to quickly conduct subconscious analysis. Then a decision is made.

Predisposed Decision Model

A manager who decides on a solution and then collects material to support the decision uses the predisposed decision model approach. Decision makers using this approach don't search out all possible alternatives. Rather, they identify and evaluate alternatives only until an acceptable decision is found. Having found a satisfactory alternative, the decision maker stops searching for additional solutions. Other, and potentially better, alternatives may exist, but will not be identified or considered because the first workable solution has been accepted. Therefore, only a fraction of the available alternatives may be considered due to the decision maker's information-processing limitations. A manager with this tendency is likely to dismiss critical information and may face the same decision again afterwards.

DECISION MAKING WITH QUANTITATIVE TOOLS

Quantitative techniques aids a manager improve the overall quality of decision making. These techniques are most commonly used in the rational/logical decision model, but they can apply in any of the other models as well. Among the most general techniques are decision trees, payback analysis, and simulations.

Decision Trees

A decision tree shows a complete picture of a potential decision and permits a manager to graph alternative decision paths. Decision trees are a useful way to analyze employing, marketing, investments, equipment purchases, pricing, and similar decisions that involve a progression of smaller decisions. Generally, decision trees are used to evaluate decisions under conditions of risk. The term decision tree comes from the graphic appearance of the skill that starts with the initial decision shown as the base. The several alternatives, based upon possible future statuses, and the payoffs associated with each of the decisions branch from the trunk.

Decision trees force a manager to be explicit in analyzing considerations associated with future decisions and in determining the outcome of several alternatives. The decision tree is a flexible method. It can be used for many situations in which emphasis can be placed on sequential decisions, the probability of several conditions, or the highlighting of alternatives.

Payback Analysis

Payback study is useful if a manager calls for to determine whether to buy a piece of equipment. Let us say, for instance, that a manager is purchasing cars for a rental car company. Though a less-expensive car may take less time to pay off, some clients may want more luxurious models. To decide which cars to purchase, a manager ought to consider some factors, for example the expected useful life of the car, its warranty and repair record, its cost of insurance, and, of course, the rental demand for the car. Based on the information gathered, a manager can then rank alternatives based on the cost of each car. A higher-priced car may be more appropriate because of its longer life and customer rental demand. The strategy, of course, is for the manager to choose the substitute that has the quickest payback of the initial cost.

Many individuals use payback analysis when they decide whether they ought to go on with their education. They decide how much courses will cost, how much salary they will earn as a result of each course completed and perhaps, degree earned, and how long it will take to recoup the investment. If the gains outbalance the costs, the payback is worthwhile.

Simulations

Simulation is a broad term suggesting any type of activity that attempts to simulate an existing system or situation in a simplified manner. Simulation is fundamentally model building, in which the simulator is trying to gain understanding by replicating something and then manipulating it by adjusting the variables used to build the model. Simulations have great potential in decision making. In the fundamental decision-making steps, Step 4 is the evaluation of alternatives. If a manager could simulate alternatives and predict their outcomes at this point in the decision process, he or he would carry off much of the guesswork from decision making.

Note: For a very good study of Decision making Process see: de Alwis, Shrianjani Marie (Gina) & Higgins, Susan Ellen (2001) "Information as a tool for management decision making: a case study of Singapore." Information Research, 7(1) [Available at http:// InformationR.net/ir/7-1/paper114.html]

5

Organizational Planning

Among all the five management functions; planning, organizing, staffing, leading and controlling, planning is the most fundamental. All other functions stem from planning. Nevertheless, planning does not always get the attention that it deserves; when it does, many managers discover that the planning process is not as easy as they thought it would be - or that even the best-laid plans can go awry.

DEFINING PLANNING

Before a manager can tackle any of the other functions, he or he must first devise a plan. A plan is a blueprint for objectives achievement that specifies the necessary resource allocations, schedules, jobs, and other actions.

An aim is a required future state that the establishment attempts to realize. Aims are significant because an organization exists for a function, and aims fix and state that purpose. Aims specify future ends; plans specify today's means. The word planning incorporates both ideas: It means determining the establishment's aims and defining the means for achieving them. Planning allows managers the chance to adjust to the environment instead of merely reacting to it. Planning increases the possibility of survival in business by actively anticipating and managing the risks that may occur in the future.

In brief, planning is like preparing for tomorrow. It is the action that allows managers to decide what they want and how they will attain it. Not only does planning provide direction and a unity of goal for organizations, it also replies to six fundamental questions in regard to any activity:

- What needs to be attained?
- When is the deadline?

- Where will this be done?
- Who will be accountable for it?
- How will it get done?
- How much time, energy, and resources are called for to attain this aim?

NATURE AND PURPOSE OF ORGANIZATIONAL PLANNING

Organizations that fail to plan are in principle planning to fail, discuss this statement. In your answer, consider types of organizational plans, and the link between planning and the strategic management process. Support your answer with instances drawn from real organizations, using textbooks, journals, newspapers, business magazines, and periodicals. Managing organizations in the 21st century has changed in many ways compared to the managing system used in the olden days. Starting from the structure of the establishment itself, how they plan, how they make decision, up until now while doing things; but one thing that has not changed is that organizations which perform with an outstanding result, never neglect their planning.

Each establishment contends with each other to perform better in accordance to others. These changes are made in order to form a better establishment each day as well as better results at the end of all progress. This essay will examine why organizations that fail to plan are in essence planning to fail, as well the types of organizational plans; hence the link between planning and strategic management process. "Organizations that fail to plan are in essence planning to fail". From this statement it is clearly understood that organizations which don't plan their future organizational ends are more likely to fail. Not only is this applicable in the perspective of management. Anything that is done without planning is very unlikely to succeed.

A well defined plan in academic term means "a drawing or diagram showing the arrangement in horizontal section of a structure, piece of ground" (Webster's Dictionary). In planning, the very first step is to set an aim which is defined as "statements of intended results that are general in nature and are measurable on a naming or ranking scale of measurement".

It is crucial to plan every single step and thing that is needed to be done to avoid failure. Therefore, the importance to understand the purposes to plan; which is allowing for a direction about what the establishment does, and what and why it needs to be attained in order that the organization, as a whole, knows exactly what they are demanded to do. Hence when they know what to do, they can work together with other staff to attain the aims that been set. For example when the plan is set, the staff can easily refer to the master plan and remind themselves what each of them are necessitated to do.

Planning cuts down doubt and makes sure everybody is committed to the fulfilling the aim. It also forces the staff to expect any changes so they can construct an appropriate response. In simpler terms, planning makes it easier to deal with uncertainty. For example, where there is uncertainty or any problem in an establishment, they know what to do and are faster to react. To minimize waste or redundancy is another one of the vital reasons to plan. This mean that the organization makes sure that nothing is left out or wasted in order to reach an efficient result at the end of the day. These include time and financial resources. For instance when dealing with the food industry where the stocks are bound to the expiry date, organizations have to make sure of the amount necessitated in a certain period of time so it doesn't result in waste of stock, dropped dead food stock.

The last reason is to set a standard. This keeps affairs on track, or in the terms of a managerial role it is known as controlling, as well as being a reference in competing with other companies. This ensures us of what we are trying to attain, and whether or not we attained it yet. For example, organizations keep track of the progress of their plan by determining their position in accordance to the plan daily, weekly, monthly or annually. Even although many cases show that performance organizations that plan are mostly do well, cannot be said that organizations that didn't plan always fail.

Generally terms, planning can be referred to in two ways: formal and informal. Formal planning means concentrating on the accomplishment of the aims. Simple thing for example setting a period of time to attain that aim and writing down a list can be shared by all through the organizational structure so everyone knows what they have to do, where they have to go also have something to refer back to while they are at it.

Informal planning is the opposite of the formal planning which is generally present in a small commercial enterprise or establishment. Informal planning isn't as well organized because it isn't written and there is limited sharing among individuals due to an abstract form of it. This shows that formal planning is addressed for a bigger organizational structure that wants to attain their future organizational purpose positively because it assists them in formalizing and systemizing all the processes being made. There are several types of organizational plans. However, this essay will only discuss the three major types of planning in an establishment: budget planning, project planning, and strategic planning. The best way to categorise each of the organizational plans is via its breadth, time-frame, specificity and frequency of use.

In specific terms, a budget is a plan of action matched by resources required to implement the plan. Put differently, a budget is a plan. Budgets in general separate between two extensive categories: the operating budget, occasionally known as the "expense" budget and the capital budget. Budget in simpler terms mean a sum of money allocated for a particular purpose. Budget is in everyone's life, be it a small or a big one. Budget is a tool which helps in controlling and planning the functions of an establishment. It is a formalized statement of the aims of an establishment stated in financial terms and accomplishes several important functions for managers. It states future projections of revenues, expenses and expected profits. Planning, evaluating performance, coordinating activities, implementing plans, communicating, motivating and authorising actions are the main functions of a budget. The budget period depends upon the action plan; it might be for a short or long duration. A budget compels the managers to think ahead by formalizing their responsibilities for planning, and is best framework for judging later performance and aids managers in co-ordinating their efforts, in order that the plans of an establishment meets the objectives of the establishment as a whole.

To design a project a team ought to have a target and ought to act as one unit to carry out certain objectives. In project planning, team members ought to enforce inventive ideas that would serve their aim in a resourceful way. Each individual on a team ought to take part in the planning process, because the diversity of team members and their several views can produce more than one approach to initiate a project. Project planning can be explained as determining the aims and objectives of a project through a co-ordination of processes and determination of courses of action before initiating a project. Project planning is a rational determination of how to initiate, sustain, and finalize a project. There are many steps to be taken when planning a project within a team. To have a successful plan when working with a team, set a role of conduct for the team members.

Define what each individual's responsibility is and what to be anticipated from them. Each project ought to be broken down into specific jobs; it is important to find ways to divide the work into manageable parts. All projects encounter problems and conflicts. In order to have an early solution to those problems, team members ought to discuss each potential problem that they might face. Team members ought to have a logical approach to problem solving.

All problems must be predefined. Also, a deadline for the project is of the essence. If time to get done with the project isn't controlled then the project itself can't be controlled. Team members have to prioritize and work on a certain pace. They might also have a set schedule on when each job within the project ought to be done. Another important point in project planning is communication. Team members ought to always give each other a feedback on the progress of their jobs or roles and what have they carried out. The process of communication and its result helps diminish the conflict of change. Discussing ideas within team members is a process where each individual ought to contribute in. Having different ideas will make the project unique and will produce more than one method acting to reach the project's aim.

There is a connection between planning and strategic management process. Planning is one part, although small, of the strategic management process. This can be shown using the roles of corporate managers. One of the four major roles of a manager is to plan. This planning plays a crucial part in determining the success of an organization as mentioned earlier. But first, we have to ask: What is "strategic management process?" and "What are the steps in the process". There isn't just one definition of the phrase "strategic management process".

The definition, although similar, differs in accordance with individual's personal opinions. For instance, Johnson views it as a six-step process. Though the first six steps describe the planning that must take place, implementation and evaluation are just as important. Even the finest strategies can fall short if management doesn't put into practice or assess them the right way.

The first step in strategic management process is identifying the organization's current mission, objective and strategies. Every organization necessitates a statement of the purpose of the organization, also called a mission. The mission verifies the reason for which the company is in the business. To do this, managers must vigilantly recognize the range of its products and services.

It is also vital for managers to identify the aims and strategies presently being pursued in the company. Aims are a foundation of planning which provide the measurable performance targets that the organization as a whole strives to reach. By being aware of current aims allows managers to decide whether or not these current aims need to be altered. This can also be applied to strategies presently in place.

The second step is analyzing the environment. Analyzing the environment is a vital step in the scheme process. Robbins describes the extraneous environment as a significant basis on a manager's actions. To outline a successful strategy, it must be supported well by the environment. In this step, managers need to know what is going on outside the organization. Information for example what the competitors are doing, what on-going laws might affect the organization and what degree of labour supply is available around the area where the company is located. Aside from analysing the external environment, managers must also examine specific and general environments to observe and be conscious of the trends and changes which are taking place. This step of the process can be considered complete when the manager has an accurate understanding of what is occurring in the external environment and the developments which could possibly involve the organization.

Following this, managers need to evaluate the results they have attained in step 2 and determine the opportunities which the company can utilize and threats it encounters. This is all part of the SWOT analysis. Robbins defines opportunities as a positive development in the external environment and threats as negative trends. After identifying threats and opportunities, managers must now look inside the organization by analysing the organization's resources and capabilities. This comprises employees' skills, the organization's resources, success at innovating products, quality of products, the organization's financial position, and the way customers distinguish the organization. All of these show that no matter how large or how small an organization is, the organization is bound to the availability of resources and capabilities. This analysis of the internal environment allows managers to recognize specific capabilities and resources. When these capabilities and resources are outstandingly unique, they can be used as competitive weapons. This fundamental value-generating technique is referred to as core competencies.

From the former step, the organization now ought to have a comprehensible assessment of its inner resources as well as its potentialities in carrying out several practical activities. Strengths are any strong capabilities the organization possesses or unique resource materials. Weaknesses are the activities which the organization doesn't perform well or the want of resources which they need. Robbins states that different strengths and drawbacks have different outcomes on the strategy being pursued. An organization's culture is its personality or characteristics. It is a sign of the organization's mutual beliefs and values. When an organization has a strong culture, it becomes more straightforward for managers to convey the organization's core competencies and strengths to new employees.

However, strong cultures are difficult to change. It then becomes a barrier to acknowledging any alterations in the organization's strategies. "Successful organizations with strong cultures may become prisoners of their own success". Strategies need to be formulated in all levels of an organization, be it a corporate, business or functional level. This follows a decision-making process. Strategic alternatives must first be assessed. Managers must select strategies which harmonize with each other and bring out the best of the organization in terms of its strengths and environmental opportunities. A successful strategy would be one that puts the organization at a relative merit over its competitors and the most favourable aggressive edge. The organization must try and maintain this merit to call the strategy a victory.

As cited earlier, the first six steps are the designing of strategies. After an organization comes up with strategies, they must apply it. The same efforts put into planning the strategies must be put into implementing it. No matter how effectual the strategies are, if the organization fails to apply it properly, these strategies will be deemed useless. Implementing strategies expeditiously frequently means that the organization has to hire new individuals with different skills, relocating a portion of current employees to new positions, or in the worst case, make redundant some employees. Most organizations now-a-days run their management using teams. Therefore, building and managing effectual teams is power in implementing strategies efficiently. Top-management leadership is every bit as important. So is a inspired group of middle and lower-managers who perform the organization's specific scheme needs.

The final step in the strategic management process is measuring the results of the strategies in terms of effectiveness, and adjustments that need to be made to improve the success of strategies. In conclusion, the four key factors for success when implementing change within an organization are: pressure for change; a clear, shared vision; capacity for change; and action. The numerous types of organizational plans as well as the implementation of strategic management process play an important role in planning and managing change. Change management entails thoughtful planning and sensitive implementation, and above all, consultation with, and involvement of, the individuals pretended by the changes. The four key factors for success when implementing change within an organization are: pressure for change; a clear, shared vision; capacity for change; and action.

THE STRATEGIC MANAGEMENT PROCESS

Three ongoing process- analysis, decisions, and actions-that are central to strategic management. In practice, these three process-often referred to as strategy analysis, strategy formulation, and strategy implementation-are highly interdependent. Further, these three processes do not take place one after the other in a sequential fashion in most companies. Henry Mintzberg, a very influential management scholar at McGill University, argues that conceptualizing the strategic management process as one in which analysis is followed by optimal decisions and their subsequent meticulous implementation neither describes the strategic management process accurately nor prescribes ideal practice. In his view, the business environment is far from predictable, thus limiting our ability for analysis. Further, decisions in an organization are seldom based on optimal rationality alone, given the political processes that occur in all organizations.

Taking into consideration the limitations discussed above, Mintzberg proposed an alternative model of strategy development. For a variety of reasons, the intended strategy rarely survives in its original form. Unforeseen environmental developments, unanticipated resource constraints, or changes in managerial preferences may result in at least some parts of the intended strategy remaining unrealized. On the other hand, good managers will want to take advantage of new opportunity presented by the environment even if it was not part of the original set of intentions. The SARS crisis in Southeast Asia is a completely unexpected environmental development. If managers of pharmaceutical firms redeploy their R&D capabilities to develop a drug to fight SARS, that would be an emergent strategy. The final realized strategy of any firm is thus a combination of deliberate and emergent strategies.

ADVANTAGES OF PLANNING

There is a well known military saying, "If you fail to plan, you plan to fail," is very true. Without a plan, managers are set up to encounter errors, waste, and delays. A plan, alternatively, helps a manager organize resources and activities expeditiously and effectively to attain aims.

The merits of planning are numerous. Planning fulfils the following goal:

- Gives an establishment a sense of direction. Without plans and aims, organizations simply react to daily occurrences without considering what will happen in the long run. For instance, the solution that makes sense in the short term does not always make sense in the long term. Plans avoid this drift situation and ensure that short-range efforts will support and harmonize with future aims.
- Focuses attention on objectives and results. Plans keep the individuals who carry them out focused on the anticipated results. Additionally, keeping sight of the aim also motivates employees.
- Establishes a basis for teamwork. Diverse groups cannot effectively cooperate in joint projects without an integrated plan. Examples are numerous: Plumbers, carpenters, and electricians cannot build a house without blueprints. Additionally, military activities require the co-ordination of Army, Navy, and Air Force units.
- Helps anticipate problems and cope with change. When management plans, it can help forecast future problems and make any necessary changes up front to avoid them. Of course, surprises - for example the 1973 quadrupling of oil prices - can always catch an establishment short, but many changes are easier to forecast. Planning for these potential problems helps to minimize mistakes and reduce the "surprises" that inevitably occur.
- Provides guidelines for decision making. Decisions are future-oriented. If management does not have any plans for the future, they will have few guidelines for making current decisions. If a company knows that it wants to introduce a new product three years in the future, its management must be mindful of the decisions they make now. Plans help both managers and employees keep their eyes on the big picture.
- Serves as a prerequisite to employing all other management functions. Planning is basic, because without knowing what an establishment wants to accomplish, management can not intelligently contract any of the other fundamental managerial activities: organizing, staffing, leading, and/or controlling.

Using Plans to Attain Aims

Planning is an essential activity, for it intends the map that lays the foundation for the other purposes. The plan itself specifies what ought to be done, by whom, where, when, and how. All businesses - from the smallest restaurant to the largest multinational corporation - need to develop plans for achieving success. But before an establishment can plan a course of action, it must first determine what it wants to attain. Aims, the end results required by the establishment, are deduced from the establishment's mission statement. The mission statement explains what the organization stands for and why it exists. A strong mission statement symbolizes legitimacy to outside audiences, for example investors, customers, and suppliers. Similarly, a strong mission statement permits employees to identify with the overall purpose of the establishment and commit to preserving it.

The mission statement is the foundation for all aims and plans outlined all through the establishment. Therefore, managers must use effectual planning and aim-setting techniques to ensure that internal policies, roles, performances, structures, products, and expenditures are in line with the mission of the establishment.

Criteria for Effectual Aims

To make sure that aim setting gains the establishment, managers must adopt certain characteristics and guidelines. The following describes these criteria:

- Aims must be particular and computable: When possible, use quantitative terms, for example increasing profits by two percent or decreasing learner enrolment by one percent, to express aims.
- Aims ought to cover up key end result areas: Because aims cannot be set for every aspect of employee or organizational performance, managers ought to identify a few key result areas. These key areas are those activities that contribute most to company performance - for instance, customer relations or sales.
- Aims ought to be ambitious but not too hard: When aims are unrealistic, they set employees up for failure and lead to low employee morale. However, if aims are too easy, employees may not feel inspired. Managers must be sure that aims are determined based on existing resources and aren't beyond the team's time, equipment, and financial resources.

- Aims ought to define the time period over which they will be attained: Deadlines give team members something to work toward and help ensure continued progress. At the same time, managers ought to set short-term deadlines along the way in order that their subordinates aren't overwhelmed by one big, seemingly non-accomplishable aim. It would be more proper to provide a short term aim for example, "Establish a customer database by June 30."
- Aims ought to be related to rewards: Individuals who attain aims ought to be rewarded with something meaningful and related to the aim. Not only will employees feel that their efforts are valued, but they will also have something tangible to prompt them in the future.

SETTING OBJECTIVES

At all the levels, management ought to have projects that work together to attain the organization's goal. The plans of the top-, middle-, and first-level managers of an establishment ought to work together to attain the main aim.

All managers plan fundamentally the same way, but the sorts of plans they develop and the amount of time they spend on planning vary. Here are some examples:

- Top-level managers are concerned with longer time periods and with plans for larger organizational units. Their planning comprises developing the mission for the organizational units, the organizational objective, and major policy areas. These aims are called strategic aims or objectives.
- Middle-level managers' planning responsibilities centre on translating broad objectives of top-level management into more specific aims for work units. These aims are called tactical aims or objectives.
- First-level managers are involved in day-to-day plans, for example scheduling work hours, deciding what work will be done and by whom, and developing structures to reach these aims. These aims are called operational aims or objectives.

If a first-level manager develops a set of plans that contradicts that of a middle-level manager, conflicts will result. Therefore, all managers must work together when planning their activities and the activities of others.

MANAGEMENT BY OBJECTIVES

Management by Objectives isn't a new concept, but its implementation is new in industrial set-up. The concept of 'Management by Objectives' (MBO) was first given by Peter Drucker in 1954. It can be defined as a process whereby the employees and the superiors come together to identify common aims, the employees set their aims to be attained, the standards to be taken as the criteria for measurement of their performance and contribution and deciding the course of action to be followed. The essence of MBO is participative aim setting, choosing course of actions and decision making. An important part of the MBO is the measurement and the comparison of the employee's real performance with the standards set. Ideally, when employees themselves have been involved with the aim setting and the choosing the course of action to be followed by them, they are more likely to fulfil their responsibilities.

Policies and Planning

The principle behind Management by Objectives (MBO) is to create empowered employees who have clarity of the roles and responsibilities expected from them, understand their objectives to be attained and therefore help in the achievement of organizational as well as personal aims.

Some of the significant features and merits of MBO are:

- Clarity of aims - With MBO, came the concept of SMART aims i.e. aims that are:
  - — Specific
  - — Measurable
  - — Achievable
  - — Realistic
  - — Time bound

The aims therefore set are clear, motivating and there is a linkage between organizational aims and performance targets of the employees.

- The focussing is on future tense instead of on past. Aims and standards are set for the performance for the future with periodic reviews and feedback.
- Motivation - Taking employees in the entire process of aim setting and increasing employee empowerment increases employee job satisfaction and commitment.

- Better communicating and Classification - repeated reviews and interactions between superiors and subordinates helps to maintain harmonious relationships within the enterprise and also solve many problems faced all through the period.

DETAILING TYPES OF PLANS

Plans devote people, departments, organizations, and the resources of each to specific actions for the time to come. Effectively designed organizational aims fit into a hierarchy in order that the achievement of aims at low levels permits the attainment of high-level aims. This process is called a means-ends chain because low-level aims lead to accomplishment of high-level aims. Three major types of plans can help managers attain their establishment's aims: strategic, tactical, and operational. Operational plans lead to the achievement of tactical plans, which in turn lead to the attainment of strategic plans. Additionally to these three types of plans, managers ought to also formulate a contingency plan in case their original plans fail.

Operational Plans

The specific results anticipated from departments, work groups, and individuals are the operational aims. These aims are precise and measurable. "Process 150 sales applications each week" or "Publish 20 books this quarter" are examples of operational aims.

An operational plan is one that a manager uses to come upon his or his task responsibilities. Supervisors, team leaders, and facilitators develop operational plans to support tactical plans. Operational plans can be a single-use plan or an ongoing plan.

- Single-use plans utilize activities that don't reoccur or recur. A one-time happening, for example a special sales program, is a single-use plan because it deals with the who, what, where, how, and how much of an activity. A budget is also a single-use plan because it predicts sources and amounts of income and how much they are used for a specific project.
- Continuing or ongoing plans are generally made once and keep their value over a period of years while undergoing periodic revisions and updates. The following are examples of ongoing plans:
- A policy allows for a broad guideline for managers to follow when dealing with significant areas of decision making. Policies

are general statements that explain how a manager ought to attempt to handle routine management responsibilities. Typical human resources policies, for instance, address such matters as employee employing, terminations, performance appraisals, pay increases, and discipline.

- A process is a set of bit-by-bit directions that explains how activities or projects are to be carried out. Most organizations have processes for purchasing supplies and equipment, for instance. This process in general begins with a supervisor completing a purchasing requisition. The requisition is then sent to the next level of management for approval. The sanctioned requisition is forwarded to the purchasing department. Depending on the amount of the request, the purchasing department may place an order, or they may need to secure quotations and/or bids for several vendors before placing the order. By defining the steps to be taken and the order in which they are to be done, processes provide a standardized way of responding to a repetitious problem.
- A rule is an expressed statement that tells an employee what he or he can and cannot do. Rules are "do" and "do not" statements put into place to promote the safety of employees and the uniform treatment and behaviour of employees. For instance, rules about tardiness and absenteeism permit supervisors to make discipline decisions rapidly and with a high degree of fairness.

Tactical Plans

A tactical plan is related with what the lower level units within each division must do, how they must do it, and who is in charge at different levels. Tactics are the means needed to activate a strategy and make it work. Tactical plans are concerned with shorter time frames and narrower scopes than are strategic plans. These plans in general span one year or less because they are considered short-term aims. Long-term aims, alternatively, can take several years or more to accomplish. Usually, it is the middle manager's responsibility to take the broad strategic plan and identify specific tactical actions.

Strategic Plans

A strategic plan is a draft of steps planned with the aims of the whole organization in mind, rather than with the ends of specific sections or departments. Strategic planning begins with an establishment's mission. Strategic plans look ahead over the next two, three, five, or even more years to move the establishment from where it presently is to where it wants to be. Requiring multilevel involvement, these plans demand harmony among all levels of management within the establishment. Top-level management develops the directional objectives for the entire establishment, while lower levels of management develop compatible objectives and plans to attain them. Top management's strategic plan for the whole establishment becomes the framework and sets dimensions for the lower level planning.

Contingency Plans

Sound and productive management depends upon a constant pursuit of adjustment, flexibleness, and mastery of changing conditions. Strong management requires a "keeping all options open" approach at all times - that's where contingency planning comes in.

Contingency planning necessitates identifying alternative courses of action that can be implemented if and when the original plan proves poor because of changing circumstances. Keep in mind that events beyond a manager's control may cause even the most carefully prepared alternative future scenarios to go awry. Unexpected problems and events often occur. When they do, managers may need to change their plans. Anticipating change during the planning process is best in case things do not go as expected. Management can then develop alternatives to the existing plan and ready them for use when and if conditions make these alternatives appropriate.

ROADBLOCKS TO PLANNING

Numerous barriers can inhibit successful planning. In order for plans to be effectual and to yield the required results, managers must identify any potential barriers and work to get over them. The common barriers that bottle up successful planning are as follows:

- Inability to plan or inadequate planning: Managers aren't born with the power to plan. Some managers aren't successful planners because they lack the background, education, and/or ability. Others may have never been taught how to plan. When these two types of managers take the time to plan, they may not know how to conduct planning as a process.
- Want of commitment to the planning process: The development of a plan is hard work; it is much easier for a manager to claim that he or she does not have the time to work through the expected planning process than to actually devote the time to developing a plan. (The latter, of course, would save them

more time in the long run) Another possible reason for want of commitment can be fear of failure. As a result, managers may choose to do little or nothing to help in the planning process.

- Inferior information: Facts that are out-of-date, of poor quality, or of insufficient amount can be major barriers to planning. No matter how well managers plan, if they are basing their planning on inferior information, their plans will probably fail.
- Focusing on the present at the expense of the future: Failure to consider the long-term effects of a plan because of emphasis on short-term problems may lead to trouble in preparing for the future. Managers ought to try to keep the big picture - their long-term aims - in mind when developing their plans.
- Too much reliance on the establishment's planning department: Many organizations have a planning department or a planning and development team. These departments conduct studies, do research, build models, and project probable results, but they don't implement plans. Planning department results are aids in planning and ought to be used only therefore. Inventing the plan is still the manager's responsibility.
- Concentrating on controllable variables: Managers can find themselves concentrating on the things and events that they can control, such as new product development, but then fail to consider outside factors, such as a poor economy. One reason may be that managers demonstrate a decided preference for the known and an averting to the unknown.

The good thing about these barriers is that they can all be get over. To plan successfully, managers need to use effectual communication, assume quality information, and solicit the involvement of others.

Note: In Organizational planning, there is no better example than Toyota Motor Corporation. Toyota's management doctrine has developed from the company's origins and has been reflected in the terms "Lean Manufacturing" and Just in Time Production. The Toyota Way has four components: 1) Long-term thinking as a basis for management decisions, 2) a process for problem-solving, 3) adding value to the establishment by developing its individuals, and 4) recognizing that continuously solving root problems drives organizational learning. The Toyota Way incorporates the Toyota Production System. For further knowledge, reader can visit Toyota's site: http://www.toyota.co.jp/en/vision/code_of_conduct/index.html

6

Perception Process

In the management view perception is reality. Organizations are accountable to their stakeholders and stakeholders hold certain perceptions of these companies, based on their actions, words and behaviours. Perceptions vary from stakeholder group to stakeholder group but however must be recognized and understood before they can be managed and leveraged. In conventional public relations practice, insufficient attention is given to the view from the external environment. Leadership may not be sensitive enough to perceptions that exist in the marketplace. Public relations and communications campaigns frequently address the needs of the enterprise through inside-out one-way messaging initiatives. To be truly effectual, messages must consider the needs of the stakeholder and be strategic, i.e. they must be aimed towards helping to shape or change perceptions.

As per Millicent Danker, Managing perceptions means communicating with an outside-in view. He believes messages must be measured by their power to change or enhance perceptions held by the stakeholder group towards the enterprise, company or brand. In moving from Perception to Reality, organizations can manage and turn around negative perceptions of their organizations. Meanwhile, organizations can also build value and enhance reputational assets by managing positive perceptions to advantage.

Organizations must recognise perception gaps where they exist, and address them through appropriate change programmes. Finally, organizations can then begin the job of communicating messages founded on truth and fact. Over time, organizations can grow their organizations into enterprises whose values represent those sought by their key stakeholder groups. The perception management process is a continuum and it begins and ends with research. The role of communication is an indispensable part of the process.

MANAGING THE PERCEPTION PROCESS

Successful managers understand the importance of perception as an influencing factor on behaviour, and they act consequently. They are aware of perceptual distortion and they know that perceptual divergences are likely to exist in any situation. And the end result is that they make decisions and take appropriate action as and when required. A manger that is skilled in the perception process will have:

- A successful manager is able to influence the perception of others in order that the work events and situations are interpreted as accurately as possible and to the advantage of all the concerned individuals.
- Avoid common perceptual distortions that bias the views of individuals and situations. These distortions include the use of stereotypes and halo effects.
- Avoid inappropriate attributions. Everyone has a tendency to try and explain why events happen the way they did or why individuals behaved as they did. A successful manager is able to establish the real reason why these things happened and avoid these things from repeating themselves in the future.
- Be emphatic - that is able to see a situation properly and not as it is perceived by others.
- Have a high level of self-awareness. Individual necessitates experience and expectations can all affect perception. The successful manager knows this and is able to identify when he or he is inappropriately distorting a situation because of such perceptual tendencies.
- Seeks information from numerous sources to confirm personal impressions before making a difficult decision. A successful manager minimizes the influence of personal perception by taking the views of all the individuals around him. The insights gained by taking the views are used to the advantage of his decision making and solve the problems then and there.
- The successful manager rises above the personal impressions to understand the problems seen by others. Influence perception of other individuals when they are drawing incorrect or incomplete impressions of events in the work settings. Individuals act as per their own perceptions.

PERCEPTUAL CONSTANCY

A more subtle part of perceptual organization is constancy, our power to comprehend certain characteristics of an object as remaining constant. Despite vibrations in the stimuli that provides us the conflicting information. Such constancy amidst changing stimuli is essential.

Perceptual Set: Previously held beliefs about objects, influence an individual's perception of similar objects is called the perceptual set. For instance, a manger may have developed perception of his own, that workers are lazy and shirkers and they without doing any work expect everything from the management. His subsequent perceptions will be influenced by this preset mindset when he meets a different group of workers.

Perceptual perspective: The perspective in which an object is placed influence perception. Contextual influence on perception: the visual stimulus by itself is meaningful only when the object is placed in front but in the verbal perspective it goes meaningless to the listener.

The organizational culture and structure provide the basic perspective in which the workers and managers do their perceiving. Therefore a verbal order, a memo, a new policy, a suggestion, a raised eyebrow or a pat on the back takes on special meaning and value when placed in the perspective of the work organization.

Perceptual Defence: As per the principle of the perceptual defence, an individual is likely to defend himself when confronted with conflicting, unacceptable or threatening stimuli. The defence mechanism put up by the perceiver may assume any of the forms given below;

- Outright denial
- Modification of the data received
- Change in perception but refusal to change.

PERCEPTUAL SELECTIVITY

Perceptual selection is the process by which individuals filter out irrelevant or less important information in order that they can deal with the most important matters. Perceptual Selection is determined by:

1. External Factors
2. Internal Factors

External Factors Affecting Perceptual Selection

Size: The larger the size, the more likely it is to be perceived. The tallest person in the office will invariably be noticed.

Intensity: The more intense an external factor (bright light, loud noise, high pitch sound etc.) the more likely it is to be perceived. One may notice that the TV commercials always have high pitch as compared to normal telecast.

Contrast: External factors that stand out against the background or things that aren't which individuals expect are more likely to be perceived.

Motion: A moving factor is more likely to be perceived than stationary factor. Films (motion pictures) attract individuals more than a static picture.

Repetition: A repeated factor is more likely to be noticed. Marketing managers use this principle in trying to get attention of the prospective customers.

Novelty and familiarity: Either novelty or familiarity can attract attention. Individuals would quickly notice a person riding an elephant on a busy street in Delhi. Alternatively, one is likely to spot a familiar face in a crowd or a familiar voice even if there is a lot of noise and confusion.

A combination of these or similar factor may be operating at any time to affect perception. Along with the internal factors, they determine whether any particular stimulus is more or less likely to be noticed.

Internal Factors Affecting Perceptual Selection

Personality: Personality has an interesting influence on what and how individuals perceive. For example, conscientious individuals tend to pay more attention to external environmental cues than does a less conscientious person. Less conscientious persons are impulsive, careless, and irresponsible. They see their environment as hectic and unstable which affects the way they make perceptual selections. Alternatively, more conscientious individuals organize their perceptions into neat categories, allowing themselves to retrieve data quickly and in an organized manner. In other words, they are careful, methodical, and disciplined in constructing perceptual selections.

Learning: Learning determines the development of perceptual sets. A perceptual set is an expectation of a particular interpretation based on past experiences with the same or an identical object. In organizational settings, past experiences of the managers and employees influence their perceptions to a great extent.

Motivation: A person's most urgent needs and desires at any particular time can influence perception. Individuals perceive things that promise to help satisfy their needs and that they have found rewarding in the past. Also, as per Pollyanna principle, individuals process pleasant event more efficiently and accurately than they do unpleasant events. For instance, an employee who receives both positive and negative feedback during the appraisal meeting may more easily and clearly remember the positive statements than the negative ones.

Perceptual Organization

Figure-ground: Comprehended objects stand out as severable from their general backdrop. In the setting of organizations, a company may import a new technology in order to compete in the globalized economy. Here import of a new technology is a figure and universal competitive environment is the background. The employees will immediately notice the installation of new technology whereas the universal competitive environment isn't visible by naked eyes.

Perceptual grouping: There is a global trend among individuals to group several stimuli together into a recognisable pattern. There are certain underlying uniformities in grouping. When simple constellations of stimuli are presented to individuals, they tend to group them together by closure, persistence, proximity, and similarity.

Closure: An individual may comprehend a whole while one really doesn't subsist. The person's perceptual process closes the gaps that are unfilled by from sensory inputs. In a formal establishment, employees may either see a 'whole' that doesn't exit or not be able to put the pieces together into a 'whole' that does exist. For instance, head of a project team may take the view that the entire team agrees to his plan of action whereas there are differing views among the team members, which remain unarticulated in a formal manner. Alternatively, a functional team might view/perceive that their objectives are the objectives of the whole company.

Continuity. A person tends to comprehend continuous lines/forms. This leads to unbending thinking on the part of organizational members (both managers and employees). Therefore, only the obvious, continuous patterns or relationships are perceived. For example, a new design for some production process or product may be limited to obvious flows or continuous lines/patterns. New innovative ideas or designs may not be perceived.

Proximity: A group of stimulants that are approximate will be perceived as a altogether pattern of parts going together. For instance, several employees in an establishment may be identified as a single group because of physical proximity. Several workers who work on a particular process may be viewed as a single whole. If the output is low and the supervisor reports a number of grievances from the group, the management may perceive that all the workers working on that particular process are trouble makers whereas in some of them might be loyal and dedicated employees.

Similarity: The larger the similarity of stimuli, the larger is the tendency to perceive them as a mutual group. Similarity is conceptually related to proximity but in most cases stronger than proximity. In an establishment, all employees who wear blue collars may be perceived as a common group, when in reality, each employee is a unique individual. This might also lead to perceptual error termed as stereotyping.

Perceptual Constancy: There are two issues. While object reality of stimuli remains unchanged, individual's subjective reality also remains constant. That is, the individual is likely to give meaning to stimuli in the same way whenever exposed to them unless and until objective reality has been revealed more broadly by way of undoing the perceptual errors. For instance, a manager in the company who believes that female employees are poor performers would continue to have the same perception until and unless the latter prove that they are better than their male colleagues.

Perceptual Perspective: It gives importance and value to simple stimuli in the environment. The organizational culture and structure provide the basic perspective in which workers and managers perceive things. Therefore, a verbal order, an e-mail message, a new policy, a suggestion, a raised eyebrow, a pat on the back takes on special meaning and value when placed in the perspective of work establishment. Organizing raw sensory stimuli into meaningful experiences involves cognition, a set of mental activities that comprises thinking, knowing, and remembering. Knowledge and experience are highly important to perception, because they help us make sense of the input to our sensory systems.

Gestalt Laws of Grouping

An interesting topic in Gestalt psychology is how individuals comprehend a well-co-ordinated form or whole, instead of many different parts. As per Gestalt psychologists, the whole is different than the sum of its parts. Gestalt is a German word meaning configuration or pattern. A major aim of Gestalt theory in the 20th century was to specify the brain processes that might account for the establishment of perception. Gestalt theorists, main among them the German-U.S. psychologists and philosophers, the founder of Gestalt theory, Max Wertheimer and the German-U.S. psychologists Kurt Koffka and Wolfgang Köhler, rejected the earlier assumption that perceptual establishment was the product of learned relationships (associations), the constituent elements of which were called simple sensations. Though Gestaltists agreed that simple sensations logically could be understood to include organized percepts, they argued that percepts themselves were introductory to experience. One doesn't perceive so many discrete dots (as simple sensations), for example; the percept is that of a dotted line.

Without denying that learning can play some role in perception, many theorists took the position that perceptual establishment reflects congenital properties of the brain itself. Indeed, perception and brain functions were held by Gestaltists to be formally identical (or isomorphic), so much in order that to study perception is to study the brain. Much contemporary research in perception is directed toward inferring specific features of brain function from such behaviour as the reports (introspections) individuals give of their centripetal experiences. More and more such inferences are gratifyingly being matched with physiological observations of the brain itself.

Many investigators relied heavily on introspective reports, treating them as although they were objective descriptions of public events. Serious doubts were raised in the 1920s about this use of introspection by the U.S. psychologist John B. Watson and others, who argued that it yielded only subjective accounts and that percepts are inevitably private experiences and lack the objectivity commonly required of scientific disciplines. In response to objections about subjectivism, there arose an approach known as behaviourism that restricts its data to objective descriptions or measurements of the overt behaviour of organizms other than the investigator himself.

Not only does perception necessitate establishment and grouping, it also involves distinguishing an object from its surroundings. Notice that once you perceive an object, the area around that object becomes the background. Gestalt psychologists have devised ambiguous figure-ground relationships - that is, drawings in which the figure and ground can be reversed - to illustrate their point that the whole is varied from the sum of its parts.

The "figure and ground" illusion is commonly experienced when one gazes at the illustration of a black vase the outline of which is created by two white profiles. At any moment one will be able to see either the black vase (in the centre area) as "figure" or the white profiles on each side (in which case the black is seen as "ground"). The fluctuations of figure and ground may occur even when one fails intentionally to shift attention, appearing without witting effort. Seeing one aspect apparently excludes seeing the other.

Though such illustrations may fool our visual systems, individuals are seldomly confused about what they see. In real world, vases don't change into faces as we look at them. Instead, our perceptions are outstandingly stable.

SOCIAL PERCEPTION

Perception is the process of acquiring, interpreting, selecting and organizing sensory information. The word perception arrives from the Latin capere, meaning "to take", the prefix per- meaning "completely". Methods of studying perception range from essentially biological or psychological approaches through the philosophy of mind or in Merleau-Ponty's affirmation of perception as the basis of all sciences and knowledge. Perception is the faculty of acquiring sensory experience. Study of the processes by which humans gather and interpret visual information is largely the province of social psychologists, who have identified numerous general principles of perception, and also some effects upon it of motivation and attention. Perception refers both to the experience of gaining sensory information about the world of individuals, things, and events, and to the psychological processes by which this is achieved. Krech and Crutchfield divide the determinants of perception into two major categories; structural factors and functional factors.

Structural Factors

By structural factors we intend those constituents driving exclusively from the nature of the forcible stimuli and the natural effects they evoke in the nervous system of the person. Therefore for the Gestalt psychologist, perceptual organizations are determined primarily by the psychological events happening in the nervous system of the individual in direct reaction to the stimulation by the physical objects. They would insist that those sensory factors which are independent of the perceiving individual's needs and personality and which force certain organizations in his cognitive field are referred to as "Structural factors in perception".

Functional Factors

The functional factors of perceptual establishment, alternatively are those, which derive mainly from the needs, moods, past experience, and memory of the individual. All functional factors in perception are social in the usual sense of the term. In one experiment, for instance, Levine, Chein and Murphy presented a series of ambiguous drawings to hungry college learners and found a marked tendency for such drawings to be perceived as food objects - sandwiches, salads, roasts, etc. There was no such consequence when the same drawings were shown to learners who had just finished eating. The different perceptions of the hungry and not-hungry learners couldn't be due to "structural" factors, since the same pictures were presented to both groups but could be due only to the differences in need or motivation of the members of the two groups. While quantitative laws of how these "functional" factors actually operate in perception are lacking a great deal of experimental work is uncommitted that demonstrates their pervasive influence in perception.

IMPRESSION MANAGEMENT

Impression Management (IM) is a tool to manage the notion held by important others of one's competence and commitment, in other words, one's reputation. Most individuals use IM to some extent during situations such as task interviews and performance appraisals, but others more consciously use it regularly. Even if you don't actively manage the process, you are still sending signals.

Upwardly visible and organizationally applicable activities frequently bring career rewards and power because they demonstrate the power and willingness to get things done. The achievement and maintenance of a reputation for leadership potential are important not just for the individual's career, but from that public image stem the power and resources for the whole team. Visibility is the key to enhanced reputation, but gaining this is becoming more difficult as organizations get flatter, and managers have dispersed teams and frequently scarcely enough contact with direct reports to know their individual accomplishments. This is particularly the case in knowledge industries like consulting. Nonetheless, some individuals believe that the character of their performance will shine through, and this is frequently the case for female managers.

Types of Impression Management

Self-focused IM: Self-advancement is the promotion of one's strengths, especially useful where the person isn't well known to those who control resources such as advancement. Nevertheless, self-promotion of successes is seen as risky, because it can be interpreted as bragging, which may result in a negative reaction by the target. Self-promotion of ambition is essential for career management, in order that managers are aware of this need - they may be too busy to read your mind. But self-promotion is a catch 22 situation for ambitious women - they are damned if they do it and damned if they do not.

Manager-Focused IM: Communicating upwards and outward and building a good kinship with your manager are self-assertive tactics to gain approval of senior managers controlling important rewards. Early use of IM by subordinates in a supervisory relationship, especially where they are of the same gender as the supervisor is likely to result in enhanced performance ratings, which is of importance for females managed by males, putting them at a disadvantage. Cranfield's research shows that women tend to be less instrumental than their male peers in initiation and maintenance of such relationships.

Task-Focused IM: Many prefer to strike through delivery of extra high functioning and high commitment, but these have to be visible to attain the rewards.

Implications for Practice

Impression management indicates ambition and drive which when coupled with professionalism and commitment could be a key to organizational resource. It is a tool which can benefit the individual, their team, their manager and the organization, through extremely professional and committed performance, good organizational citizenship and aim delivery, relationship-building and political/cultural awareness. Nevertheless, males seem more willing than females to use upward influence IM as part of their career management. If women aren't noticed, then they may not extend their potential to the full advantage of their employer or themselves.

There is a growing business case for organizations to develop their resource pool of women, as some investors start to move their funds into organizations with visible senior female representation. Women directors bring new ideas and different perspectives to corporate decision-making on previously all-male boards, as well as act as role models for those below, enhancing the recruitment and retention of talented women. Nevertheless, both males and females need to be noticed in order for organizations to invest in development for more senior levels. Managers ought to not assume that females who don't push themselves forward aren't as ambitious or able as their male peers.

Some men and women trust the formal HRM systems to provide career opportunities, underestimating the importance of informal networks for information about senior posts. Some individuals with potential don't always realise the importance of "branding" their values and core strengths to their senior managers. Managers could help their junior staff by clarifying the kind of performance and commitment which get rewarded, in order that they can make better-informed choices. Perhaps individuals don't want to use IM, but they ought to know the unwritten penalties for not bearing and being seen to deliver what the organization wants and demands.

Note: For perception process in working atmosphere, BAE Systems is a very good example. BAE Systems is a worldwide company engaged in the development, delivery and support of progressing defence and aerospace. Reader can find more information from their site http://www.baesystems.com/CorporateResponsibility/Casestudies/Supplychain/index.htm.

7

Personality and Attitudes

Every human being might have different perception, attitude and meaning for this broad terminology "personality", as we, human beings, are said to be social animal and the only animal having something powerful tool called mind which other animals don't possess in this entire planet. Other animals also got brain but its potential is limited. But our brain and its capacity are simply unlimited. Because of this tool, we are ruling the entire universe. I have mentioned all of this because, with external and internal beauties, this organ of human also plays important role in developing, enriching and boosting our personality as a whole.

Now, what actually Personality means?

MEANING OF PERSONALITY

The foremost thing or the main thing for which we can determine or perceive another stranger is via his external or physical outfit, as no one can know how he is? His behaviour, character at a glance so personality at a glance goes for "looks". But, most of the individuals only think that if a person has good looks, then he/she has got personality. He/she only possess looks, external personality but not personality as a whole. So to analyze or determine somebody's total personality we have to understand him/her which needs time. Someone might not be good looking but he/she can have his/her behaviour, character prominent and vice-versa.

Personality traits aren't inborn or genetically underlying. We have to develop or enhance these traits after landing on earth. We are the only one who can develop our whole personality. There are others like our parents who are always there to help us but the real hero is with us. If we are interested to develop our personality we need to learn many things and might be more and more and more things. Apart from academic education we must have to learn many extra curricular things like:

1. Public Speaking Skills.
2. Body language Skills.
3. Handwriting analysis Skills.
4. Behavioural Skills.
5. Anger Management Skills.
6. Fitness Skills.
7. Yoga and Exercise.
8. Food habit.
9. Communication Skills.
10. Friends making Skills.
11. Relationship Skills.
12. Super learning Skills.
13. Dealing with problems.
14. Self or Auto-Suggestions skills.

A person can only be real person when he/she can be cent percent successful in fulfilling his/her whole responsibility and the above mentioned points are the key points and landmarks to make one accountable, rational, bold, brave and smart.

DEVELOPMENT OF PERSONALITY

Just a few years back the Management scientists have not for some time given much credence to the idea that task attitudes or job satisfaction "causes" item-by-item productivity at work. Nevertheless, it has been suggested by Organ that job satisfaction might well have something to do with other forms of contribution to work organizations. The effects of satisfaction would register in contributions unconstrained by ability, technology, or workflow, and not otherwise elicited by formal incentives or literal task requirements. Why ought to this be the case? Because attitudes predict behaviour only to the extent that behaviour isn't bound by situational constraints or forces. Furthermore, general attitudes (and job satisfaction is arguably a general attitude) seldom predict specific behaviours of the sort implied by productive performance. Rather, they predict aggregations of thematically related (as opposed to topographically similar) behaviours over time and across varied situations.

A 1988 review of then-extant evidence (Organ, 1988) supported the position that job satisfaction is related to constructive, spontaneous, optional, non-compensated contributions that several writers have called "organizational citizenship behaviour" (OCB). Further development of research along these lines has strongly suggested that participant assessments of fairness--fairness of supervision, of policies and processes, of pay--goes far to account for the relationship between satisfaction and OCB (Organ & Konovsky, 1989; Farh, Podsakoff & Organ, 1990; Moorman, 1990). Of course, measures of perceived fairness are basically attitudinal measures, and much of what we call and measure as job satisfaction falls down to conceptions of fair outcomes, treatment, and processes.

Interestingly, the theoretical basis for predicting behaviour from personality leans on very much the same considerations as the prediction of behaviour from general attitudes. That is, measures of personality seldom account for much variance in specific behaviours in tightly controlled situations. Personality has predictive power only in what Mischel (1977) calls "weak situations." Weak situations are those devoid of compelling external incentives and lacking in "demand characteristics" for behaviour. Moreover, Epstein (1980) demonstrated that measures of personality attain maximum predictive power when the behavioural criterion is a total of thematically related behaviours across time and situations.

It would seem that OCB by its very nature would represent behaviour that occurs in weak situations (some, e.g., Davis-Blake & Pfeffer, 1989, would suggest that work organizations feature predominantly strong rather than weak situations, but we will defer for the moment discussion of this issue). Furthermore, if OCB is measured by ratings of how participants characteristically respond to such situations--i.e., the extent to which they spontaneously respond in cooperative, altruistic, and conscientious fashion--we would expect that such ratings would operationally capture aggregation trends across many instances and opportunities for so responding. In sum, we ought to expect to find in OCB the kind of "performance" that is attributable to personality.

PERSONALITY, TASK ATTITUDES, & OCB

There is an even more pressing reason for assessing the role of personality as a determinant of OCB.

Recent evidence (e.g., Staw & Ross, 1985; Staw, Bell & Clausen, 1986; Arvey, Bouchard, Segal & Abraham, 1989) provides a case for thinking of task attitudes as substantially dispositional in origin. Some individuals are more satisfied, willy-nilly. To be sure, the research in question has not gone unchallenged (Davis-Blake & Pfeffer, 1989; Cropanzano & James, 1990), and debate continues as to the relative contribution of disposition and situation in accounting for work attitudes. Nonetheless, we must reckon with the possibility that some dimension or dimensions of personality underlie both satisfaction and OCB and therefore account for the consistent relationship between satisfaction and OCB. This possibility exists so long as some appreciable part of the variance in task attitudes is dispositional in nature.

Assume for the moment that OCB is functionally related to variance in task attitudes (such as fairness assessments) that aren't dispositional expressions, but reactions to the perspective of work. We would take this to mean that contributions in the form of OCB are responses to judgments individuals make about the fairness with which they have been treated. We would, in consequence, take serious interest in pursuing a general model relating social justice to workplace behaviour, a model taking shape in the work of Bies and Moag (1986), Folger and Greenberg (1985), Greenberg and Tyler (1987), and Organ and Moorman (1993), and a model quite consistent with the view of organizations as collective effort based on implicit contract (Rousseau & Parks, 1992). Furthermore, from a purely pragmatic view, we would infer that leaders of organizations must take pains to manage the perspective of work in such a way as to meet with widely prevalent norms of fairness, if their organizations require volumes of discretionary contributions for survival.

If, alternatively, the statistical record of associations between work attitudes and OCB is an artefact of their common but independent linkage to underlying dispositions, then both theory and application would have to accord a more central position to "the person." Such an approach is one with which management science has not traditionally felt comfortable. Not only is it a paradigm in general viewed as having been empirically unavailing, but which would invite all manner of distasteful and invidious distinctions among individuals (Davis-Blake & Pfeffer, 1989). Nevertheless, there is also the view that management scientists have little to show from organizational research based on dispositional constructs because such research has been theoretically impoverished; it has tended "to draw on personality variables in isolation, lifting them out of their networks, neither building upon nor feeding back to their theoretical underpinnings" (Weiss & Adler, 1990).

At this point some readers may object that this discussion amounts to yet another fruitless form of the "person versus situation" debate, one to be eschewed in favour of the "interactional" approach. Nevertheless, even to specify a coherent form of such interactions (which are potentially numerous and subtle; Bowers, 1973; Buss, 1987; George, 1992), let alone to implicate the relevant dispositional constructs, is a job that surely could be informed by a review of the available evidence.

While it is statistically possible to obtain an important interaction between two variables without either variable showing even a hint of a main effect, this type of interaction is exceedingly rare in psychological research and when found is even more seldomly replicated. Non-statistical forms of interaction--e.g., when two variables feedback upon each other in a dynamic process--ought to be glimpsed even in cross-sectional research, if it can be assumed that cross-sections varying in time and place capture different stages of the dynamic process. If dispositional constructs are to be given serious analysis in the study of organizations, the rationale for this ought to not be some inscrutable interaction that lies beyond our power to divine it (which, like any proposition incapable of being refuted, would be unscientific on its face). The case ought to rest on some patterning of the empirical record.

In any case, the purpose of this review and discussion isn't to see if we can "throw out contextual variables," but to see if it is defensible to believe that reported attitudes about certain dimensions of work perspective are related to OCB mainly by virtue of some underlying disposition(s). Failing that, we are interested in seeing whether the logic that so far has correctly predicted an association between work attitudes and OCB fares as well in predicting a relationship between personality and OCB; and if not, then, why not?

While quite a few analyses have looked at personality and OCB, no one personality measure (e.g., extraversion) has figured in very many studies. A meta-analysis that collapses across theoretically different dispositional constructs would not be interpretable, since it might average a very few promising predictors with a greater number of non-predictors. Furthermore, among the measures used in OCB research, there is varying degree of overlap among them with respect to personality referents, and it would be difficult to effect a reliable sorting of measures by underlying concepts. The intent here isn't to derive an estimate of population relationships, but to derive some sense of just how well personality measures generally have fared in predicting in OCB and, if possible, to see if there are signs of convergence upon those personality constructs that offer most encouragement for a dispositional basis of OCB.

NATURE AND DIMENSION OF ATTITUDE

An individual's personality is influenced by factors like heredity, external environment, and person-situation interaction. Some of the personality attributes that have an impact on an individual's behaviour are the venue of control, Machiavellianism, self-esteem, self-monitoring, propensity to risk-taking, and Type A personality. The locus of control refers to the degree to which individuals believe that they can determine their own fate. Individuals high on the venue of control (called internals) tend to move up the career ladder rapidly.

Machiavellianism (Mach) denotes the degree to which an individual is pragmatic, maintains emotional distance, and believes that the ends justify the means. High-Mach individuals are most productive in jobs which impose minimum restrictions on the employee, involve persuading others, and offer high rewards. Self-monitoring refers to the power of an individual to adjust his behaviour to external situational factors. High self-monitors are capable of changing their behaviour and expressions as per the situation. They build up faster in their careers than low self-monitors.

People diverge in their willingness to take chances or risks. High risk-taking individuals perform well in jobs such as stock brokers and currency traders. Individuals who have a Type A personality are continuously involved in the struggle to attain more in less time in the face of opposition from other individuals. But because of their emphasis on quantity than quality and their poor decision-making skills, they frequently don't make good managers. Type B individuals lay more emphasis on quality of outcome rather than quantity and have good analytical skills. They therefore make good managers.

Many personality theorists have attempted to explain the development of human personality. As per Daniel Levinson, an individual's life can be divided into adult, mid-life and late adult stages. The personality of an individual, Levinson argues, develops to some extent at each stage of his lifecycle. Another theorist, Hall, suggested that the personality development of an employee takes place in four stages: exploration, establishment, maintenance and decline.

Chris Argyris (Immaturity-Maturity model) proposed that human personality moves along a continuum from immaturity (infancy) to maturity (adulthood). John Harrold proposed the personality-task fit theory in which he founded a relationship among personality characteristics, the necessities of a task, and task performance.

Attitudes are evaluative statements (favourable or unfavourable) about objects, individuals or events. Attitudes are assumed from parents, teachers and members of the peer group, apart from the predispositions acquired at birth. The three task-related attitudes are job satisfaction, task involvement, and organizational commitment. As per Edwin A. Locke, job satisfaction is the pleasurable or positive emotional state that results when an individual evaluates his task or task experience. Task involvement refers to the degree to which a person psychologically identifies with his task, actively participates in it, and believes that his performance in the task contributes to his self-worth.

Organizational commitment refers to the extent to which an individual identifies with a particular establishment, and its aims and wishes to stay a member of that establishment. Organizations can reduce turnover by taking steps to enhance the job satisfaction of their employees and increase their task participation and organizational commitment.

Attitudes enable individuals to adjust to their work environment. They are also used by individuals to defend their ego, express their values, and to interpret events. The cognitive dissonance theory refers to the incompatibility that an individual may perceive between two or more of his attitudes, or between his behaviour and attitudes. The efforts made by an individual to reduce dissonance depend on the importance of the elements that give rise to the dissonance, the extent to which they can be controlled, and the honours that the individual is likely to lose by not overcoming the dissonance.

JOB SATISFACTION

As much the individuals are happier within their task, the more satisfied they are said to be. Job satisfaction isn't the same as motivation, though it is clearly linked. Task design aims to enhance job satisfaction and performance; methods include task rotation, task enlargement and task enrichment. Other influences on satisfaction include the management style and culture, employee involvement, empowerment and autonomous work groups. Job satisfaction is a very important attribute which is often measured by organizations. The most general way of measurement is the use of rating scales where employees report their reactions to their jobs. Questions relate to rate of pay, work responsibilities, variety of jobs, promotional opportunities, the work itself and co-workers. Some questioners ask yes or no questions while others ask to rate satisfaction on 1-5 scale (where 1 represents "not at all satisfied" and 5 represents "highly satisfied").

The Job satisfaction has been defined as a pleasurable emotional state resulting from the appraisal of one's task; an affective reaction to one's task; and an attitude towards one's task. Weiss (2002) has indicated that job satisfaction is an attitude but points out that researchers ought to clearly distinguish the objects of cognitive evaluation which are affect (emotion), beliefs and behaviours. This definition suggests that we figure attitudes towards our jobs by taking into account our feelings, our beliefs, and our behaviours.

Measuring Job Satisfaction

There are numerous methods for measuring job satisfaction. By far, the most common method for collecting data concerning job satisfaction is the Likert scale (named after Rensis Likert). Other less common methods of for gauging job satisfaction include: Yes/No questions, True/False questions, point systems, checklists, and forced choice answers. This data is normally collected using an Enterprise Feedback Management (EFM) system.

The Job Descriptive Index (JDI), created by Smith, Kendall, & Hulin (1969), is a specific questionnaire of job satisfaction that has been sparsely used. It measures one's satisfaction in five facets: pay, promotions and promotion opportunities, co-workers, supervision, and the work itself. The scale is simple, participants answer either yes, no, or can not decide (indicated by '?') in response to whether given statements accurately depict one's task.

The Job in General Index is an overall mensuration of job satisfaction. It is an improvement to the Task Descriptive Index because the JDI focuses too much on individual facets and not adequate on work satisfaction in the main.

ORGANIZATIONAL COMMITMENT

Now the question arises that what constitutes commitment in organizations? In one view, commitment is the total capacity to act in ways that meet the establishment's aims and interests. Though a simple enough definition, it is inadequate. The problem is that commitment has now been defined in a number of widely varying ways. The sociologist Etzioni argues that commitment-and the authority that organizations have over members-is rooted in the nature of employee participation in the establishment.

Participation takes one of three forms, ranging from total commitment to no commitment at all. Moral engagement, based on positive and intense orientation to the establishment, results from internalization of the establishment's values, aims, and norms. Calculative involvement is less intense and rests on an exchange relationship between the individual and the establishment. Individuals become committed to an establishment to the extent that they perceive some beneficial or just exchange relationship. Alienative involvement is a want of commitment, occurring when members feel constrained by conditions to belong to the establishment but don't identify with it.

The management guru Kanter takes a different view of commitment, arguing that different types of commitment result from varied behavioural requirements placed on members by the establishment. Again, participation takes three forms, but here the forms may be interrelated. Continuance commitment has to do with a member's dedication to the survival of the establishment and results from having individuals make sacrifices for and investments in the establishment. Cohesion commitment is attachment to social relations in an establishment; it can be enhanced by having employees publicly renounce previous social ties or engage in ceremonies that enhance group cohesion. Control commitment is a member's attachment to the norms of an establishment that shape behaviour in required ways. It exists when employees believe that the establishment's norms and values are important guides to their behaviour.

Social psychologists and organizational researchers view commitment quite differently. Organizational researchers study attitudinal commitment, focusing on how employees identify with the aims and values of the establishment. This is commitment viewed mainly from the standpoint of the establishment. Social psychologists study behavioural commitment, focusing on how a person's behaviour serves to bind him to the establishment. Once behaviour shows commitment, individuals must adjust their attitudes accordingly, which then influence their subsequent behaviour. Therefore a cycle begins: behaviour shapes attitudes and the shaped attitudes in turn shape behaviour.

Hence, we have at least three different ways to view organizational commitment. If we accept all three notions, we will look in different places for evidence of commitment. We will look at exchange relationships as behaviours evidencing commitment, and acceptance of organizational norms and values as attitudes showing commitment. A broad view of commitment ought to lead managers to many different sources and manifestations of it. Most views of commitment treat it as a universal concept: one is or isn't committed to the establishment as an entity. A more differentiated view, in which employees are thought to be more or less committed to numerous facets of the workplace, might be more helpful.

The previous discussion of occupational communities suggests that managers must consider employees' other commitments as well. Employees aren't only committed to the establishment to a greater or lesser degree, but as individuals with multiple roles also have other commitments. These include such obvious connections as those of family or community, but they also embrace membership in occupational communities or in other associations. Managers need to be sensitive to these other motivations that may determine an employee's behaviour or attitudes.

Another interesting expression of commitment is the phenomenon known as whistle-blowing, or publicizing unethical, illegal, or immoral behaviour. For the individual, whistle-blowing may be the last resort, the only step left open; for the establishment it is highly threatening when negative information reaches the press. Whistle-blowing may occur because the whistle-blower feels tremendously committed to the establishment; it is, after all, borne of an impulse to reform an evil and few individuals are willing to risk punishment to reform what they don't value. In this view the whistle blower is the defender of the establishment's true values and the management that punishes the behaviour is the deviant. Whistle-blowing may have the beneficial effect for the establishment, then, of spawning change, particularly when it can be made to overseeing bodies, as with all the government instances of whistle-blowing. Most of the work on whistle-blowing is descriptive and philosophical. Organizations are probably more apt to retaliate against whistle-blowers they value, perhaps because of their potential threat. They may also retaliate against those who are vulnerable because they lack public support. Individuals frequently fail to blow the whistle when organizational conditions suggest they ought to. This hesitancy undoubtedly results from fear of reprisal and agnosticism that their organizations will take ameliorative stairs.

Note: Personality & Attitudes play an important part in growth of a company. Best practical example is Infosys. In 2001 it was rated Best Employer in India by Business Today. Infosys won the Global MAKE (Most Admired Knowledge Enterprises) award, for the years 2003, 2004 and 2005. Infosys was rated best employer to work for in 2000, 2001, and 2002 by Hewitt Associates. For detailed information, reader may visit this site: http://www.infosysblogs.com/oracle/2008/10/key_factors_for_success_of_erp.html

8

Learning Process

To learn is to gain knowledge or technique. Learning also may demand a change in attitude or behaviour. Children learn to identify objects at an early age; teenagers may learn to improve study habits; and adults can learn to solve complicated problems. The managers necessitate to gain the higher levels of knowledge and technique, comprising the power to exercise judgment and solve problems. The challenge for the aviation instructor is to understand how individuals learn, and more importantly, to be able to enforce that knowledge to the learning environment.

Learning may be described as a body of principles advocated by psychologists and educators to explicate how individuals acquire skills, knowledge, and attitudes. Several branches of learning theory are used in formal training programs to improve and accelerate the learning process. Fundamental concepts such as required learning outcomes, objectives of the training, and depth of training also apply. When properly integrated, learning principles, derived from theories, can be useful to aviation instructors and developers of instructional programs for both pilots and maintenance technicians.

Over the years, many theories have attempted to explain how individuals learn. Even although psychologists and educators aren't in complete agreement, most do agree that learning may be explicated by a combination of two fundamental approaches: behaviourism and the cognitive theories.

BEHAVIOURISM

Behaviourists believe that animals, comprising humans, learn in about the same way. Behaviourism stresses the importance of having a particular form of behaviour reinforced by someone, other than the learner, to shape or control what is learned. In aviation training, the instructor provides the reinforcement. Frequent, positive reinforcement and rewards accelerate learning. This theory provides the instructor with ways to manipulate learners with stimuli, induce the required behaviour or response, and reinforce the behaviour with appropriate rewards. Generally, the behaviourist theory emphasizes positive reinforcement rather than no reinforcement or punishment.

Other features of behaviourism are substantially more complicated than this simple explanation. Instructors who need more details ought to refer to psychology texts for a better understanding of behaviourism. As an instructor, it is important to keep in mind that behaviourism is still widely used today, because controlling learning experiences helps direct learners toward specific learning results.

COGNITIVE THEORY

Much of the current psychological thinking and experimentation in education lets in some facets of the cognitive theory. This is true in fundamental as well as more advanced training programs. Unlike behaviourism, the cognitive theory focuses on what is going on inside the learner's mind. Learning isn't just a change in behaviour; it is a change in the way a learner thinks, understands, or feels. There are several branches of cognitive theory. Two of the major theories may broadly be classified as the information processing model and the social interaction model. The first says that the learner's brain has internal structures which select and process incoming material, store and retrieve it, use it to create behaviour, and receive and process feedback on the effects.

This demands a number of cognitive processes, comprising executive purposes of recognizing expectancies, planning and monitoring performance, encoding and chunking information, and creating internal and external responses. The social interaction theories gained prominence in the 1980s. They stress that learning and subsequent changes in behaviour take place as a result of interaction between the learner and the environment. Behaviour is modelled either by individuals or symbolically. Cultural influences, peer pressure, group dynamics, and film and television are some of the important factors. Therefore, the social environment to which the learner is exposed demonstrates or models behaviours, and the learner cognitively processes the observed behaviours and consequences. The cognitive processes constitute attention, retention, motor responses, and motivation. Techniques for learning admit direct modelling and verbal instruction. Behaviour, personal factors, and environmental consequences all work together to create learning.

Both models of the cognitive theory have general principles. For example, they both acknowledge the importance of reinforcing behaviour and measuring changes. Positive reinforcement is important, particularly with cognitive concepts such as knowledge and understanding. The need to evaluate and measure behaviour remains because it is the only way to get a clue about what the learner understands. Evaluation is frequently limited to the kinds of knowledge or behaviour that can be measured by a paper-and-pencil exam or a performance test. Though psychologists agree that there frequently are errors in evaluation, some means of measuring learner knowledge, performance, and behaviour is requisite.

COMBINED APPROACH

Both the behaviouristic and the cognitive approaches are utilitarian learning theories. A reasonable way to plan, manage, and conduct aviation training is to include the best features of each major theory. This provides a way to measure behavioural outcomes and promote cognitive learning. The combined approach isn't dim-witted, but neither is learning.

PRINCIPLES OF LEARNING

Educational psychologists have identified many principles of learning, also referred to as laws of learning, which seem generally applicable to the learning process. These principles have been discovered, tested, and used in practical situations. They provide additional insight into what makes individuals learn most effectively. Edward Thorndike developed the first three "Laws of learning:" readiness, exercise, and effect. Since Thorndike set down his fundamental three laws in the early part of the twentieth century, three additional principles have been added to it afterward are: primacy and recency, and intensity.

These principles are widely applied in aerospace instruction, and many other fields, as defined below:

Readiness

Readiness means a degree of single-mindedness and eagerness. Individuals learn best when they are physically, mentally, and emotionally ready to learn, and they don't learn well if they see no ground for learning. Getting learners ready to learn, producing interest by showing the value of the subject matter, and providing continuous mental or physical challenge, is in general the instructor's responsibility. If learners have a strong purpose, a clear objective, and a definite reason for learning something, they make more progress than if they lack motivation. Since learning is an active process, learners must have adequate rest, health, and physical ability. Under certain circumstances, the instructor can do little, if anything, to inspire in learners a preparedness to learn. Fundamental needs of learners must be satisfied before they are prepared or capable of learning.

Exercise

The principle of exercise lands that those things most frequently repeated are best remembered. It is the basis of drill and practice. It has been proven that learners learn best and retain information longer when they have meaningful practice and repetition. The key here is that the practice must be meaningful. It is clear that practice leads to improvement only when it is followed by positive feedback. The human memory is fallible. The mind can seldom retain, evaluate, and apply new concepts or practices after a single exposure. Learners don't learn complicated jobs in a single session. They learn by applying what they have been told and shown. Every time practice occurs, learning continues. These let in learner recall, review and summary, and manual drill and physical applications. All of these serve to produce learning habits. The instructor must repeat important items of subject matter at reasonable intervals, and offers opportunities for learners to practice while making sure that this process is directed toward an objective.

Effect

The principle of effect is based on the emotional reaction of the learner. It has a direct relationship to motivation. The principle of effect is that learning is strengthened when accompanied by a pleasant or satisfying feeling, and that learning is weakened when associated with an unpleasant feeling. The learner will strive to continue doing what provides a pleasant effect to continue learning. Positive reinforcement is more apt to lead to success and motivate the learner, so the instructor ought to recognize and commend improvement. Whatever the learning situation, it ought to contain elements that affect the learners positively and give them a feeling of satisfaction. Therefore, instructors ought to be cautious about using punishment in the classroom.

One of the important responsibilities of the instructor is to set up the learning situation in such a manner that each trainee will be able to see evidence of progress and attain some degree of success. Experiences that create feelings of defeat, frustration, anger, confusion, or futility are unpleasant for the learner. If, for instance, an instructor attempts to teach advanced concepts on the initial engagement, the learner is likely to feel inferior and be frustrated. Impressing upon learners the difficulty of a job to be learned can make the teaching job difficult. Generally it is better to tell learners that a problem or job, though difficult, is within their capability to understand or perform. Every learning experience doesn't have to be entirely successful, nor does the learner have to master each lesson completely. Nevertheless, every learning experience ought to contain elements that leave the learner with some good feelings. A learner's chance of success is definitely increased if the learning experience is a pleasant one.

Primacy

Primacy, the state of being first, frequently produces a strong, almost unshakable, belief. Things learned first produce a strong impression in the mind that is difficult to erase. For the instructor, this means that what is taught must be right the first time. For the learner, it intends that learning must be right. "Unteaching" wrong first impressions is harder than teaching them right the first time. If, for example, a learner learns a faulty skill, the instructor will have a hard job correcting bad habits and "reteaching" correct ones.

The learner's first go through ought to be positive, functional, and lay the foundation for all that is to follow. What the learner learns must be procedurally correct and applied the very first time. The instructor must present subject matter in a logical order, step by step, making sure the learners have already learned the preceding step. If the job is learned in isolation, isn't initially applied to the overall performance, or if it must be relearned, the process can be confusing and time consuming. Preparing and following a lesson plan helps delivery of the subject matter right the first time.

Recency

The principle of recency says that things most recently learned are best remembered. Conversely, the further a learner is removed time-wise from a new fact or understanding, the more difficult it is to remember. For instance, it is fairly easy to recall a telephone number dialled a few minutes ago, but it is in general impossible to recall a new number dialled last week. The closer the training or learning time is to the time of real need to employ the training, the more apt the learner will be to perform successfully. Information gained last in general is remembered best; frequent review and summarization help fix in the mind the material covered. Instructors recognize the principle of recency when they carefully plan a summary for a lesson or learning situation. The instructor repeats, restates, or reemphasizes important points at the end of a lesson to help the learner remember them.

Intensity

The more intense the material instructed, the more probably it will be retained. A sharp, clear, vivid, dramatic, or exciting learning experience teaches more than a routine or boring experience. The principle of intensity implies that a learner will learn more from the real thing than from a substitute. For instance, a learner can get more understanding and appreciation of a movie by watching it than by reading the script. Similarly, a learner is likely to gain greater understanding of jobs by performing them rather than merely reading about them. The more immediate and dramatic the learning is to a real situation, the more impressive the learning is upon the learner. Real world applications that integrate processes and jobs that learners are capable of learning will make a vivid effect on them.

In contrast to practical instruction, the classroom enforces limitations on the amount of realism that can be brought into teaching. The instructor needs to use imagination in approaching reality as closely as possible. Classroom instruction can benefit from a wide variety of instructional aids, to improve realism, motivate learning, and challenge learners.

Instructors ought to emphasize important points of instruction with gestures, showmanship, and voice. Demonstrations, skits, and function playing do much to increase the learning experience of learners. Examples, analogies, and personal experiences also make learning come to life. Instructors ought to make full use of the gumptions (hearing, sight, touch, taste, smell, equilibrium, rhythm, depth perception, and others).

ORGANIZATIONAL REWARD SYSTEM

This discussion examines the role of monetary rewards in encouraging knowledge sharing in organizations through four mechanisms of knowledge sharing. We argue that the system of contributing knowledge to databases is the most amenable to rewards contingent on knowledge sharing behaviours because of opportunities for the reward allocator to measure the knowledge sharing behaviours. In the case of formal interactions within or across teams and work units, while rewards could be made partly contingent on knowledge sharing behaviours as in merit pay, rewards based on collective performance are also probably to be effectual in creating a feeling of cooperation, ownership, and commitment among employees.

Additionally, we propose that team-based rewards and company wide inducements (profit sharing, gain sharing, and employee stock options) would be particularly instrumental in enhancing knowledge sharing within teams and across work units, respectively. In the case of knowledge sharing through informal interactions, the key enabling factor is trust between the individual and the establishment. In this case, the role of rewards is indirect, that is, procedural and distributive fairness of organizational rewards are important factors in the development of trust. We also consider knowledge sharing in communities of practice and theorize that intrinsic rewards and factors that build expertise and provide recognition are the most appropriate means of fostering feeling of competence. Finally, we discuss the research implications.

Several organizations have introduced reward systems to encourage employees to share their knowledge with others. For example, Buckman Laboratories recognizes its 100 top knowledge sharers with an annual conference at a resort. Lotus Development, a division of IBM, devotes 25% of the total performance evaluation of its customer support workers on the extent of their knowledge sharing activities. Although knowledge management systems have emerged in the last two decades, employee suggestion programs have been present for a much farseeing time even although these are narrower in focus. Normally, employees receive monetary or non-monetary awards for their valuable suggestions in such programs.

Rewards could range from monetary incentives such as bonuses to non-monetary awards such as dinner girl certificates to awards such as praise and public recognition that don't have a monetary tantamount value. Rewards could also be intrinsic, such as pleasure derived from performing the job itself. The focus of our paper is primarily on extrinsic rewards although we acknowledge the situations in which intrinsic rewards are of main importance. For the purpose of our discussion, and in order to use a uniform metric, we consider only the monetary rewards for their effect on knowledge sharing. We consider two sets of complementary factors on which rewards could be contingent: first, knowledge sharing behaviours and second, outcomes other than knowledge sharing, such as performance. Hence, we include in our discussion the pecuniary awards that are contingent on knowledge sharing behaviours and incentives that are contingent on performance at individual, group, and establishment levels.

Bartol and Locke (2000) identified numerous important aspects of organizational reward systems that are useful for motivating individuals to perform the targeted behaviours. These factors include, but aren't limited to, perceived fairness of rewards, employees setting challenging aims in order to attain the attractive rewards, and practices that insure that employees possess high self-efficacy for performing the jobs. In order to reward systems meet these criteria and are effectual, two fundamental prerequisites are that it ought to be possible for the reward giver to observe or record the objective behaviour and to assess its value.

Individual Level Rewards

In the case of formal meetings of teams and work units, it is possible to reward individuals for their knowledge sharing behaviour because the leader has the opportunity to judge the contributions made by individuals over a period of time. Therefore, knowledge sharing behaviours could be one of the criteria in performance evaluation, and decisions on merit pay and promotions could be related to the scale of knowledge sharing by individuals in formal interactions. Bonuses might be possible, but they tend to be more properly tied to specific outcomes or linked to special acquirements.

Unless a manager is actually part of the team, it will normally be more cumbersome to evaluate ongoing knowledge sharing at the team level for purposes of allocating rewards. One possible solution is to institute peer ratings, perhaps as part of a 360 degree performance appraisal. While rewarding individuals for knowledge is one potential approach to promoting knowledge sharing, another approach is to foster knowledge sharing at the team level. These extra information mechanisms may make it possible to reward knowledge sharing behaviour amongst teams and across teams/work units.

Rewards at the Team Level

At the team level, it may be possible to encourage knowledge sharing exercised indirect rewards--that is, rewards that are contingent on factors other than knowledge sharing, but which are probably to call for knowledge sharing for successful performance. For example, when outcomes such as performance are rewarded at the individual level, an individual who shares knowledge with others may be likely to think that the knowledge he/she shares will improve the performance of others rather than his/her own performance.

Since knowledge sharing behaviour necessitates effort away from the job, an individual may, in fact, perceive knowledge sharing behaviour to be detrimental to self-performance. Alternatively, team metrics have the advantage of furthering cooperation and co-ordination and motivating group members to focus on group aims and performance. It may be remarked that team incentives may also suffer from the problem of free riding. Notwithstanding, as Lawler (1971) argued, there could be a positive effect on individual perceptions of instrumentality if the belief is that individual behaviour will facilitate cooperation and co-ordination, which, in turn, would lead to advance in collective performance.

On equilibrium, we would expect individuals to believe that their knowledge sharing behaviour helps others in improving performance and it might also develop a sense of cooperation and reciprocity in which everyone shares knowledge thereby improving team performance. Past research has indeed argued and empirically found support for the convinced relationship between knowledge sharing and team performance. Therefore, team-based rewards are likely to encourage knowledge sharing by individuals within teams assuming individuals perceive the linkage between their knowledge sharing behaviour and team performance, and rewards.

Rewards Across Teams/Work-units

In the case of organizations with several businesses or operations in several countries, there are merits to be gained by sharing knowledge between businesses or subsidiaries. The role of rewards has been acknowledged in such organizations and systems that reward heads of business divisions/subsidiaries on the basis of performance of the firm as a whole (e.g., profits) or that of a large number of clusters, as opposed to just the individual unit's performance, have been empirically found to be more effectual in encouraging knowledge sharing. Likewise, in Nucor Steel, plant general managers tend to share their best practices with one another because their bonuses depend not only on the performance of their individual plants, but also on the basis of performance of the whole company.

Durham and Bartol (2000) argue that a likely limitation of profit sharing plans is that they don't establish a clear link between individual behaviour and its affect on profits. Nevertheless, if a link does exist between individual knowledge and profits, such reward systems can be effectual. For example, as a person goes up in hierarchy, the perceived link between one's behaviours and company profits may strengthen. Profit sharing could help individuals sharing their knowledge for the benefit of the establishment as altogether and for teams (e.g., consulting project teams) sharing knowledge with one another.

An area that relates to share is gain sharing, a compensation plan in which an establishment shares with employees a portion of the added earnings obtained through their collective increases in productivity. Gainsharing plans have been in existence for more than hundred years and normally include the whole establishment or an important portion. Welbourne and Gomez-Mejia (1995) presented eleven different theoretical perspectives on why gain sharing might lead to the contribution of ideas by employees in a work unit. Authors also cited several studies that found a positive effect of introduction of gain sharing on productivity. Gain sharing programs, such as Scanlon and Rucker plans, have specific provisions for employee involvement in terms of contribution of suggestions and a committee affording awards to employees with valuable idea, even although the principal focus of the plans is on group level rewards.

Another type of pay for performance plan operating at the organizational level that is belike to have a positive effect on knowledge sharing is employee stock ownership. Lawler, Mohrman, and Ledford (1995) found that 71 percent of Fortune 1000 organizations had stock ownership programs of some kind or the other. Employee stock option plans are one of the most popular forms of stock ownership, which gives employees the choice to purchase a specific amount of stock at a particular price over a period of time. The underlying premise is that employees will be more involved in the long-term success of the establishment. In a long-term relationship, a temporary mismatch between one's contributions and rewards is accommodated as the person hopes to balance the two over a period of time. Alternatively, a short-term relationship is likely to set up a quid pro quo attitude in which the individual, generally, would want quick monetary incentives or knowledge reciprocated by someone else.

There could be numerous situations in organizations where the nature of knowledge that is being shared is complex; meaning it is difficult to codify or communicate or it takes a long time and great effort for the source to transmit and the recipient to absorb that knowledge. Normally, such knowledge tends to be tacit in nature. An example of such situations could be a senior R&D scientist mentoring a new scientist on firm-specific technology or a new technology in its nascent stage. Another example could be one top manager grooming a successor. It might require long periods of time of observations and discussions by the successor. The person who shares the knowledge not only has to set aside the time and spend effort that could possibly be a distraction from the current task on hand, but also it is possible that this source of knowledge may feel a sense of losing his or his worth in the establishment because the unique knowledge that this person possessed is now being shared with other persons. The commitment to the establishment and a sense of ownership, nurtured in part by employee stock option plans, is likely to be useful in encouraging such knowledge sharing behaviours.

Profit sharing plans will have a positive effect on knowledge sharing all through teams and work units.

Gain sharing plans will have a positive effect on knowledge sharing all through teams and work units. Stock ownership plans are in particular suited to motivate employees to share their complicated knowledge.

As in the earlier case of knowledge sharing between teams, in the case of formal interactions across teams and work units, it might be possible to monitor the knowledge sharing behaviour and include this criterion in individual evaluations. Multinationals and diversified organizations may hold conferences where managers of several divisions may present their best practices, in the presence of top managers, for everyone to share. While opening a new subsidiary in a foreign country, managers of other countries in that region may be directed by the universal company head office to share their expertise and experience in helping the new subsidiary take off. The corporate head office may have sources of monitoring such behaviours on the basis of resubmit received from the managers of the new supplementary, for example.

BEHAVIOURAL MANAGEMENT

Organizational studies cover the study of organizations from multiple point of views, methods, and levels of analysis. For example, some divides these multiple point of views into three perspectives: modern, symbolic, and post-modern. Another conventional distinction is between the study of "micro" organizational behaviour -- which refers to individual and group dynamics in an organizational setting -- and "macro" organizational theory which studies whole organizations, how they adapt, and the strategies and structures that guide them. To this distinction, some scholars have contributed an interest in "meso" -- primarily interested in power, culture, and the networks of individuals and units in organizations -- and "field" level analysis which study how whole populations of organizations act.

Whenever individuals interact in organizations, many components come into play. Modern organizational studies attempt to understand and model these factors. Like all modernist social sciences, organizational studies seek to control, predict, and explain. There is some argument over the ethics of controlling workers' behaviour. Therefore, organizational behaviour or OB (and its cousin, Industrial psychology) have at times been accused of being the scientific tool of the powerful. Those accusations however, OB can play a major role in organizational development and success.

After the First World War, the focus of organizational studies changed to analysis of how human factors and psychology impressed organizations, a transformation propelled by the identification of the Hawthorne Effect. This Human Relations Movement focused on teams, motivation, and the actualization of the aims of individuals within organizations.

The Second World War further changed the field, as the invention of large-scale logistics and operations research led to a renewed interest in rationalist approaches to the study of organizations. Interest grew in theory and methods native to the sciences, comprising systems theory, and the study of organizations with a complexity theory perspective and complexity strategy. Influential work was done by Herbert Alexander Simon and James G. March and the so-called "Carnegie School" of organizational behaviour.

In the 1960s and 1970s, the field was powerfully determined by social psychology and the emphasis in academic study was on quantitative research. An explosion of theorizing, much of it at Stanford University and Carnegie Mellon, produced Bounded Rationality, Informal Establishment, Contingency Theory, Resource Dependence, Institutional Theory, and Organizational Ecology theories, between many others. Beginning in the 1980s, cultural explanations of organizations and change became an important part of study. Qualitative methods of study became more satisfactory, informed by anthropology, psychology and sociology.

Organizational behaviour is presently a growing field. Organizational studies departments generally form part of business schools, though many universities also have industrial psychology and industrial economics programs. The field is extremely authoritative in the business world with practitioners like Peter Drucker and Peter Senge, who turned the academic research into business practices. Organizational behaviour is becoming more important in the universal economy as individuals with diverse backgrounds and cultural values have to work together effectively and efficiently. It is also under increasing criticism as a field for its ethnocentric and pro-capitalist assumptions.

During last 20 years organizational behaviour study and practice has developed and flourished through producing integrations with other domains:

- Anthropology became an interesting prism to understanding firms as communities, by bringing in concepts like 'Organizational culture,' 'organizational rituals' and 'symbolic acts' enabling new ways to understand organizations as communities.
- Leadership Understanding the crucial role of leadership at numerous level of an establishment in the process of change management.
- Ethics and their importance as pillars of any vision and one of the most important driving forces in an establishment.

Note: For detailed information and understanding more on learning process, reader may visit this site: http://www.infosys.com/instepweb/

9

Motivating and Rewarding Employees

The job of a manager in the workplace is to get things done through employees. To do this the manager should be able to motivate employees. But that's easier said than done. Motivation practice and theory are difficult subjects, touching on several disciplines. Human nature can be very simple, yet very complex too. An understanding and appreciation of this is a prerequisite to effective employee motivation in the workplace and therefore effective management and leadership.

Quite apart from the benefit and moral value of an altruistic approach to treating colleagues as human beings and respecting human dignity in all its forms, research and observations show that well motivated employees are more productive and creative. The inverse also holds true.

DEFINING MOTIVATION

Many individuals wrongly view motivation as a personal trait-that is, some individuals have it, and others do not. But motivation is defined as the force that causes an individual to behave in a specific way. Simply put, a extremely motivated person works hard at a task; an unmotivated person doesn't. Managers frequently have difficulty in motivating employees. But motivation is really an internal process. It is the result of the interaction of a person's needs, his or his power to make choices about how to meet those needs, and the environment created by management that appropriates these needs to be met and the choices to be made. Motivation isn't something that a manager can "do" to an individual.

MOTIVATION THEORIES

Motivation is a composite phenomenon. Numerous theories attempt to explain how motivation works. In management circles, probably the most popular explanations of motivation are based on the needs of the individual. The fundamental needs model, referred to as content theory of motivation, highlights the specific factors that motivate an individual. Though these factors are found within an individual, things outside the individual can affect him or his as well.

In short, all individuals have needs that they want satisfied. Some are basic needs, such as those for food, sleep, and water-needs that deal with the physical aspects of behaviour and are regarded unlearned. These needs are biological in nature and relatively stable. Their influences on behaviour are generally obvious and therefore easy to identify.

Secondary needs, alternatively, are psychological, which means that they are learned mainly through experience. These demands vary importantly by culture and by individual. Secondary needs consist of internal states, such as the wish for power, achievement, and love. Identifying and interpreting these needs is more difficult because they are founded in a variety of ways. Secondary needs are accountable for most of the behaviour that a supervisor is concerned with and for the rewards a person seeks in an establishment. Numerous theorists, comprising Abraham Maslow, Frederick Herzberg, David McClelland, and Clayton Alderfer, have furnished theories to help explain motives as a source of motivation.

Motivation Theories: Needs

Abraham Maslow's Theory of Hierarchy Need

The great management scientists Abraham Maslow defined need as a physiological or psychological deficiency that a person feels the obsession to satisfy. This demand can produce tensions that can influence a person's work attitudes and behaviours. Maslow formed a theory based on his definition of need that proposes that humans are encouraged by multiple demands and that these needs exist in a hierarchical order. His premise is that only an unsatisfied need can influence behaviour; a satisfied motive isn't a motivator.

Maslow's theory is based on these two principles:

- Deficit principle: A satisfied need no more motivates behaviour because individuals act to satisfy deprived needs.
- Progression principle: The five needs he identified exist in a hierarchy, which means that a need at any stage only comes into play after a lower-level need has been satisfied.

In his theory, Maslow identified five levels of human needs. Table below illustrates these five levels and provides suggestions for satisfying each need.

Higher Level Needs	**To Satisfy, Offer:**
Self-actualization needs	Creative and challenging work
Participation in decision making	
	Task flexibility and autonomy
Esteem needs	Responsibility of an important task
	Promotion to higher position task
	Praise and recognition from boss
Lower Level Needs	**To Satisfy, Offer:**
Social needs	Friendly co-workers
	Interaction with customers
	Pleasant supervisor
Safety needs	Safe working conditions
	Task security
	Base compensation and benefits
Physiological needs	Rest and refreshment breaks
	Physical comfort on the task
	Reasonable work hours

Though research has not asserted the strict deficit and progression principles of Maslow's theory, his ideas can help managers understand and satisfy the demands of employees.

Herzberg's Two-factor Theory

Frederick Herzberg offers another framework for understanding the motivational significances of work environments.

In his two-factor theory, Herzberg identifies two sets of factors that affect motivation in the workplace:

- Hygiene factors let in salary, task security, working conditions, organizational policies, and technical quality of supervision.

Though these factors don't motivate employees, they can cause dissatisfaction if they are missing. Something as simple as adding music to the office place or implementing a no-smoking policy can make individuals less dissatisfied with these faces of their work. Nevertheless, these improvements in hygiene factors don't inevitably increase satisfaction.

- Satisfiers or motivators include such things as responsibility, accomplishment, growth opportunities, and feelings of recognition, and are the key to job satisfaction and motivation. For example, managers can find out what individuals actually do in their jobs and make improvements, therefore increasing job satisfaction and performance.

Following Herzberg's two-factor theory, managers involve to ensure that hygiene factors are adequate and then build satisfiers into jobs.

Alderfer's ERG Theory

Clayton Alderfer's ERG (Existence, Relatedness, Growth) theory is rested on Maslow's hierarchy of needs theory. To begin his theory, Alderfer collapses Maslow's five levels of demands into three categories.

- Existence needs are desires for physiological and material well-being. (In terms of Maslow's model, existence needs include physiological and safety needs).
- Relatedness needs are desires for satisfying interpersonal relationships. (In terms of Maslow's model, relatedness corresponds to social needs).
- Growth needs are desires for continued psychological growth and development. (In terms of Maslow's model, growth needs include esteem and self-realization needs).

This approach proposes that unsatisfied needs motivate behaviour, and that as lower level needs are satisfied, they become less important. Higher level needs, although, become more important as they are satisfied, and if these needs aren't met, a person may move down the hierarchy, which Alderfer calls the frustration-regression principle.

What he means by this term is that an already satisfied lower level need can become reactivated and determine behaviour when a higher level need cannot be satisfied. As a result, managers ought to provide opportunities for workers to capitalize on the importance of higher level demands.

McClelland's Acquired Needs Theory

David McClelland's acquired needs theory recognizes that everyone prioritizes demands differently. He also believes that individuals aren't born with these needs, but that they are really learned through life experiences. McClelland identifies three specific needs:

- Need for achievement is the drive to excel.
- Need for power is the wish to cause others to behave in a way that they would not have behaved otherwise.
- Need for affiliation is the wish for friendly, close interpersonal relationships and conflict avoidance.

McClelland associates each demand with a distinct set of work preferences, and managers can help tailor the environment to meet these needs.

High achievers differentiate themselves from others by their desires to do things better. These individuals are strongly inspired by task situations with personal responsibility, feedback, and an intermediate degree of risk. Additionally, high achievers frequently exhibit the following behaviours:

- Seek personal responsibility for finding solutions to problems.
- Want rapid feedback on their performances in order that they can tell easily whether they are improving or not.
- Set moderately challenging aims and perform best when they perceive their probability of success as 50-50.

An individual with a high need of power is likely to follow a path of continued promotion over time. Individuals with a high need of power frequently demonstrate the following behaviours:

- Enjoy being in charge.
- Want to influence others.
- Prefer to be placed into competitive and position-oriented situations.
- Tend to be more concerned with prestige and gaining influence over others than with effectual performance.

Individuals with the motive for affiliation seek companionship, social approval, and satisfying interpersonal relationships. Individuals needing affiliation exhibit the following behaviours:

- Take a special interest in work that provides companionship and social approval.

- Strive for friendship.
- Prefer cooperative situations rather than competitive ones.
- Desire relationships involving a high degree of mutual understanding.
- May not make the best managers because their wish for social approval and friendship may complicate managerial decision making.

Interestingly enough, a high need to attain doesn't inevitably lead to being a good manager, especially in large organizations. Individuals with high achievement needs are generally interested in how well they do personally and not in influencing others to do well. Alternatively, the best managers are high in their needs for power and low in their needs for association.

Motivation Theories: Behaviour

Process theories explain how workers select Behavioural actions to meet their needs and determine their choices. The following theories each offer advice and insight on how individuals actually make choices to work hard or not work hard based on their individual preferences, the available rewards, and the possible work outcomes.

Equity Theory

As per the equity theory, based on the work of J. Stacy Adams, workers compare the reward potential to the effort they must expend. Equity exists when workers perceive that rewards equal efforts.

Fig. The Equity Theory

But employees just do not look at their potential rewards, they consider the rewards of others as well. Inequities occur when individuals feel that their rewards are inferior to the rewards offered to other persons sharing the same workloads.

Employees who feel they are being covered inequitably may show the following behaviours:

- Put less effort into their jobs.
- Ask for better treatment and/or rewards.
- Find ways to make their work seem better by comparison.
- Transfer or quit their jobs.

The equity theory makes a good point: Individuals act as per their perceptions. What a manager thinks is irrelevant to an employee because the real issue is the way an employee perceives his or her situation. Rewards perceived as equitable ought to have positive results on job satisfaction and functioning; those rewards perceived as inequitable may produce task dissatisfaction and make performance problems. Every manager needs to see that any negative consequences from equity comparisons are annulled, or at least minimized, when rewards are allocated. Informed managers anticipate perceived negative inequities when especially visible rewards, such as pay increases or promotions, are allocated. Instead of letting equity concerns get out of hand, these managers carefully communicate the intended values of rewards being given, clarify the performance appraisals upon which these rewards are based, and suggest appropriate comparison points.

Expectancy Theory

Victor Vroom brought in one of the most widely consented explanations of motivation. Very simply, the expectancy theory says that an employee will be inspired to exercise a high level of effort when he believes that:

- Effort will lead to a good performance appraisal.
- A good appraisal will lead to organizational rewards.
- The organizational rewards will satisfy his personal aims.

The key to the expectancy theory is an understanding of an individual's aims and the relationships between attempt and performance, between performance and rewards, and finally, between the rewards and individual aim satisfaction. When an employee has a high level of expectancy and the reward is attractive, motivation is generally high.

Hence, to motivate workers, managers must strengthen workers' perceptions of their efforts as both possible and worthy, clarify expectations of performances, tie rewards to performances, and make a point that rewards are desirable.

Reinforcement Theory

The theory of reinforcement is based on E. L. Thorndike's law of effect, simply looks at the relationship between behaviour and its consequences. This theory focuses on modifying an employee's on-the-task behaviour through the appropriate use of one of the following four techniques:

- Avoidance is an attempt to show an employee what the consequences of improper behaviour will be. If an employee doesn't engage in improper behaviour, he or she will not experience the consequence.
- Extinction is fundamentally ignoring the behaviour of a subordinate and not providing either positive or negative reinforcement. Classroom teachers frequently use this skill when they ignore learners who are "acting out" to get attention. This proficiency ought to only be used when the supervisor perceives the behaviour as temporary, not typical, and not dangerous.
- Positive reinforcement rewards desirable behaviour. Positive reinforcement, such as a pay raise or promotion, is provided as a reward for positive behaviour with the purpose of increasing the probability that the required behaviour will be repeated.
- Punishment (threats, docking pay, suspension) is an effort to decrease the likelihood of a behaviour recurring by applying negative consequences.

The reinforcement theory has the following significances for management:

- Learning what is acceptable to the establishment determines inspired behaviour.
- Managers who are trying to motivate their employees ought to be sure to tell individuals what they are doing wrong and be careful not to reward all individuals at the same time.
- Managers must tell individuals what they can do to receive positive reinforcement.
- Managers must be sure to administer the reinforcement as closely as possible to the occurrence of the behaviour.

- Managers must recognize that failure to reward can also modify behaviour. Employees who believe that they deserve a reward and don't receive it will frequently become disillusioned with both their manager and company.

Goal-setting Theory

The goal-setting theory was brought in the late 1960s by Edwin Locke, who proposed that intentions to work toward an aim are a major source of work motivation. Aims, in essence, tell employees what needs to be done and how much effort ought to be expanded. Generally, the harder the aim, the higher the level of performance expected. Managers can set the aims for their employees, or employees and managers can develop aims together. One advantage of employees participating in aim setting is that they may be more likely to work toward an aim they aided to accomplish.

No matter who sets the aim, however, employees do better when they get feedback on their progress. Additionally to feedback, four other factors act upon the aims-performance relationship:

- The employee must be committed to the aim.
- The employee must believe that he is capable of performing the job.
- Jobs involved in achieving the aim ought to be simple, familiar, and independent.
- The aim-setting theory is culture bound.

If the aim-setting theory is followed, managers need to work with their employees in determining aim objectives in order to provide targets for motivation. Additionally, the aims that are based ought to be specific rather than general in nature, and managers must furnish feedback on performance.

MANAGEMENT PHILOSOPHIES AND MOTIVATION

Management philosophy can set the foundation for a positive work climate and influence a manager's approach to motivation. The way a manager views employees and communicates with employees affects their behaviour.

Two most popular theories are Douglas McGregor's Theory X and Theory Y, which talk about how managers produce self-fulfilling prophecies based on how they treat their employees. Another theory by

Chris Argyris centres on what he refers to as the mature worker. In his book, Personality and Establishment, Argyris contrasts the management practices discovered in conventional organizations with the demands and capabilities of the mature adult personality.

For instance, the concept of work specialization is supposed to make individuals work more efficiently because the works are much defined. Argyris believes that this concept may actually be counterproductive because it will limit an employee from reaching self-actualization.

Like McGregor, Argyris is concerned about how managers treat individuals. He believes that if managers treat their employees in a positive manner-as accountable adults-their employees will be more productive. However, Argyris takes this conception one step further. He believes that mature workers want additional responsibilities, a variety of jobs, and the power to participate in decisions. If not, he believes that the outcome will be employee absenteeism, apathy, and even alienation.

MOTIVATION STRATEGIES

To some extent, a high level of employee motivation is deduced from effectual management practices. To develop inspired employees, a manager must treat individuals as people, empower workers, provide an efficient reward system, redesign jobs, and produce a flexible workplace.

Empowering Employees

Empowerment occurs when individuals in an establishment are given autonomy, authority, trust, and encouragement to attain a job. Empowerment is designed to unshackle the worker and to retrace a task the worker's responsibility.

In an attempt to empower and to change some of the old bureaucratic ideas, managers are encouraging corporate intrapreneurships. Intrapreneurship promotes employees to pursue new ideas and gives them the authority to promote those ideas. Obviously, intrapreneurship isn't for the timid, because old structures and processes are ploughed upside down.

Providing an Effectual Reward System

Managers frequently use rewards to reinforce employee behaviour that they want to go forward. A reward is a work outcome of positive value to the individual. Organizations are rich in rewards for individuals whose performance achievements help meet organizational objectives.

Individuals receive rewards in one of the following two ways:

- Extrinsic rewards are outwardly administered. They are valued outcomes given to someone by another person, normally a supervisor or higher level manager. Common workplace examples are pay bonuses, promotions, time off, special assignments, office fixtures, awards, verbal praise, and so forth. In all cases, the motivational stimulus of extrinsic rewards originates outside the individual.
- Intrinsic rewards are self-administered. Think of the "natural high", a person may experience after completing a task. That person feels good because he has a feeling of competency, personal development, and self-control over his work. In contrast to extrinsic rewards, the motivational stimulus of intrinsic rewards is internal and does not depend on the actions of other individuals.

To prompt behaviour, the establishment needs to provide an effectual reward system. An effectual reward system has four elements:

- Rewards need to satisfy the fundamental demands of all employees.
- Rewards need to be comprised in the system and be comparable to ones offered by a competitive establishment in the same area.
- Rewards need to be available to individuals in the same positions and be distributed fairly and equitably.
- The overall reward system needs to be multifaceted. Because all individuals are different, managers must provide a range of rewards-pay, time off, recognition, or promotion. Additionally, managers ought to provide many different ways to earn these rewards.

This last point deserves to be noted. With the widely developing trend toward empowerment in industry, many employees and employers are beginning to view conventional pay systems as inadequate. In a conventional system, individuals are paid as per the positions they hold, not the contributions they make. As organizations adopt approaches built upon teams, customer satisfaction, and empowerment, workers need to be paid differently. Many organizations have already responded by designing many pay plans, designed by employee design teams, which base rewards on technique levels. Rewards demonstrate to employees that their behaviour is reserve and ought to be repeated. If employees do not feel that their work is valued, their motivation will decay.

Redesigning Jobs

Many individuals go to work every day and go through the same, half-hearted activities to perform their jobs. These individuals frequently refer to this condition as burnout. But smart managers can do something to improve this condition before an employee becomes bored and loses motivation. The concept of task redesign, which requires knowledge of and concern for the human qualities individuals bring with them to the establishment, applies motivational theories to the structure of work for amending productivity and satisfaction.

When redesigning jobs, managers look at both task scope and task depth. Redesign efforts may include the following:

- Task enlargement. Frequently referred to as horizontal task loading, task enlargement increases the form of jobs a task comprises. Though it does not increase the quality or the challenge of those jobs, task enlargement may reduce some of the monotony, and as an employee's boredom decreases, his or his work quality generally increases.
- Task rotation. This practice assigns individuals to different jobs or jobs to different individuals on a temporary basis. The idea is to add form and to expose individuals to the dependence that one task has on other jobs. Task rotation can encourage higher levels of contributions and renew interest and enthusiasm. The establishment benefits from a cross-trained manpower.
- Task enrichment. Also called vertical task loading, this application comprises not only an increased variety of jobs, but also provides an employee with more responsibility and authority. If the skills needed to do the task are skills that match the jobholder's abilities, task enrichment may improve morale and performance.

Creating Flexibility

Today's employees evaluate personal time. Because of family wants, a conventional nine-to-five workday may not work for many individuals. Hence, flextime, which permits employees to set and control their own work hours, is one way that organizations are accommodating their employees' needs. Here are some other options organizations are trying as well:

- A compressed workweek is a form of flextime that allows a full-time task to be completed in less than the standard 40-hour, five-day workweek. Its most common form is the 4/40 schedule, which gives employees three days off.each week. This schedule benefits the individual through more leisure time and lower commuting costs. The establishment ought to gain through lower absenteeism and improved performance. Of course, the danger in this type of scheduling is the possibility of increased fatigue.
- Task sharing or twinning occurs when one full-time task is split between two or more persons. Task sharing frequently involves each person working one-half day, but it can also be done on weekly or monthly sharing arrangements. When jobs can be split and shared, organizations can gain by hiring talented individuals who would otherwise be unable to work full-time. The qualified employee who is also a parent may not want to be in the office for a full day but may be willing to work a half-day. Though adjustment problems occasionally occur, the arrangement can be good for all concerned.
- Telecommuting, occasionally called flexiplace, is a work arrangement that allows at least a portion of scheduled work hours to be completed outside of the office, with work-at-home as one of the options. Telecommuting frees the jobholder from necessitating to work fixed hours, wearing special work attire, enduring the normal constraints of commuting, and having direct contact with supervisors. Home workers frequently demonstrate increased productivity, report fewer distractions, enjoy the freedom to be their own boss, and appreciate the profit of having more time for themselves.
- Naturally, when there are positives, there are also negatives. Many home workers feel that they work too much and are isolated from their family and friends. Additionally to the feelings of isolation, many employees feel that the want of visibility at the office may outcome in the loss of promotions.

Note: Employee satisfaction plays an important role in success of a company, as can be seen in the case of Google. In 2007 and 2008, Fortune Magazine placed Google at the top of its list of the hundred best places to work. Google's corporate philosophy embodies such casual principles as "you can make money without doing evil," "you can be serious without a suit," and "work ought to be challenging and the challenge ought to be fun." Reader can visit their site: http://www.google.org/about.html

10

Stress Management

Stress management covers techniques meant to equip a person with effectual coping mechanisms for dealing with psychological stress, with stress defined as a person's physiological response to an internal or external stimulus that triggers the fight-or-flight response. Stress management is effectual when a person utilizes strategies to meet or alter stressful situations. Walter Cannon and Hans Selye used animal studies to base the earliest scientific basis for the study of stress. They measured the physiological responses of animals to external pressures, such as heat and cold, prolonged restraint, and surgical processes, then generalized from these studies to human beings.

CONCEPT OF STRESS

Subsequent studies of stress in human being by Richard Rahe and others demonstrated the view that stress is caused by distinct, measurable life stressors, and further, that these life stressors can be ranked by the median degree of stress they create (leading to the Holmes and Rahe Stress Scale). Therefore, stress was traditionally conceptualized to be a result of external insults beyond the control of those experiencing the stress. More recently, nevertheless, it has been argued that external considerations don't have any intrinsical capacity to create stress, but instead their effect is mediated by the individual's perceptions, capacities, and understanding. Stress is a psychological and physiological response to events that upset our personal equilibrium in some way.

When faced with a threat, whether to our physical safety or emotional equilibrium, the body's defences kick into high gear in a rapid, automatic process known as the "fight-or-flight" response. We all know what this stress reaction feels like: heart pounding in the chest, muscles tensing up, breath coming faster, all sense on red alert.

The Body's Stress Response

The "fight-or-flight" stress response involves a cascade of biological changes that prepare us for emergency action. When danger is sensed, a small part of the brain called the hypothalamus sets off a chemical alarm. The sympathetic nervous system responds by releasing a flood of stress hormones, comprising adrenaline, nor-epinephrine, and cortisol. These stress hormones race through the bloodstream, readying us to either flee the scené or battle it out.

Heart rate and blood flow to the large muscles increase, so we can run faster and fight harder. Blood vessels under the skin constrict to prevent blood loss in case of injury, pupils dilate, so we can see better, and our blood sugar ramps up, giving us an energy boost and speeding up reaction time. At the same time, body processes not essential to immediate survival is suppressed. The digestive and reproductive systems slow down, growth hormones are switched off, and the immune response is inhibited.

The biological stress response is meant to protect and support us. It is what helped our stone age ancestors survive the life-or-death situations they commonly faced. But in the modern world, most of the stress we feel is in response to psychological rather than physical threats. Caring for a chronically-ill child or getting audited by the IRS qualifies as stressful situations, but neither calls for either fight or flight. Regrettably, our bodies do not make this distinction. Whether we're stressed over a looming deadline, an argument with a friend, or a mountain of bills, the warning bells ring. And just like a caveman confronting a sabre-toothed tiger, we go into automatic overdrive.

If you have a lot of responsibilities and worries, you may be running on stress a good portion of the time-launching into emergency mode with every traffic jam, phone call from the in-laws, or segment of the evening news. But the problem with the stress response is that the more it is activated, the harder it is to shut off. Instead of levelling off once the crisis has passed, your stress hormones, heart rate, and blood pressure remain elevated.

Moreover, extended or repeated activation of the stress response takes a heavy toll on the body. Prolonged exposure to stress increases your risk of everything from heart disease, obesity, and infection to anxiety, depression, and memory problems. Because of the widespread damage it can cause, it is essential to learn how to deal with stress in a more positive way and reduce its impact on your daily life.

Signs and Symptoms of Stress

To get a handle on stress, you first need to learn how to recognize it in yourself. Stress affects the mind, body, and behaviour in many ways-all directly tied to the physiological changes of the fight-or-flight response. The specific signs and symptoms of stress vary widely from person to person. Some individuals primarily experience physical symptoms, such as low back pain, stomach problems, and skin outbreaks. In others, the stress pattern centres around emotional symptoms, such as crying jags or hypersensitivity. For still others, changes in the way they think or behave predominates.

The following table lists some of the common warning signs and symptoms of stress. Use it to identify the symptoms you normally experience when you're under stress. If you know your red flags, you can take early steps to deal with the stressful situation before it-or your emotions-spiral out of control.

Stress Warning Signs and Symptoms:

Cognitive Symptoms

- Memory problems
- Indecisiveness
- Inability to concentrate
- Trouble thinking clearly
- Poor judgment
- Seeing only the negative
- Anxious or racing thoughts
- Constant worrying
- Loss of objectivity
- Fearful anticipation

Emotional Symptoms

- Moodiness
- Agitation
- Restlessness
- Short temper
- Irritability, impatience
- Inability to relax
- Feeling tense and "on edge"

- Feeling overwhelmed
- Sense of loneliness and isolation
- Depression or general unhappiness

Physical Symptoms

- Headaches or backaches
- Muscle tension and stiffness
- Diarrhoea or constipation
- Nausea, dizziness
- Insomnia
- Chest pain, rapid heartbeat
- Weight gain or loss
- Skin breakouts (hives, eczema)
- Loss of sex drive
- Frequent colds

Behavioural Symptoms

- Eating more or less
- Sleeping too much or too little
- Isolating yourself from others
- Procrastination, neglecting responsibilities
- Using alcohol, cigarettes, or drugs to relax
- Nervous habits (e.g. nail biting, pacing)
- Teeth grinding or jaw clenching
- Overdoing activities (e.g. exercising, shopping)
- Overreacting to unexpected problems
- Picking fights with others

Keep in mind that the signs and symptoms of stress can also be caused by other psychological and medical problems. If you're experiencing any of the warning signs of stress, it is important to see a doctor for a full evaluation. Your doctor can help you determine whether or not your symptoms are stress-related.

SOURCES OF STRESS

The potential causes of stress are varied and extremely individual. What you consider stressful depends on many factors, comprising your personality, general outlook on life, problem-solving abilities, and social support system. Something that's stressful to you may not faze someone else, or they may even enjoy it. For example, your morning commute may make you anxious and tense because you worry that traffic will make you late.

Others, nevertheless, may find the trip relaxing because they allow more than enough time and enjoy listening to music while they drive. The pressures and demands that cause stress are known as stressors. We generally think of stressors as being negative, such as an exhausting work schedule or a rocky relationship. Nevertheless, anything that forces us to adjust can be a stressor. This comprises positive events such as getting married or receiving a promotion. Irrespective of whether an event is good or bad, if the adjustment it commands strains our coping skills and adaptive resources, the end effect is stress.

Major Life Changes

Many a times a few major life events are stressors. Whether it be a divorce, a child leaving home, a planned pregnancy, a move to a new town, a career change, graduating from college, or a diagnosis of cancer, the faster or more dramatic the change, the greater the strain. Furthermore, the more major life changes you're dealing with at any one time, the more stress you'll feel.

Daily Hassles and Demands

While major life changes are stressful, they are also proportional rarities. After all, it is not every day that you file for divorce or have a baby. Nevertheless, you may battle traffic, argue with your family members, or worry about your finances on a daily basis. Because these small disturbs take place so on a regular basis, they end up affecting us the most.

The daily causes of stress include:

- Environmental stressors: Your physical surroundings can set off the stress response. Examples of environmental stressors include an unsafe neighbourhood, pollution, noise (sirens keeping you up at night, a barking dog next door), and uncomfortable living conditions. For individuals living in crime-ridden areas or war-torn regions, the stress may be persistent.
- Family and relationship stressors: Problems with friends, romantic partners, and family members are common daily stressors. Marital disagreements, dysfunctional relationships,

rebellious teens, or caring for a chronically-ill family member or a child with special needs can all send stress levels skyrocketing.

- Work stressors: In our career-driven society, work can be an ever-present source of stress. Work stress is caused by things such as task dissatisfaction, an exhausting workload, insufficient pay, office politics, and contravenes with your boss or co-workers.

Internal Causes of Stress

Not all stress is induced by external pressures and demands. Your stress can also be self-generated. Internal causes of stress include:

- Uncertainty or worries
- Pessimistic attitude
- Self-criticism
- Unrealistic expectations or beliefs
- Perfectionism
- Low self-esteem
- Excessive or unexpressed anger
- Want of assertiveness

EFFECTS OF STRESS

The presence of a stressor does not mechanically result in disabling stress symptoms. The degree to which any stressful situation or event impacts your daily operating depends partly on the nature of the stressor itself and partly on your own personal and extraneous resources.

Chronic stress wears you down day after day and year after year, with no visible get away. Under sustained or severe stress, even the most well-adjusted person loses the power to adapt. When stress gets over our coping resources, our bodies and minds suffer.

Health Effects

Current research suggests that anywhere from 60 to 90 percent of illness is stress-related. The physical wear and tear of stress comprises damage to the cardiovascular system and immune system suppression. Stress compromises your power to fight off disease and infection, throws your digestive system off equilibrium, makes it difficult to conceive a baby, and can yet stunt growth in children.

Many medical conditions are caused or exacerbated by stress, including:

- Chronic pain
- Migraines
- Ulcers
- Heartburn
- High blood pressure
- Heart disease
- Diabetes
- Asthma
- PMS
- Obesity
- Infertility
- Autoimmune diseases
- Irritable bowel syndrome
- Skin problems

Emotional Effects

Chronic stress grinds away at your mental health, causing emotional impairment additionally to physical ailments. Long-term stress can even rewire the brain, leaving you more vulnerable to everyday pressures and less able to cope. Over time, stress can lead to mental unhealthinesses such as:

- Anxiety
- Depression
- Eating disorders
- Substance abuse

Severe stress reactions can outcome from sudden, catastrophic events or traumatic experiences such as a natural disaster, sexual assault, life-threatening accident, or participation in combat. After the initial shock and emotional fallout, many trauma victims gradually begin to recover from its effects. But for some individuals, the stress symptoms do not go away, the body does not regain its equilibrium, and life does not return to normal. This severe and persisting reaction to trauma is known as post-traumatic stress disorder (PTSD).

Common symptoms of PTSD include:

- Avoidance of places and things associated with the trauma
- Chronic irritability and tension
- Depression
- Flashbacks, intrusive thoughts, or nightmares about the trauma
- Hyper vigilance for signs of danger

MODELS OF STRESS MANAGEMENT

It happens to all of us and sometimes, we feel there is no way out. I'm talking about stress which is one of the leading challenges that the human kind is constantly grappling with trying to understand and deal with it effectively. There might be simple words to describe stress and sometimes it does not need any definition because we all go through it. Experts have been working on effective stress management methods which would seek to remedy all harmful effects that stress is associated with and eradicate it all together. So far, some models have been devised and, they might hold the key to deal with stress and they include the following.

Transactional Model

In 1984, Richard Lazarus and Susan Folkman suggested that stress can be thought of as resulting from an "imbalance between demands and resources" or as occurring when "pressure exceeds one's perceived power to cope". Stress management was developed and premised on the idea that stress isn't a direct response to a stressor but rather one's resources and power to cope mediate the stress response and are amenable to change, therefore allowing stress to be controllable. In order to develop an effectual stress management programme it is first necessary to identify the factors that are central to a person controlling his/her stress, and to identify the intervention methods which in effect target these factors.

Lazarus and Folkman's interpretation of stress focuses on the transaction amongst individuals and their external environment (known as the Transactional Model). The model conceptualizes stress as a result of how a stressor is appraised and how a person appraises his/her resources to cope with the stressor. The model breaks the stressor-stress link by proposing that if stressors are perceived as positive or challenging rather than a threat, and if the stressed person is confident that he/she possesses enough rather than deficient coping strategies, stress may not inevitably follow the presence of a potential stressor. The model proposes that stress can be reduced by helping stressed individuals change their perceptions of stressors, providing them with strategies to help them cope and improving their assurance in their power to do so.

Health Realization Health Model

The health realization/innate health model of stress is also founded on the idea that stress doesn't necessarily follow the presence of a potential stressor. Instead of focusing on the individual's appraisal of so-called stressors in relation to his or his own coping skills (as the transactional model does), the health realization model focuses on the nature of thought, stating that it is ultimately a person's thought processes that determine the reaction to potentially stressful external circumstances. In this model, stress results from appraising oneself and one's circumstances through a mental filter of insecurity and negativity, whereas a feeling of well-being comes from approaching the world with a "quiet mind," "inner wisdom," and "common sense". This model proposes that helping stressed individuals understand the nature of thought--especially providing them with the power to recognize when they are in the grip of unsafe thinking, disengage from it, and access natural positive feelings--will cut down their stress.

TECHNIQUES OF STRESS MANAGEMENT

There are numerous ways of coping with stress. Some techniques of time management may help a person to control stress. In the face of high demands, effectual stress management involves learning to set limits and to say "No" to some demands that others make. Techniques of stress management will change as per the theoretical paradigm adhered to, but may include some of the following:

- Autogenic training
- Cognitive therapy
- Conflict resolution
- Exercise
- Masturbation
- getting a hobby
- Meditation
- Deep breathing
- Nootropic
- Relaxation techniques

- expressing it in art
  - — Fractional relaxation
  - — Progressive relaxation
  - — Stress balls
- Natural medicine
- Clinically validated alternative treatments
- Time management
- Listening to certain types of relaxing music, particularly:
  - — New Age music
  - — Classical music

Levels of stress can be assessed. One way is through the use of the Holmes and Rahe Stress Scale to rate stressful life events. Changes in blood pressure and galvanic skin response can also be measured to test stress levels, and changes in stress levels. A digital thermometer can be used to evaluate changes in skin temperature, which can indicate activation of the fight or flight response drawing blood away from the extremities. Stress management has physiological and immune gain effects.

We all face several types of challenges and obstacles, and occasionally the pressure is hard to handle. When we feel overwhelmed, under the gun, or unsure how to meet the demands placed on us, we experience stress. In small doses, stress can be a good thing. It can give you the push you need, motivating you to do your best and to stay focused and alert. Stress is what keeps you on your toes during a presentation at work or drives you to study for your midterm when you'd rather be watching TV. But when the going gets too tough and life's demands outstrip your power to cope, stress becomes a threat to both your physical and emotional well-being.

Note: Recent estimates suggest that task stress costs business more than $600 billion a year in absenteeism, compensation claims, increased health insurance costs, and lowered productivity. For a detailed example in stress management visit: http://www.lge.gov.uk/lge/core/page.do?pageId=119917

11

Understanding Teams

As part of a team, an employee is required to give his or her all for the team, professionally speaking. Ideally, working toward a common goal should be the most important reward for any employee. And as a team member, an employee should be proud and motivated to be a part of the team's effort toward organizational goals. When a team achieves a goal, each team member is unlikely to forget his or her experience of being a part of a successful team. In the new world of business, many tasks are completed through teamwork, but very few teams work all that well. In this chapter, methods ordinary team members can use to achieve extraordinary results are discussed. Also examined in this chapter are the different types of work teams, the stages of team development, the benefits of teams, and the strategies that management can use to resolve team conflicts.

GROUP DYNAMICS AND TEAMS

Generally the term 'Team building' refers to the process of establishing and developing a greater sense of collaboration and trust between team members. Interactive exercises, team assessments, and group discussions enable groups to cultivate this more cracking sense of teamwork.

Characteristics of Good Team Building

- Each team member is willing to contribute
- Each team member knows he can influence the team agenda
- High level of interdependence among team members
- Team and individuals are prepared to take risks
- Team develops a relaxed climate for communication
- Team has capacity to produce new ideas

- Team is clear about aims and establishes targets
- Team leader has good individuals skills and is committed to team approach
- Team member roles are defined
- Team members develop a mutual trust
- Team members know how to examine team and individual errors without personal attacks

Team Effectiveness

When evaluating how well team members are working in concert, the following statements can be used as a guide:

- Team aims are developed through a group process of team fundamental interaction and agreement in which each team member is willing to work toward achieving these aims.
- Participation is actively shown by all team members and roles are shared to facilitate the achievement of jobs and feelings of group togetherness.
- Feedback is asked for by members and freely given as a way of evaluating the team's performance and clarifying both feelings and interests of the team members. When feedback is given it is done with a wish to help the other person.
- Team decision making involves a process that encourages active participation by all members.
- Leadership is distributed and shared among team members and people willingly lead their resources as required.
- Problem solving, discussing team issues, and critiquing team effectiveness are promoted by all team members.
- Conflict isn't suppressed. Team members are allowed to express negative feelings and confrontation within the team which is managed and dealt with by team members. Dealing with and handling conflict is seen as a way to improve team performance.
- Team member resources, talents, skills, knowledge, and experiences are fully identified, acknowledged, and used whenever appropriate.
- Risk taking and creativity are encouraged. When mistakes are made, they are treated as a source of learning rather than reasons for punishment.

After evaluating team performance against the above rules of thumb, determine those areas in which the team members need to amend and develop a strategy for doing so.

THEORIES OF GROUP FORMATION

Kurt Lewin's Individual Change Process

The first systematic study of group development was carried out by Kurt Lewin, who introduced the term "group dynamics". His ideas about mutual, cross-level influence and quasi-stationary equilibria, although uncommon in the traditional empirical research on group development, have resurged recently. His early model of individual change, which has served as the basis of many models of group development, described change as a three-stage process: unfreezing, change, and freezing.

Unfreezing:	This phase involves overcoming inertia and dismantling the existing "mind set". Defence mechanisms have to be bypassed.
Change	In the second stage change occurs. This is typically a period of confusion and transition. One is aware that the old ways are being challenged but does not have a clear picture to replace them with yet.
Freezing	In the third stage the new mindset is crystallizing and one's comfort level is returning to previous levels. This is often misquoted as "refreezing".

Tuckman's Stages

Bruce Tuckman reviewed about fifty studies of group development (including Bales' model) in the mid-sixties and synthesized their commonalities in one of the most frequently cited models of group development. The model describes four linear stages that a group will go through in its unitary sequence of decision making. A fifth stage was added in 1977 when a new set of studies were reviewed.

Forming:	Group members learn about each other and the task at hand. Indicators of this stage might include: Unclear objectives, Uninvolvement, Uncommitted members, Confusion, Low morale, Hidden feelings, Poor listening, etc.
Storming:	As group members continue to work, they will engage each other in arguments about the structure of the group

	which often are significantly emotional and illustrate a struggle for status in the group. These activities mark the storming phase: Lack of cohesion, Subjectivity, Hidden agendas, Conflicts, Confrontation, Volatility, Resentment, anger, Inconsistency, Failure.
Norming:	Group members establish implicit or explicit rules about how they will achieve their goal. They address the types of communication that will or will not help with the task. Indicators include: Questioning performance, Reviewing/clarify objective, Changing/confirming roles, Opening risky issues, Assertiveness, Listening, Testing new ground, Identifying strengths and weaknesses.
Performing:	Groups reach a conclusion and implement the conclusion. Indicators include: Creativity, Initiative, Flexibility, Open relationships, Pride, Concern for people, Learning, Confidence, High morale, Success, etc.
Adjourning:	As the group project ends, the group disbands in the adjournment phase. This phase was added when Tuckman and Jensen's updated their original review of the literature in 1977.

Each of the five stages in the Forming-storming-norming-performing-adjourning model proposed by Tuckman involves two aspects: interpersonal relationships and task behaviours. Such a distinction is similar to Bales' (1950) equilibrium model which states that a group continuously divides its attention between instrumental (task-related) needs and expressive (socioemotional).

As Gersick (1988) has pointed out, some later models followed similar sequential patterns. Examples include: define the situation, develop new skills, develop appropriate roles, carry out the work (Hare, 1976); orientation, dissatisfaction, resolution, production, termination (LaCoursiere, 1980); and generate plans, ideas, and goals; choose & agree on alternatives, goals, and policies; resolve conflicts and develop norms; perform action tasks and maintain cohesion (McGrath, 1984).

Tubbs' Systems Model

Stewart Tubbs "systems" approach to studying small group interaction led him to the creation of a four-phase model of group development:

Orientation:	In this stage, group members get to know each other, they start to talk about the problem, and they examine the limitations and opportunities of the project.
Conflict:	Conflict is a necessary part of a group's development. Conflict allows the group to evaluate ideas and it helps the group avoid conformity and groupthink
Consensus:	Conflict ends in the consensus stage, when group members compromise, select ideas, and agree on alternatives.
Closure	In this stage, the final result is announced and group members reaffirm their support of the decision.

Fisher's Theory of Decision Emergence in Groups

Fisher outlines four phases through which task groups tend to proceed when engaged in decision making. By observing the distribution of act-response pairs (a.k.a. "interacts") across different moments of the group process, Fisher noted how the interaction changed as the group decision was formulated and solidified. His method pays special attention to the "content" dimension of interactions by classifying statements in terms of how they respond to a decision proposal (e.g. agreement, disagreement, etc.).

Orientation:	During the orientation phase, group members get to know each other and they experience a primary tension: the awkward feeling people have before communication rules and expectations are established. Groups should take time to learn about each other and feel comfortable communicating around new people.
Conflict:	The conflict phase is marked by secondary tension, or tension surrounding the task at hand. Group members will disagree with each other and debate ideas. Here conflict is viewed as positive, because it helps the group achieve positive results.
Emergence:	In the emergence phase, the outcome of the group's task and its social structure become apparent. Group members soften their positions and undergo and attitudinal change that makes them less tenacious in defending their individual viewpoint.

Reinforcement:	In this stage, group members bolster their final decision by using supportive verbal and nonverbal communication.

Based on this categorization, Fisher created his "Decision Proposal Coding System" that identifies act-response pairs associated with each decision-making phase. Interestingly, Fisher observed that the group decision making process tended to be more cyclical and, in some cases, almost erratic. He hypothesized that the interpersonal demands of discussion require "breaks" from task work. In particular, Fisher observed that there are a number of contingencies that might explain some of the decision paths taken by some groups. For instance, in modifying proposals, groups tend to follow one of two patterns. If conflict is low, the group will reintroduce proposals in less abstract, more specific language. When conflict is higher, the group might not attempt to make a proposal more specific but, instead, because disagreement lies on the basic idea, the group introduces substitute proposals of the same level of abstraction as the original.

Poole's Multiple-sequences Model

Marshall Scott Poole's model suggests that different groups employ different sequences in making decisions. In contrast to unitary sequence models, the multiple sequences model addresses decision making as a function of several contingency variables: task structure, group composition, and conflict management strategies. Poole developed a descriptive system for studying multiple sequences, beyond the abstract action descriptions of previous studies. From Bales' Interaction Process Analysis System and Fisher's Decision Proposal Coding System, Poole proposes 36 clusters of group activities for coding group interactions and 4 cluster-sets: proposal development, socioemotional concerns, conflict, and expressions of ambiguity. However, in his latter work, Poole rejected phasic models of group development and proposed a model of continuously developing threads of activity. In essence, discussions are not characterized by blocks of phases, one after another, but by intertwining tracks of activity and interaction.

Poole suggests three activity tracks: task progress, relational, and topical focus. Interspersed with these are breakpoints, marking changes in the development of strands and links between them. Normal breakpoints pace the discussion with topic shifts and adjournments. Delays, another breakpoint, are holding patterns of recycling through information. Finally, disruptions break the discussion threads with conflict or task failure.

Task track:	The task track concerns the process by which the group accomplishes its goals, such as dealing doing problem analysis, designing solutions, etc.
Relation track:	The relation track deals with the interpersonal relationships between the group members. At times, the group may stop its work on the task and work instead on its relationships, share personal information or engage in joking.
Topic track:	The topic track includes a series of issues or concerns the group have over time
Breakpoints:	Breakpoints occur when a group switches from one track to another. Shifts in the conversation, adjournment, or postponement are examples of breakpoints.

McGrath's Time, Interaction, and Performance (TIP) Theory

McGrath's (1991) work emphasized the notion that different teams might follow different developmental paths to reach the same outcome. He also suggested that teams engage in four modes of group activity: inception, technical problem solving, conflict resolution, and execution According to this model, modes "are potential, not required, forms of activity" resulting in Modes I and IV (inception and execution) being involved in all group tasks and projects while Modes II (technical problem solving) and III (conflict resolution) may or may not be involved in any given group activity (Hare, 2003 uses the terms meaning, resources, integration, and goal attainment for these four modes).

McGrath further suggested that all team projects begin with Mode I (goal choice) and end with Mode IV (goal attainment) but that Modes II and III may or may not be needed depending on the task and the history of the group's activities. McGrath contended that for each identified function, groups can follow a variety of alternative "time-activity paths" in order to move from the initiation to the completion of a given function. Specifically, TIP theory states that there is a "default path" between two modes of activity which is "satisfying" or "least effort" path, and that such default path will "prevail unless conditions warrant some more complex path".

Mode I: Inception	Inception and acceptance of a project (goal choice)

Mode II: Technical Problem Solving	Solution of technical issues (means choice)
Mode III: Conflict Resolution	Resolution of conflict, that is, of political issues (policy choice)
Mode IV: Execution	Execution of the performance requirements of the project (goal attainment)

This model also states that groups adopt these four modes with respect to each of three team functions: production, well-being, and member support. In this sense, groups are seen as "always acting in one of the four modes with respect to each of the three functions, but they are not necessarily engaged in the same mode for all functions, nor are they necessarily engaged in the same mode for a given function on different projects that may be concurrent". The following table illustrates the relationship between modes and functions.

TEAMWORK DEFINED

The conventional workplace, with its emphasis on internal competition and individual star performers, is undergoing a transformation. Management experts and researchers suggest that a successful establishment is characterized by effectual teamwork and leadership rather than management. Organizations are realizing the importance of developing teams that can work in a co-ordinated, efficient, and creative fashion.

As a result, managers are accountable for creating, developing, and supporting the cooperative efforts of individuals under their influence. Compiling honest, clear-eyed evaluations of how these individuals interact is a critical first step to building cohesive, long-term working relationships. Interactions among employees can be qualified in three ways:

- Groups: A group exists almost anywhere two or more individuals interact or coexist. A group doesn't have a unified purpose. Many individuals mistakenly expect that simply working in close proximity to others is enough to allow an effectual team to emerge. Not so. Though individuals may be close physically, do not assume that their thought processes or levels of commitment are in sync. Remember that an individual may work simply for a pay check and show a want of concern for the establishment, its activities, its mission, and its individuals that is obvious to even the most casual observer. These individuals do just enough to get by, but not enough to make a difference.

- Mobs: Unlike groups, mobs have a unified purpose. Mobs of employees frequently form with the focused intent to challenge, malign, or even sabotage the recognized order. Though many individuals think of mobs as chaotic, disorganized, and unstructured, they are actually very purposeful in their actions.
- Team: Teams share a common aim. A team is composed of two or more individuals who interact on a regular basis and co-ordinate their work to attain a mutual objective. Some management experts believe that highest productivity results only when groups become teams.

The major difference between groups and teams centres more or less around how work gets done. Work groups emphasize individual work products, individual accountability, and even individual-centred leadership. In contrast, work teams share leadership roles, have both individual and mutual accountability, and produce collective work products. In other words, a work group's performance is a function of what its members do as people, while a team's performance is based on collective results-what two or more workers attain jointly.

TYPES OF TEAMS

The development of teams and teamwork has developed dramatically in all types of organizations for one simple reason: No one person has the power to deliver the kinds of products and services required in today's extremely competitive marketplace. Organizations must depend on the cooperative nature of numerous teams to produce successful ventures and outcomes. Teams can be vertical (functional), horizontal (cross-functional), or self-directed (self-managed) and can be used to produce new products, complete specific projects, insure quality, or replace operating departments.

- Functional teams perform specific organizational functions and include members from several vertical levels of the hierarchy. In other words, a functional team is composed of a manager and his or his subordinates for a special functional area. Accounting, personnel, and purchasing departments are examples of functional teams.
- Cross-functional teams are made up of experts in several specialties (or functions) working together on many

organizational tasks. Team members come from such departments as research and development, design, engineering, marketing, and distribution. These teams are frequently empowered to make decisions without the approval of management. For instance, when Nabisco's executives concluded that the company needed to improve its relationship with customers and better satisfy customers' needs, they created cross-functional teams whose assignments were to find ways to do just that. Though functional teams are generally permanent, cross-functional teams are frequently temporary, lasting for as little as a few months or as long as several years, depending on the group tasks being performed.

- Self-directed work teams, or self-managed teams, operate without managers and are accountable for complete work processes or segments that deliver products or services to external or internal customers. Self-directed work teams (SDWTs) are designed to give employees a feeling of "ownership" of a whole task. For instance, at Tennessee Eastman, a division of Eastman Kodak Company, teams are accountable for whole product lines-admitting processing, lab work, and packaging. With shared team responsibilities for work outcomes, team members frequently have broader task assignments and cross-train to master other jobs. This cross-training lets greater team flexibility.

No matter what type of team is formed, the benefits of teamwork are many, comprising synergy and increased skills, knowledge, productivity, flexibility, and commitment. Among the other benefits are changed job satisfaction, employee empowerment, and improved quality and organizational effectiveness.

EFFECTIVENESS OF TEAMS

High-performance teams do not just appear; they are developed and raised. By themselves, leaders with vision cannot guarantee the development of such high-performance teams, nor can members who wish to be part of such teams. The development of high-performance teams takes the mixed efforts of visionary leaders and inspired team members. Additionally, facilitators with expertise in team building are needed. The following lists the characteristics that constitute high-performance teams:

The team has a common focus, comprising clear and graspable aims, plans of action, and ways to measure success.

- Each member has clearly defined expectations of other members.
- Each member is able to give, receive, and elicit essential feedback.
- Members value each other's deviations in healthy and productive ways.
- Roles and responsibilities are clearly defined for each team member.
- The team fully utilizes its resources-both internal and external.
- The team is able to reach aims by achieving the requisite results.
- The team members manage their meetings in a productive way.

To build an effectual team, a leader necessitates to establish an organizational environment in which individual team members can reflect upon and analyze relationships with other team members. A leader ought to encourage the solution of any conflicts through healthy, professional confrontation, and willingly and openly negotiate necessary changes. In short, effectual leaders are cheerleaders for the team; they encourage and support members who are committed and actively demanded with their teams and engage those members who are not participating. Several factors within an establishment itself influence team effectiveness, comprising its organizational culture, level of autonomy, and types of feedback mechanisms. But the factors that determine the effectiveness of a team most directly stem from its internal structure and processes.

- Structural factors include team or group type, size, and composition of skills and abilities.
- Team processes include stages of team development, cultural norms, functions cohesiveness, and interpersonal processes such as trust development, facilitation, influence, leadership communication, and conflict solution.

To judge the effectiveness of their teams, leaders need to examine their teams' performances and personal results. Performance outcomes may be measured by products made, ideas generated, customers served, numbers of defects per thousand items produced, overtime hours, items sold, and customer satisfaction levels. Personal outcomes may be measured by employee satisfaction, commitment, and willingness of members to stay on the team. Both results are important for the long-term viability as well as the short-term success of the team.

TEAM BUILDING

Team building demands managers to follow a systematic planning and implementation process to assess whether teams can improve the establishment's aim attainment; to remove barriers to team building; and to build effectual teams through training, empowerment, and feedback. Managers must also decide on team size and member roles to gain the level best contribution for all members.

To produce effectual teams, managers need to avoid the following six deadly sins of team building:

1. Lack of a model. A team leader frequently focuses on a single aspect of team operating, such as communication practices. But many other elements are critical to team success and effectiveness, and a team is only as strong as its weakest component. A single-dimensional team-building process may cause frustration and destroy the believability of the process.

   Fix: A model of how teams function is needed to address all the components that result in reduced team effectiveness. At a minimum, the following must be considered for team effectiveness:

   — A system of reinforcement and celebration
   — Clear understanding of team members' roles and functions
   — Clear understanding of the team's relationship to the establishment
   — Clearly stated and commonly held vision and aims
   — Effectual and skilled interpersonal relations
   — Efficient and shared understanding of processes and norms
   — Talent and skills needed to cope with the aims
2. Lack of diagnosis. Each team has distinct strengths and weaknesses, which team building, must bear in mind. The team leader must be aware of these strengths and weaknesses.

   Fix: The leader must assess his team's strength and weaknesses. Though assessment and diagnostic instruments can be purchased, employing an outside consultant to complete a thorough team assessment is advisable.

3. Short-term intervention. Some managers think that a one-day retreat or team-building exercise will resolve issues causing tension and frustration. One day, no matter how good it is, isn't going to makc much of a change in the norms, culture, or practices of a team. A one-day retreat may bring to light issues that cannot be solved during that day and are left to fester, leading in team members mistrusting the process.

   Fix: Plan a long-term strategy for team building. One year is a good time frame for this plan.

4. No evaluation of progress. Because team building is a long-term process, both management and team members need to know whether it is succeeding. A mechanism for evaluation of team functioning needs to be in place in order that the team leader can name barriers and eliminate them.

   Fix: Plan regular evaluations of team progress. The diagnostic instrument used initially can be used at regular intervals to gauge progress.

5. Leadership detachment. The detached manager looks at team development as something that will help others change in order that the team will function more effectively. Nevertheless, the most significant person in most teams is the formal leader or manager who sets the tone for the team, whether deliberately or unintentionally.

   Fix: A manager must be willing to hear from employees about how his or his behaviour impacts the team, whether negatively or positively. The worst thing that an establishment can do is to begin the process and refuse to acknowledge that a manager is a key player in the process.

6. Addressing all problems internally. Team building cannot succeed unless conflicts and problems are brought into the open and dealt with properly. Poorly functioning teams are characterized by climates of blame, defensiveness, and a want of power to deal with conflict. These teams cannot amend themselves.

   Fix: Consider employing an outside consultant to help if a team is very negative or has undecided conflicts. The most important reason for using an outside consultant is that an "outsider" has no preconceptions or agenda.

Remember that poor team building is worsen than doing nothing. Poorly thought-out efforts are likely to increase negativity, reduce team functioning, and reduce management credibility. A manager's personal reputation and the degree to which employees have confidence in him are at stake.

STAGES IN TEAM DEVELOPMENT

Team building requires a manager to follow a systematic planning and implementation process to assess whether his or his team can improve the establishment's aim attainment; remove barriers to team building; and build an effectual team through training, empowerment, and feedback. Managers must also decide on team size and member roles to gain the maximum share from all members.

By and large, when organizations form teams, these organizations have specific projects or aims in mind. A team is simply a tool that accomplishes a project or aim. But no matter what the reason teams are formed, they go through four stages, as per a 1965 research paper by Bruce Tuckman of the Naval Medical Research Institute at Bethesda. Tuckman's four stages are:

Stage 1: Forming

All through the forming stage, team members not only get to know each other but also familiarize themselves with their task and with other individuals interested in the project, such as supervisors. At the close of the forming stage, team members ought to know the following:

- A fundamental set of team rules
- A rough project schedule
- Each member's project responsibilities
- The main phases of the mission
- The project's overall mission
- The resources at their disposal

Keep in mind that no one person demands to be accountable for the team. Project management duties can be shared, with different members taking responsibilities for each stage of the project.

Stage 2: Storming

Storming is qualified by competition and conflict within the team as members learn to bend and mould their feelings, ideas, attitudes, and beliefs to suit the team establishment. Though conflicts may or may not surface as group issues, they do exist. Questions about who is accountable for what, what the rules are, what the reward system is, and what the valuation criteria are arising.

These questions reveal conflicts over leadership, structure, power, and authority. Because of the discomfort generated during this stage, some members may remain completely silent, while others attempt to dominate. Members have a modified wish for structural clarification and commitment. In order to progress to the next stage, team members must move from a testing-and-proving mentality to a problem-solving mentality. Listening is the most helpful action team members and the team leader can take to settle these issues.

Stage 3: Norming

In Tuckman's norming stage, team relations are qualified by cohesion. Team members actively acknowledge all members' contributions, build community, maintain team focus and mission, and work to solve team issues. Members are willing to change their preconceived ideas or opinions on the basis of facts presented by other members, and they actively ask questions of one another. Leadership is shared, and cliques dissolve. As members begin to know and identify with one another, the trust that individuals place in their colleagues fosters cohesion within the team. During this stage of development, team members begin to experience a sense of group belonging to and a feeling of relief as a result of resolving interpersonal conflicts.

Stage 3 is characterized by the flow of data between team members: They share feelings and ideas, solicit and give feedback to one another, and explore actions related to the task. Creativity is high. If this stage of data flow and cohesion is attained by the group members, their interactions are characterized by openness and sharing of information on both a personal and task level. They feel good about being part of an effectual group. The major pull back of the norming stage is that members may begin to fear the inevitable future break-up of the group; they may resist exchange of any form.

Stage 4: Performing

Again, the performing stage isn't reached by all teams. Those teams that do reach this stage not only enjoy team members who work independently but also support those who can come back together and work interdependently to solve problems. A team is at its most productive all through this stage.

Team members are both extremely task-oriented and extremely individuals-oriented during this stage. The team is unified: Team identity is complete, team morale is high, and team loyalty is intense. The task function becomes genuine problem solving, leading to optimal solutions and optimum team development. There is support for experimentation in solving problems, and an emphasis on achievement. The overall aim is productivity through problem solving and work.

Bruce Tuckman revised his original and described another final stage:

Stage 5: Adjourning

Teams assembled for particular project or for a finite length of time go through a fifth stage, called adjourning , when the team breaks up. A planned conclusion in general comprises recognition for participation and achievement and an opportunity for members to say personal goodbyes. Disbanding a team can produce some apprehension, and not all team members handle this well. The termination of the team is a regressive movement from giving up control to the team to giving up inclusion in the team. This last stage focuses on wrapping up activities rather than on task execution.

MANAGING TEAM CONFLICT

Conflict is not always negative; conflict is inevitable, natural, and even healthy whenever individuals work unitedly. Conflict can be an effectual means for everyone to grow, learn, and become more productive and satisfied in the workplace. What is unhealthy, nevertheless, is unresolved conflict that is allowed to fester and become a hindrance to an otherwise productive team. Common causes of conflict include employee competition; differences in objectives, values, or perceptions; disagreements about roles, work activities, or individual styles; and breakdowns in communication.

As an outcome, conflict management is a big part of managing individuals or teams. To manage conflict, a manager must analyze the conflict situation to determine the cause and severity, and then develop a strategy for action. Strategy options include the following:

- Avoidance-withdrawing from or ignoring conflict.
- Smoothing-playing down differences to ease conflict.
- Compromise-giving up something to gain something.
- Collaboration-mutual problem solving.

- Confrontation-for verbalization of disagreements.
- Appeal to team objectives-highlighting the mutual demand to reach a higher aim.
- Third-party intervention-asking an objective third party to mediate.

Remember that conflict ought to be looked upon as an opportunity. When conflict is identified early, managers can prevent small issues from escalating into major, long-term wars in the workplace.

Managing Conflict in Work Teams

The role of conflict in work teams is decided by the manner in which it is managed. Conflict is a driving force of change that can result in improved decision-making processes and progressive team development.

However, teams must learn to be confrontational without destroying the team process. Teams are able to handle conflict and perform at a high level by following a framework of communication required for managing conflict constructively. Teams capable of mediating their own conflicts, improve both productivity and member relationships.

Teams are normally built up of a diverse group of people; each member possessing different capabilities and skills. This element is what makes the use of teams so advantageous; nevertheless, diversity can also produce conflict. Hence, it is important for teams to understand the dynamics of conflict and to regulate its natural flow. The following discussion presents several conflict resolution methods and skills for managing team conflict, while giving team growth, development, and an increased quality of decision-making. Contrary to the common belief that conflict is limited to a disruptive effect, a number of researchers acknowledge the significant benefits of conflict to team processes. Conflict is a driving force of change (McDaniel et al., 1998). When managed correctly, conflict produces the following results: new ideas for changing organizational processes, solving of continuous problems, a chance for workers to elaborate their capabilities, and the creation of creativity into thoughts about organizational problems.

Regrettably, these positive outcomes are often unachievable due to uneducated, reactionary efforts to eliminate the source of conflict. The consequences of poorly handled team conflict such as this are a lowering of team energy, disruption of healthy relationships, and the prevention of task achievement. Additionally, there is an avoidance of the disputed subject and the creation of an environment of fear. Too often, conflict is smoothed over by a team leader and isn't resolved; the end result is a building up of resentment between team members that degenerates the team's performance level.

The fundamental issue in dealing with team conflict is for the team to realize that the focus isn't on conflict itself, but how it is handled. The idea behind managing conflict isn't to reduce conflict, but to handle it in a constructive manner. Teams must learn to be confrontational without destroying the team process. Research suggests that high performing teams are capable of mediating their own conflicts while improving productivity and fortifying relationships.

Before the rise in the use of teams, classic literature studying group behaviour recognized the implication of conflict in groups. Coser (1956) states that both positive and negative factors contribute to the formation of a group. A group that is devoid of conflict is a group without process or structure. The life of a work group is dependent on this need for conflict for the group to thrive and prosper, just as much as the group relies on the need for cooperation. Current team research extends this outlook toward the positive aspects of conflict and proposes different methods by which teams may cultivate positive outcomes.

TEAM CONFLICT RESOLUTION METHODS

Team Mediation Process

McDaniel et al. (1998) offers a step by step mediation process for teams dealing with conflict. This mediation process provides the work team with skills and structure for mediating their own challenges. Using a simple process framework for applying communication skills to a situation, team members are able to manage conflict in a way that maintains and strengthens the team environment. Each member must learn and devote themselves to a consistent process for communicating and resolving conflicts with others.

The anticipated outcomes of this process are higher team performance levels, less stress, and a more positive work environment.

There are four prerequisites for effectual implementation of this team mediation process:

1. The first necessity is for each team member to be able to learn the appropriate communication skills and the overall mediation process. If a few team members don't make the effort to learn the skills necessary for accepted communication, then the

process is incapable of working effectively. These communication skills include learning to confront others, listening to other's concerns, acknowledging opposing perspectives, responding properly, and committing to a plan of agreed action.

2. The next requirement is the individual certification of competency for each member's use of the mediation skills and understanding of the process. Competency ratings are used in other areas of technique, such as technical competencies, and are appropriate measures of interpersonal engagement technique usage.
3. The third requirement for effectual mediation implementation is an environment in which the team is empowered to solve their own conflicts. The team must have the authority to produce and establish its system of mediation. For instance, the team commences to establish the system by brainstorming over the ideas of conflict, the negative results, and the positive outcomes for the team. Within this process, the team defines agreed upon team values, expectations, and processes. This process is referred to as setting the "path" or boundaries of acceptable behaviour for the team. It is very important for the team as a whole to enforce these behavioural boundaries when they are crossed; the process is unproductive when an outside party is expected to supply such reinforcement.
4. The fourth necessity ensures that once these first three requirements are met, team members are required to recognize and resolve conflicts jointly. Team self-reliance for conflict solution ranges from situations involving only two members, to complicated situations, involving disagreement among all team members. The proposed mediation process provides the team with the power to cover conflict at both extremes.

If a team meets the four prerequisites of this mediation process, the next step is for all team members to participate in technique development training.

Within the training, team members learn how to coach one another through the mediation process. They also practice applying communication skills to more and more difficult conflict scenarios. The training methods taken from the skills training are focused on around the conclusion that conflict can be addressed through a three step cycle of concern, vision, and action:

1. The first step teaches the responsibility of both parties participating in a dispute to understand the other person's concerns. This demands the understanding of the emotions, needs, and reasons behind the stated position of the opposition.
2. The second step illustrates the importance of both parties envisioning one another's view of a win-win solution for the team. Recognizing the perspective of the team as whole is a critical element when arriving at a fully consented solution. This becomes a meeting point amongst the two arguing parties.
3. The third step is a commitment by both disputing sides to take the appropriate actions to ensure the particular conflict will not reoccur. These actions are submitted by both parties, along with a prescribed method for mediating the problem ought to it reoccur.

CONCLUSION

The role of conflict in work teams is decided by the manner in which it is managed. Conflict pervades the core of team processes, and, if unaddressed, conflict serves to stunt the development of a team. Nevertheless, teams educated in the dynamic nature of conflict are capable of harnessing the energy created by its elements, resulting in productive outcomes. With growing emphasis, the merits of the constructive management of team conflict are becoming more evident in present day's business world.

Note: An in-depth exploration of basic principles of Team work for the purpose of gaining depth of understanding into the subject, we can take the example of Nokia Company. In 2007, Nokia was listed as number one company in Europe and number three in the world in a "Top Companies for Leaders" study carried on by Human Resources Company "Hewitt Associates" in partnership with "Fortune magazine". For detailed information, reader can visit: http://www.nokia.com/link?cid=EDITORIAL_4382

12

Communication Skills

The power to communicate is the main factor that distinguishes human beings from animals. And it is the power to communicate well that distinguishes one individual from another. The fact is that apart from the fundamental necessities, one needs to be fitted out with habits for good communication skills, as this is what will make them a happy and successful social being.

In order to develop these habits, one calls for to first acknowledge the fact that they need to improve communication skills from time to time. They need to take stock of the way they interact and the direction in which their work and personal relations are going. The only constant in life is change, and the more one accepts one's strengths and works towards dealing with their defects, especially in the area of communication skills, the better will be their interactions and the more their social quality.

SIGNIFICANCE OF COMMUNICATION

"Identification is one of the key ingredients of effectual communication. In fact, unless your listeners can identify with what you are saying and with the way you are saying it, they aren't likely to receive and understand your message."

The quote above is the fundamental factor that explicates the implication of communication skills. In fact, there are other such quotes, which are as follows that explains the importance of effectual communications skills:

Good communication is as inducing as black coffee, and just as hard to sleep after. The latest computer can merely compound, at speed, the oldest problem in the relations between human beings, and in the end the communicator will be presented with the old problem, of what to say and how to say it.

The big misunderstanding of our times is the assumption that insight will work with individuals who are uninspired to modification. Communication doesn't depend on syntax, or eloquence, or rhetoric, or articulation; but on the emotional perspective in which the message is being heard. Individuals can only hear you when they are moving toward you, and they aren't likely to when your words are pursuing them. Even the choicest words lose their power when they are used to overpower. Attitudes are the real figures of speech.

METHODS OF COMMUNICATION

Communication is generally classified into a couple of types. The classifications include:

- Verbal and non-verbal
- Technological and non-technological
- Mediated and non-mediated
- Participatory and non-participatory

The commonly known types of communications are:

Intra-personal communication skills: This means individual reflection, contemplation and meditation. One example of this is transcendental mediation. As per the experts this type of communication encompasses communicating with the divine and with spirits in the form of prayers and rites and rituals.

Inter-personal communication skills: This is direct, face-to-face communication that occurs between two persons. It is fundamentally a dialogue or a conversation between two or more individuals. It is personal, direct, as well as intimate and permits maximum interaction through words and gestures. Interpersonal communications maybe:

Focused Interactions: This primarily results from a real encounter between two persons. This implies that the two persons involved are completely aware of the communication happening between them.

Unfocused interactions: This occurs when one simply observes or listens to persons with whom one isn't conversing. This in general occurs at stations and bus stops, as well as on the street, at restaurants, etc.

Non verbal communication skills: This contains aspects such as body language, gestures, facial expressions, eye contact, etc., which also become a part of the communicating process; as well as the written and typed modes of communications.

Mass communication: This is generally identified with tools of modern mass media, which comprises: books, the press, cinema, television, radio, etc. It is a means of conveying messages to an entire populace. No matter what the different types of communication skills are, communicating is an ever-continuing process that is going on all the time. It is as significant to human life as is day-to-day existence.

INTERPERSONAL COMMUNICATION

What do we mean interpersonal communication? Read how researchers define interpersonal communication and then complete the interactive activity and quiz at the end of this section.

The Contextual View

One way of defining interpersonal communication is to equate it to other forms of communication. In so doing, we would examine how many individuals are involved, how physically close they are to one another, how many sensory channels are used, and the feedback provided. Interpersonal communication differs from other forms of communication in that there are few participants demanded, the interactants are in close physical proximity to each other, there are many sensory channels used, and feedback is immediate. An important point to note about the contextual definition is that it doesn't take into account the relationship between the interactants.

The Developmental View

We have numerous relationships with individuals. Some researchers say that our definition of interpersonal communication must account for these differences. These researchers say that interacting with a sales clerk in a store is different than the relationship we have with our friends and family members. Therefore, some researchers have proposed an alternative way of defining interpersonal communication. This is called the developmental view. From this view, interpersonal communication is defined as communication that occurs between individuals who have known each other for some time. Importantly, these individuals view each other as unique people, not as individuals who are simply enacting social situations.

This is defined as communication between two or more individuals and necessitates the transfer of information (or message) from one person to the other(s). The person transferring the information is called the sender or transmitter. The individuals receiving the message are known as receivers. The transmitter will need to send the information in a format that the receiver(s) will understand. Changing over the information into a format that the receivers will understand is known as Encoding.

Messages can be encoded into a form of formats oral, written or visual. After encoding the message is transferred via a medium called a channel, for instance a letter, fax, phone call, or e-mail. After transference the information will require to be interpreted by the receiver. This process of interpretation is known as decoding. Finally the receiver will send a message back to the transmitter confirming whether the information sent has been understood. This back check is known as feedback.

ORGANIZATIONAL COMMUNICATION

Organizations can't function without communication. Communication can take numerous forms but all forms involve the transfer of information from one party to the other. In order for the transfer of information to qualify as communication, the recipient must understand the meaning of the information transferred to them. If the recipient doesn't understand the meaning of the information conveyed to them, communication has not taken place. Communication is the life source of organizations because organizations require individuals. Individuals cannot interact with each other without communication. In the absence of communication, everything would grind to a halt. For instance;

The workers in an organization would not know the organization's objectives so they would not strive to accomplish the organization's objectives.

- The workers in an organization would not know what their roles and responsibilities were, so they would not be able to carry out their daily tasks and duties.
- The managers would not be able to train their workers reports so the workers would not possess the skills they needed to carry out their jobs.
- The managers would not be able to inform workers of changes.
- The organization would not be aware of their competitor's activities.

On the whole individuals are able to communicate with each other as this is a basic human function. Notwithstanding successful organizations strive not only for communication but effectual communication.

Broadly Speaking Organizational communication is individuals working together to attain individual or collective aims. Individuals can relate to each other only through some form of communication. The survival of an establishment depends on people and groups who are able to maintain among themselves effectual and continuing relationships. If we can understand organizational communication, we will understand the establishment itself. Communication can be defined as "the transfer of meanings between persons and groups". The purpose of communication may range from completing a task or mission to producing and keeping satisfying human relationships. The word transfer means more than the simple process of "packaging" an idea as conceived by a sender and transporting it to the mind of a receiver, where it is "unpackaged". It implies the creation of meaning in the mind of a sender followed by a re-creation of the same meaning in the mind of a receiver. If something takes place along the way to change the sender's original meaning, the communication has failed in its intent.

Communication may be believed a functional part of an organizational system, and it may be considered in an interpersonal perspective. The structure of an establishment is determined in part by the network of channels or paths along which information must flow between members or subunits.

The field draws its lineage through business information, business communication, and early mass communication studies published in the 1930s through the 1950s. Until then, organizational communication as a discipline consisted of a few professors within speech departments who had a particular interest in speaking and writing in business settings. The current field is well recognized with its own theories and empirical pertains distinct from other communication subfields and other approaches to organizations.

Several seminal publications stand out as works broadening the scope and recognizing the significance of communication in the organizing process, and in using the term "organizational communication". Nobel Laureate Herbert Simon wrote in 1947 about "establishment communications systems", saying communication is "absolutely essential to organizations".

Assumptions Underlying Early Organizational Communication

Some of the main assumptions underlying much of the early organizational communication research were:

- Humans act rationally. Sane individuals behave in rational ways, they in general have access to all of the information required to make rational decisions they could articulate, and hence will make rational decisions, unless there is some breakdown in the communication process.
- Formal logic and empirically verifiable data ought to be the foundation upon which any theory ought to rest. All we actually need to understand communication in organizations is (a) observable and replicable behaviours that can be transformed into variables by some form of measurement, and (b) formally replicable syllogisms that can extend theory from observed data to other groups and settings.
- Communication is mainly a mechanical process, in which a message is constructed and encoded by a sender, transmitted through some channel, then received and decoded by a receiver. Distortion, represented as any differences between the original and the received messages, can and ought to be identified and reduced or eradicated.
- Organizations are mechanical things, in which the parts (including employees functioning in defined roles) are interchangeable. What works in one establishment will work in another similar establishment. Individual differences can be minimized or even eradicated with careful management techniques.
- Organizations function as a container within which communication takes place. Any differences in form or function of communication between that happening in an establishment and in another setting can be identified and studied as factors impressing the communicative activity.

FORMAL AND INFORMAL COMMUNICATIONS

Formal communication is defined as communication which happens through the official organizational channels or is undertaken by an employee to do their task. For instance official meetings, letters and a manager asking an employee to carry out a particular task. Conversely informal communication is that which occurs outside the recognized communication networks such as talking in the lunchroom or hallways between employees. Informal communication can be productive or negative. It has the potential to build teams, better working relationships and generate ideas as employees are in a relaxed environment.

UPWARD AND DOWNWARD COMMUNICATIONS

Downward communication is communication produced by directors and managers and passed down the hierarchy of workers in the organization. In conventional organizations this is the preferred method of communication i.e. Managers decide what the systems, rules and processes will be and then they pass these down to employees they manage and supervise. Downward Communication can increase efficiency by synchronising organizational processes and can ensure that everybody is working towards the same overall aims and objectives. Types of downward communication constitute task descriptions, appraisals/ evaluations, organizational policy, and organizational systems.

Though there are merits to downward communication organizations have commenced to encourage upward communication. This is communication which originates at the lower level of the employment hierarchy and is then communicated up through the line. Organizations encouraging upward communication believe that everybody is capable of generating thoughts and ideas which may help the organization to build up, particularly when they are working closely in the area that the idea applies to.

Upward communication may increase motivation and make employees feel valued and respected whilst enabling managers to understand how employees are feeling. Moreover if problems occur at they are more likely to be identified earlier by those working closely in the area that they occur. Types of upward communications include suggestion schemes, feedback forums/surveys, grievance processes and employee-manager discussions.

LATERAL COMMUNICATION

This is communication that occurs among employees on the same level in the organization. As this can involve decision making it can produce efficiency as employees don't have to wait for managerial approval. Alternatively, if the manager isn't kept informed or if the manager fails to set limits there is potential for conflict.

DIAGONAL COMMUNICATION

This takes place when communication occurs between workers in a different section of the organization and where one of the workers involved is on a higher level in the organization. For instance in a bank diagonal communication will occur when a department manager in head office converses with a cashier in a branch of the bank founded on the high street.

BARRIERS TO EFFECTUAL COMMUNICATION

At each stage in the process encoding, transference, and decoding there is the possibility of interference which may hinder the communication process. This interference is known as noise. Frequently a comparison is made between communication and a leaky bucket. If you use a leaky bucket to carry water, water will be lost at several points in your journey from the water tap to your destination. It isn't possible to stop losing water because the bucket contains holes. The amount of water you will lose will be determined by the number of holes in the bucket, the size of the holes, the route you take to your final destination and length of time it takes you to get to your destination. There may also be other events that occur during your journey which increase the amount of water lost. Likewise when information is transferred from the transmitter to the receiver not all of the information may be received by the receiver because of holes called noise. Each of the noise may be affect the amount of information transferred. Just as in a leaky bucket, more holes decrease the amount of water, more noise decreases the amount of correct information received. Noise can take a variety of forms comprising

Language issues and Cultural Differences: the receiver(s) may not (fully) understand the language used by the transmitter. This may occur if the transmitter's language is foreign to the receiver. There may also be language problems (that the communication process) if the message contains technical information and the receiver's isn't familiar with the technical terms used. Cultural differences created by an individual's background and experience affect their perception of the world. Such cultural differences may affect the interpretation (decoding) of the message sent.

Environmental issues: If the environment that the transmitter or receiver are in, is noisy and full of sound, the sounds may prevent the message being fully understood. Background noise is frequently created by colleagues or machinery.

Channel issues: If the channel used to transfer the information is poor it may prevent all or some of the information being transferred. Examples include a faulty fax machine, a crackling phone, handwriting that cannot be read or in the case of oral messages incorrect facial gestures.

Receivers Attitude and behaviour: If the receiver(s) isn't interested in the message (or unable to give their full attention to decoding) this may reduce the amount of information received or the accuracy of the information transmitted to them. Likewise the receiver(s) may misunderstand the message by "jumping to conclusions" or reading the message in a manner that suits their own interests/objectives and distort the true meaning of the message.

Transmission journey: If the message is complex or there are lots of steps taken to transfer the message it may affect the accuracy or interpretation. Comparing with the leaky bucket if the leaky bucket has to carry water over a longer distance more water will probably lost than if the journey was shorter.

IMPROVING COMMUNICATION

Research shows that managers spend somewhere between 50% - 80% of their total time communicating in one way or the other. This is not surprising, since communication is so critical to everything that goes on in an establishment. Without effectual communication there can be little or no performance management, innovation, understanding of clients, co-ordination of effort, and without effectual communication it is difficult to manage the anticipations of those who are in a position to make decisions about your fate.

It can also be said that many managers don't communicate well, and don't set an organizational climate where communication inside the establishment is managed effectively. This is not surprising, since a manager who communicates ineffectively and doesn't encourage effectual organizational communication is unlikely to hear about it. Poor communication is self-sustaining, because it eliminates an important "feedback loop". Staff are loathe to "communicate" their concerns about communication because they don't perceive the manager as receptive. Both staff and management run down a little dance.

Briefly, you may be fostering poor communication, and never know it. You may see the symptoms, but unless you are looking carefully, you may not identify your own participation in the problem. What can you do about it?

Some Must do's for the Managers

1. Actively solicit feedback about your own communication, and communication inside the establishment. Ask staff questions like:

- When we talk, are you generally clear about what I am saying?
- Do you think we communicate well around here?
- Have you got any ideas about how we could communicate better?

Consider comprising these questions (or similar ones) in your performance management process, or staff meetings.

2. Assess your own communication knowledge and understanding
3. Working with your staff, define how you ought to communicate in the establishment. Develop consensus regarding:
   a. How disagreements ought to be handled.
   b. How horizontal communication ought to work (staff to staff).
   c. How vertical communication ought to work (manager to staff, staff to manager).
   d. What information ought to be available and when.

Once consensus is reached, support the achievement of these aims through positive reinforcement and coaching.

4. Look at the affect of the structure of your establishment and how it impacts on communication. Indirect communication (communication that is transferred from person to person) is notorious for inducing problems. Look at increasing direct communication where the person with the message to send does it directly with the receiver.
5. Learn about, and use combat-ready listening techniques. This will set a tone and contribute to a positive communication climate. If you do not know what active listening is, find out.

Exploring communication patterns and effectiveness can bring to the surface a number of resentments and perceptions. If the manager is not prepared to deal with these, it is best to look to an outside consultant.

Note: Communication in an establishment and skills are an important factor in working of any establishment. Take the example of Virgin group. A research study has shown that the UK public vote Virgin as their most admired brand. It is one of the world's most recognized and respected brands. Reader can visit company's site for more indepth knowledge. http://www.virgin.com/AboutVirgin/WhatWeAreAbout/WhatWeAreAbout.aspx

13

Leadership and Management

Leading is launching direction and regulating others to follow that direction. But this definition is not as simple as it sounds because leadership has many variations and different areas of vehemence. Common to all definitions of leadership is the notion that leaders are individuals who, by their actions, facilitate the movement of a group of individuals toward a common or shared aim. This definition implies that leadership is an influence process. The distinction between leader and leadership is important, but potentially confusing.

The leader is an individual; leadership is the function or activity this individual performs. The word leader is frequently used interchangeably with the word manager to describe those individuals in an establishment who have positions of formal authority, irrespective of how they actually act in those jobs. But just as a manager is supposed to be a formal leader in an establishment does not mean that he exercises leadership.

DEFINITION OF LEADERSHIP

An issue frequently argued among business professionals is whether leadership is a different function and activity from management. Harvard's John Kotter says that management is about coping with complexity, and leadership, in contrast, is about coping with change.

He also states that leadership is an important part of management, but only a part; management also involves planning, organizing, staffing, and controlling. Management produces a degree of predictability and order. Leadership produces change. Kotter believes that most organizations are under led and over managed. He sees both strong leadership and strong management as requisite for optimal organizational effectiveness.

IMPORTANCE OF LEADERSHIP

In an organization where there is faith in the abilities of formal leaders, employees will look towards the leaders for numerous things. During drastic change times, employees will expect effectual and sensible planning, confident and effectual decision-making, and regular, complete communication that are timely. Also during these times of change, employees will perceive leadership as supportive, concerned and devoted to their welfare, while at the same time recognizing that tough decisions need to be made. The best way to summarize is that there is a climate of trust between leader and the equilibrium of the team. The being of this trust, brings hope for better times in the time to come, and that makes coping with drastic change much easier.

In organizations characterized by poor leadership, employees anticipate nothing positive. In a climate of distrust, employees learn that leaders will act in undecipherable ways and in ways that don't seem to be in anyone's best interests. Poor leadership means an absence of hope, which, if allowed to go on for too long, results in an establishment becoming completely non-functioning. The establishment must deal with the practical impact of unpleasant change, but more significantly, must labour under the weight of employees who have given up, have no faith in the system or in the power of leaders to turn the establishment around. Leadership before, during and after change implementation is the fundamental thing to getting through the swamp. Regrettably, if haven't founded a track record of effectual leadership, by the time you have to deal with difficult changes, it may be too late.

DIFFERENCE BETWEEN LEADERSHIP & MANAGEMENT

Leaders and managers aren't same. By definition, a manager works within a system to exert existing aims and direction. They use individuals and equipment to meet an aim or they use a process to create results. A leader by contrast, sets the direction for projects. They bring vision to reality by deriving commitment from the individuals in the establishment.

Managers	Leaders
• Work within the existing culture	• Produce visions and excitement
• Maintain existing relationships	• Set a direction
• Plan and budget	• Align individuals
• Organize and staff	• Build new relationships and structure
• Control and problem solve	• Motivate and inspire

While people might have a talent towards one versus the other, leadership and management aren't contradictory - great leaders can be great managers and vice versa. Evidently, there is tremendous advantage for someone who possesses both leadership and management skills to attain great things. This by no means implies that management is an easy task. Mastering the skills necessary to be an effectual and efficient manager can take many years. Successful organizations need both managers and leaders. Management activities are critical to any business. Most frequently, management is providing the "what" that needs to be done in the daily operation. Leadership provides the "how" those management actions get attained. Organizations ought to have the "what" and "how" aligned for optimal results.

For example, when senior management shares the company vision with the manpower, they understand their role in the overall picture. This leads to greater employee buy-in and increased productivity. Then, the manpower is able to share feedback with senior management regarding processes/processes that support the vision. This creates collaboration and greater efficiency. The practice of leadership is a fundamental business differentiator. Organizations are looking for ways to grow their products/ services, business relationships, and market share.

There are three common traits that leaders possess:

- Inspire: Leaders produce the energy for employees to do their best. They clear roadblocks and promote creativity.
- Communicate: Leaders keep employees informed about the establishment. They build relationships at all levels in the establishment.
- Support: Great leaders produce environments where employees feel safe to speak up.

The business environment is invariably changing, but the leadership component remains steadfast. It is significant for managers to work jointly to identify and develop leaders in the establishment. The success of this collaboration has a direct affect on a company's future.

LEADERSHIP STYLES

Theories burst to explain what makes an effectual leader. The oldest theories attempt to identify the common traits or skills that make an effectual leader. Contemporary theorists and theories centre on actions of leaders rather than characteristics. A number of traits that appear on a regular basis in leaders include ambition, energy, the wish to lead, self-confidence, and intelligence. Though certain traits are helpful, these dimensions provide no guarantees that a person possessing them is an effectual leader. Underlying the trait approach is the assumption that some individuals are natural leaders and are endowed with certain traits not possessed by other people. This research compared successful and abortive leaders to see how they disagreed in physical characteristics, personality, and ability.

The six core characteristics that the majority of effectual leaders possess:

- Business knowledge: Leaders tend to have technical expertise in their businesses.
- Cognitive ability: Leaders are intelligent, perceptive, and conceptually skilled, but aren't inevitably geniuses. They show analytical ability, good judgment, and the capacity to think strategically.
- Drive: Leaders are ambitious and take initiative.
- Honesty and integrity: Leaders are truthful and do what they say they will do.
- Motivation: Leaders want to lead and are willing to take charge.
- Self-confidence: Leaders are assertive and decisive and enjoy taking risks. They admit mistakes and nurture trust and commitment to a vision. Leaders are emotionally stable rather than recklessly adventuresome.

Traits do a better task at anticipating that a manger may be an effectual leader rather than actually distinguishing between an effectual or ineffective leader. Because workplace situations vary, leadership prerequisites vary. As a result, researchers began to analyse what effectual leaders do rather than what effectual leaders are.

Irrespective of what their traits or skills, leaders carry out their roles in a wide variety of styles. Some leaders are autocratic. Others are democratic. Some are participatory, and others are hands off. Frequently, the leadership style depends on the situation, admitting where the establishment is in its life cycle.

The following are common leadership styles:

- Autocratic: The manager makes all the decisions and commands team members. This approach in general results in passive resistance from team members and requires continual pressure and direction from the leader in order to get things done. Generally, this approach isn't a good way to get the best performance from a team. Nevertheless, this style may be appropriate when urgent action is necessary or when subordinates really prefer this style.

- Participative: The manager involves the subordinates in decision making by consulting team members (while still maintaining control), which encourages employee ownership for the decisions.

A good participative leader encourages participation and delegates wisely, but never loses sight of the fact that he or she bears the crucial responsibility of leadership. The leader values group discussions and input from team members; he or he maximizes the members' specialities in order to obtain the best performance from the entire team. The participative leader motivates team members by empowering them to conduct themselves; he or she guides them with a loose rein. The downside, nevertheless, is that a participative leader may be seen as unsure, and team members may feel that everything is a matter for group discussion and decision.

MODELS AND THEORIES OF LEADERSHIP STYLES

Numerous experts believe that overall leadership style reckons largely on a manager's beliefs, values, and assumptions. How managers approach the following three elements-motivation, decision making, and task orientation-affect their leadership styles:

- Motivation: Leaders influence others to reach aims through their approaches to motivation. They can use either positive or negative motivation. A positive style uses praise, recognition, and rewards, and increases employee security and responsibility. A negative manner uses punishment, penalties, potential task loss, suspension, threats, and reprimands.
- Decision making: The second element of a manager's leadership style is the degree of decision authority the manager concedes employees-ranging from no involvement to group decision making.
- Task and employee orientation: The final element of leadership style is the manager's perspective on the most effectual way to get the work done. Managers who favour task orientation

emphasize getting work done by expending better methods or equipment, controlling the work environment, assigning and organizing work, and monitoring performance. Managers who favour employee orientation emphasize getting work done through meeting the human needs of subordinates. Teamwork, convinced relationships, trust, and problem solving are the major focuses of the employee-oriented manager. Keep in mind that managers may demonstrate both task and employee orientations to some degree.

The managerial grid model, shown in Figure below and developed by Robert Blake and Jane Mouton, keys out five leadership styles with changing concerns for individuals and production:

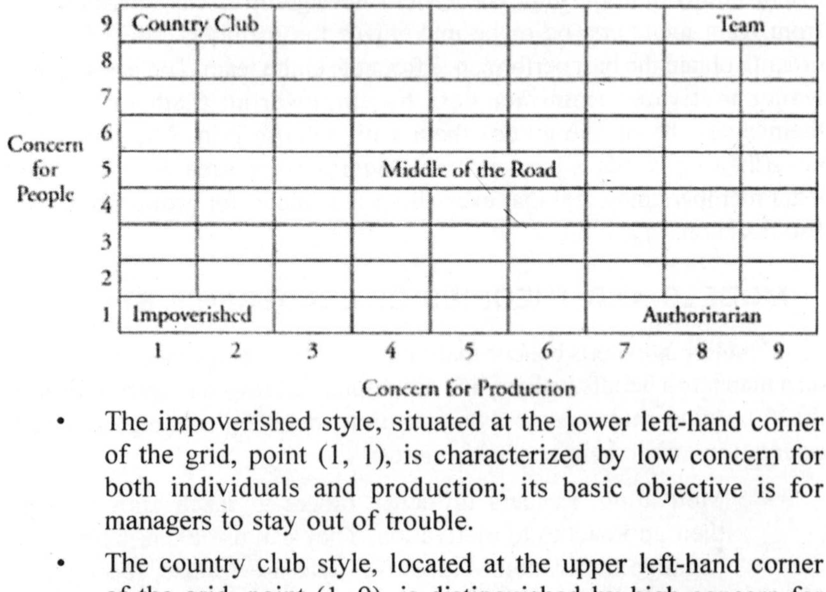

- The impoverished style, situated at the lower left-hand corner of the grid, point (1, 1), is characterized by low concern for both individuals and production; its basic objective is for managers to stay out of trouble.
- The country club style, located at the upper left-hand corner of the grid, point (1, 9), is distinguished by high concern for individuals and a low concern for production; its main objective is to produce a secure and comfortable atmosphere where managers trust that subordinates will respond positively.
- The authoritarian style, located at the lower right-hand corner of the grid, point (9, 1), is identified by high concern for production and low concern for individuals; its basic objective is to attain the establishment's aims, and employee demands aren't relevant in this process.
- The middle-of-the-road style, located at the middle of the grid, point (5, 5), maintains an equilibrium amongst workers' needs

and the establishment's productivity aims; its main objective is to maintain employee morale at a level sufficient to get the establishment's work done.

- The team style, located at the upper right-hand of the grid, point (9, 9), is characterized by high business concern for individuals and production; its basic objective is to establish cohesiveness and foster a feeling of commitment among workers.

The Managerial Grid model suggests that capable leaders ought to use a style that reflects the highest concern for both individuals and production-point (9, 9), team-oriented style.

EFFECTIVE LEADERSHIP

Effectual leaders develop and use power, or the power to regulate others. The conventional manager's power comes from his or his position within the establishment. Legitimate, reward, and coercive are all forms of power used by managers to alter employee behaviour and are defined as follows:

- Legitimate power stems from a formal management perspective in an establishment and the authority granted to it. Subordinates accept this as a legitimate source of power and follow with it.
- Reward power stems from the authority to reward others. Managers can contribute formal rewards, such as pay increases or promotions, and may also use praise, attention, and recognition to influence behaviour.
- Coercive power is the opposite of reward power and stems from the authority to punish or to propose punishment. Managers have coercive power when they have the right to fire or demote employees, criticize them, withhold pay increases, give reprimands, make negative entrances in employee files, and so forth.

Keep in mind that diverse types of position power receive different responses in followers. Legitimate power and reward power are most likely to give compliance, where workers obey orders even although they may personally differ with them. Coercive power most often gives resistance, which may lead workers to deliberately avoid carrying out instructions or to refuse orders.

Dissimilar external sources of position power, personal power most often comes from internal sources, such as a person's special knowledge or personality characteristics. Personal power is the tool of a leader. Subordinates follow a leader as of respect, admiration, or caring they feel for this individual and his or her ideas. The following two types of personal power exist:

- Expert power results from a leader's peculiar knowledge or skills regarding the tasks performed by followers. When a leader is a true expert, subordinates tend to go on quickly with his or her commendations.
- Referent power results from leadership characteristics that command identification, respect, and admiration from subordinates who then wish to emulate the leader. When workers admire a supervisor because of the way he or he deals with them, the influence is grounded on referent power. Referent power depends on a leader's personal characteristics rather than on his or his formal title or position, and is most visible in the area of charismatic leadership.

The most common follower response to expert power and referent power is allegiance. Commitment means that workers share the leader's viewpoint and enthusiastically carry out instructions. It is needless to say here, commitment is preferred to compliance or resistance. Commitment helps followers defeat fear of change, and it is particularly significant in those instances.

Keep in mind that the varied types of power described in this section are interrelated. Most leaders use a combination of these types of power, depending on the leadership style used. Authoritarian leaders, for instance, use a mixture of legitimate, coercive, and reward powers to dictate the policies, plans, and activities of a group. In comparison, a participative leader uses primarily referent power, necessitating all members of the group in the decision-making process.

SITUATIONAL APPROACHES TO LEADERSHIP

The theme in former approaches to understanding leadership was the wish to identify attributes or behaviours that effectual leaders had in common. A common set of characteristics proved to be elusive, nevertheless. Researchers were continually frustrated by the want of consistent support for their findings and conclusions. As a result, research began to focus on what style of leadership was most effectual in a particular situation. Contingency or situational theories examine the fit between the leader and the position and provide guidelines for managers to attain this effectual fit.

The theorists in this section believe that managers choose leadership styles based on leadership situations. Managers adjust their decision-making, orientation, and motivational approaches based upon a unequalled combination of factors in their situations: characteristics of employees, types of work, organizational structures, personal preferences, and upper-level management's works.

The following sections describe the three most long-familiar situational theories.

Fiedler's Contingency Theory

Fred E. Fiedler's contingency theory focuses on the belief that there is no best way for managers to lead. Different states of affairs produce different leadership style requirements for managers. The style that works in one environment may not work in another.

Fiedler looked at three elements that prescribe a leader's situational control. These elements are:

- Task structure: Is the task extremely integrated, fairly unstructured, or somewhere in between? The spelling out in detail (favourable) of what is needed of subordinates affects task structure.
- Leader-member relations: This element applies to the amount of loyalty, dependability, and support that a leader receives from his or his employees. In a favourable relationship, a manager has a extremely formed task structure and is able to reward and/or punish employees without any problems. In an unfavourable relationship, the task structure is generally poorly formed, and the leader possesses limited authority.
- Positioning power: Positioning power measures the amount of power or authority a manager comprehends the establishment has given him or his for the purpose of directing, rewarding, and punishing subordinates. Positioning powers of managers depends on the carrying away (favourable) or increasing (unfavourable) of the decision-making power of employees.

Fiedler then rated managers as to whether they were relationship pointed or task oriented. Task-oriented managers tended to do better in situations with good leader/member relationships, structured tasks, and either weak or strong position power. They also did well when the tasks were unstructured but position power was strong, as well as when the leader/member relations were moderate to poor and the tasks were unstructured. Relationship-oriented managers, alternatively, do better in all other situations.

The task-motivated style leader experiences pride and satisfaction in task achievement for his or her establishment, while the relationship-motivated style leader seeks to build interpersonal relations and extend extra help for team development in his or his establishment.

Judging whether a leadership style is good or bad can be hard. Each manager has his or her own preferences for leadership. Task-motivated leaders are at their best when their teams perform successfully-such as achieving new sales records or outperforming major competitors. Relationship-oriented leaders are at their best when greater customer satisfaction is gained and positive company effigies are laid down.

Hersey-Blanchard's Situational Model

The Hersey-Blanchard Model of Situational Leadership, shown in Figure below, is based on the amount of direction (task behaviour) and amount of socio-emotional support (relationship behaviour) a leader must provide given the state of affairs and the level of maturity of the followers.

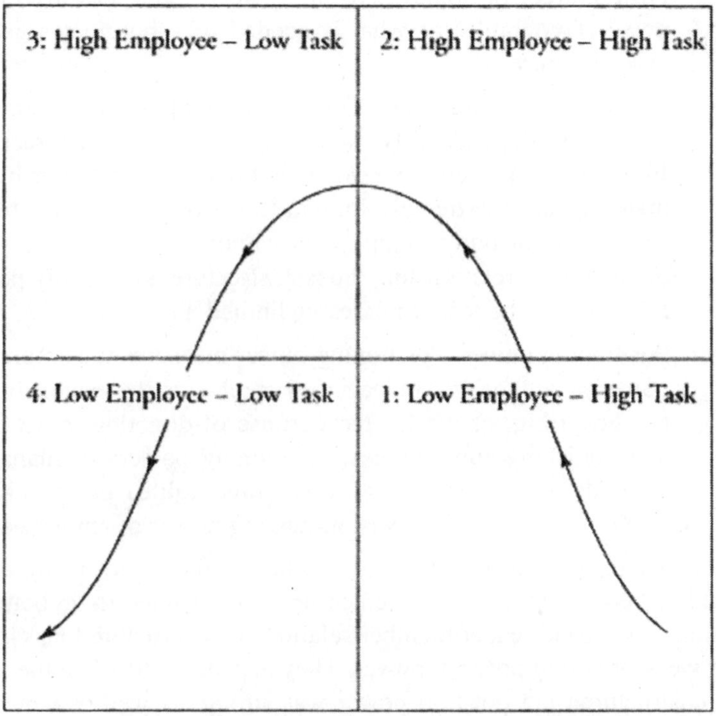

Task behaviour is the scale to which the leader engages in spelling out the duties and responsibilities to an individual or group. This behaviour contains telling individuals what to do, how to do it, when to do it, and where to do it. In task behaviour, the leader engages in one-way communication. Relationship behaviour, alternatively, is the extent to which the leader engages in two-way or multiway communications. This behaviour comprises listening to, facilitating, and supporting employees. And maturity is the willingness and power of a person to take responsibility for directing his own behaviour. Employees tend to have varying degrees of maturity, depending on the specific tasks, functions, or objectives that they undertake to carry out.

To determine the set aside leadership style to use in a given situation, a leader must first determine the maturity levels of his or his followers in relationship to the specific task. As employee maturity levels increase, a leader ought to begin to reduce task behaviour and increase relationship behaviour until his or her followers reach moderate maturity levels. As the employees move into above-average maturity levels, the leader ought to diminish not only task behaviour but also relationship behaviour.

Once maturity levels are identified, a manager can find out the appropriate leadership style: telling, selling, participating, or delegating.

- Telling: This style reflects high task/low relationship behaviour. The leader provides clear instructions and specific direction. Telling style is best matched with a low follower readiness level.
- Selling: This style reflects high task/high relationship behaviour. The leader promotes two-way communication and helps build confidence and motivation on the part of the employee, though the leader still has responsibility and controls decision making. Selling style is best matched with a moderate follower readiness level.
- Participating: This style reflects high relationship/low task behaviour. With this style, the leader and followers share decision making and no more need or expect the relationship to be directive. Participating style is best corresponded with a moderate follower readiness level.
- Delegating: This style reflects low relationship/low task behaviour. Delegating style is appropriate for leaders whose followers are ready to attain a special task and are both competent and inspired to take full responsibility. This style is best coped with a high follower readiness level.

House's Path-aim Theory

The path-aim theory, developed by Robert House, is founded on the expectancy theory of motivation. A manager's task is to coach or guide workers to choose the best paths for arriving at their aims. Based on the aim-setting theory, leaders engage in different types of leadership behaviours depending on the nature and demands of a particular situation.

A leader's behaviour is satisfactory to subordinates when viewed as a source of satisfaction. He or he is motivational when need satisfaction is contingent on performance; this leader facilitates, coaches, and rewards effectual performance. Path-aim theory identifies numerous leadership styles:

- Achievement-oriented: The leader sets challenging aims for followers, expects them to perform at their highest levels, and shows confidence in their abilities to meet these expectations. This style is set aside when followers lack task challenges.
- Directive: The leader lets followers know what is anticipated of them and tells them how to perform their tasks. This style is appropriate when followers hold equivocal jobs.
- Participative: The leader consults with followers and asks them for suggestions before making a decision. This style is appropriate when followers are using wrong processes or are making poor decisions.
- Supportive: The leader is friendly and approachable. He or he shows concern for the followers' psychological well-being. This style is set aside when followers lack confidence.

Path-aim theory assumes that leaders are flexible and that they can change their styles as situations necessitate. This theory proposes two contingency variables that moderate the leader behaviour-outcome relationship:

- Environment characteristics are outside the control of followers, task structure, authority system, and work group. Environmental components determine the type of leader behaviour expected if follower outcomes are to be maximized.
- Follower characteristics are the focus of control, experience, and perceived ability. Personal characteristics of subordinates determine how the environment and leader behaviour are understood.

Effectual leaders clarify the path to help their followers attain their aims, and make their journeys easier by reducing roadblocks and pitfalls. Research establishes that employee performance and satisfaction are positively influenced when leaders compensate for shortcomings in either their employees or the work settings.

GENDER DIFFERENCES IN LEADERSHIP

A number of women now-a-days are entering the manpower on a universal basis. This increase is construed with unprecedented increases in the diversity of the ethnic and national origin demographic makeup of organizations. As more women gain the work experience and education necessary to qualify for leadership positions, the supply of capable women grows. Organizations are subsequently called on to re-establish and expand their notions of what constitutes effectual leadership as it relates to gender, stereotyping, and role prospects. These efforts are supported by the estimate that women will outnumber men in management functions by the year 2030 as more women are earning Bachelor level degrees and taking part in graduate level education programs.

The relative scarcity of women in top leadership roles isn't a new phenomenon and can be demonstrated both in national and international terms. The percentage of women in managerial roles ranges from 25% (Germany) to 43% (Australia) while the percentage of women in positions at the senior level is between 0.3% and 5% (Japan and Germany, respectively) and 15% (Australia) with the U.S. 10%. Regarding management level women manpower percentage is approximately 40% but with women in this group holding onto only 0.5% of the highest paid management perspectives. In 1997, there wee only two female CEOs amongst the leadership of Fortune 500 organizations and only five in the next 500. Corporate board demographics continue this trend. Four years ago, only 10% of corporate board places were help by women with 150 of the Fortune 500 organizations describing no women board members whatsoever.

What explains these discrepancies? There are several arguments and a growing knowledge base of research attempting to explain these discrepancies, the epidemiology, and their potential impact on both social and organizational grounds. Boatwright and Forrest (2000) point to a phenomenon known as the 'glass ceiling' as one reason for any numerical differences in leadership positions. Patterns of favouritism and stereotype may also account for the historically low count of women leaders. Oakley

(2000) argues that gender equity in organizational leadership roles is a matter of business value orientation.

As women become more and more dominant in leadership roles, research respective to gender differences in leadership behaviours becomes more significant. One obvious reason is to further understanding and design intervention/prevention strategies to discover and eliminate any gender bias that may impact perception and rewarding of women's performance in the workplace. A second reason surrounds changes in organizational structures towards flattened hierarchical, team-based structures. To date, research regarding the issue of gender differences in leadership may leave something to be required if organizations are to use the knowledge base to alter their practices and successfully integrate the complexities of diversity in their human resource management strategies. Current leadership research has been carried on within the perspective of a Western industrialized culture that has been predominately characterized as idealizing individualism, follower duty, and rational thoughts over emotions. These ideas may lead to the valuing of masculine leadership styles and later stereotyping of a more feminine style as 'less then.

Several theoretical models have been utilized in the study of gender differences in leadership behaviour. Bolman and Deal (1991 and 1997; as cited in Thompson, 2000) believes organizational dynamics as consisting of four distinct characteristics: structural, human resource, political, and symbolic. Quinn outlines organizational dynamics against a structure of competing values with successful leadership manifesting from adequate analysis and equilibrium of the values. Social theory describes individual behaviour as driven by societal anticipations. Boatwright and Forrest (2000) further this description using attachment theory. Likewise, relational theory contributes to these views by arguing that a basic human straining is to develop and maintain relationship. Numerous organizational theories can also be used to illustrate and indicate against gender differences in leadership.

The result of gender socialization on differences in leadership behaviour commenced to scratch the surface of how a perspective or environment can affect how one acts in an organizational setting. With the advent of new technologies and organizational globalization, distance and national boundaries begin to fall away. Within these new organizational contexts manifests different national cultural differences. Countries whose cultures value masculine styles may value leadership behaviours that are more competitive, valuing and strong, and holding up male averages as 'best practice.' A study conduct by Gibson (1995) sought to illustrate these concepts using four different countries paired along like cultural dispositions for masculinity. Each country was assessed in terms of leadership behaviour, gender differences, and style preferences. Norway and Sweden were equated as a pair to the United States and Australia. Leadership was measured in terms of aim emphasis, interaction facilitation, work facilitation, support, and personnel development.

The consequences of the study described Norwegian and Swedish organizations in terms of involvement, community, expected uncertainty, minimized inequality, employee interdependence, approachable superiors, and decreased aggressive or confrontational behaviours. Conversely, U.S. and Australian organizations were characterized by increased individualism, clearly defined and separate sex roles, high initiative, decreased group interdependence, increased focus on individual accomplishment and self-interests, and increased assessing of planning and prediction.

Another study by Charles and Davies (2000) highlights the leadership outlooks of Wales, United Kingdom as compared to the gendering of senior management positions in other sections of the U.K. The author argued that because of Wales' economic history driven by largely male-dominated industry, the associated relations and stereotypes might manifest in diminished numbers of women in leadership roles. What does all this mean for individual gender differences in leadership behaviour? National culture has been argued to have important influence on leadership behaviour as per gender socialization and the expectations determined by that culture. From a systemic view, cultural gender expectations may result in organizational cultural characteristics that are also gendered. In fact, feminine and masculine styles may be less biological imperative form and more related to tacit understandings and learned behaviours driven by numerous social and national constructs. The effects of the 'gendered establishment' and its culture have been presented in research. Eagley and Johnson showed that female leaders were less likely than their male counterparts to be interpersonally oriented or use participative leadership styles (two characteristics attributed to women leaders in research literature) when they figured out within a male-dominated organization or industry.

Cultural variant can particularly be evidenced through group dynamics in organizational settings. Emergent leadership situations have been used to study how and when gender differences might naturally manifest in group organizational settings. In studying leadership as a dynamic social process, emergent leadership occurs when someone in a group setting adopts the role of 'leader' where they had not been one to begin with identified. In a study of emergent leadership in group settings, Sapp, Harrod, and Zhao (1996) sought to establish any differences in male and female group and leadership roles.

Cantor and Benay hypothesize that women leaders may react to stereotypes by suppressing normative gender behaviours or acting 'likewise to men' in order to rise through the ranks in an establishment. The perception of the 'successful leader' as male or exhibiting masculine traits may also influence employing or promotion practices. Some researchers argue that task or task-oriented leadership is quickly being replaced by employee or person-centred leadership and that this shift underscores the importance of studying employee preference for leadership styles.

In study of gender differences in organizational higher-ranking perception, Carless (1998) found that superiors may rely more on gender stereotypes and assumptions in describing and rating male and female leadership effectiveness and performance. Gardiner and Tiggemann (1999) also found that women leaders endured negative evaluations when their behaviours didn't confirm evaluators' anticipations or stereotypes of gender. In an article regarding the interplay of cultural and organizational roles, Lorenzen (1996) attempted to provide reason for the apparent 'catch-22' for gender differences in leadership and perception beaten back by stereotype. Where gender is perceived within the social position, female leaders may be perceived more negatively than male leaders. Organizational culture and ideals may also influence employee and leadership perception of self and others. Within certain organizations, women leaders may be expected not to perform as well as their male counterparts, ensuing in more favourable perceptions when they are successful.

In 1990, Eagley and Johnson conducted a meta-analysis of gender leadership research to assess the implication of gender differences in leadership styles. Their view was that the research to date demonstrated some reliable, but small conflicts in style where women in leadership emphasized personal relations versus men' focus on task achievement. Several more studies have attempted to further define these differences in leadership style. A study by Carless (1998) seeks to describe leadership styles within the confines of the definition of transformational leadership. Maher (1997) and Oakley (2000) describe women's leadership style as more transformational in both conventional and non-conventional organizational contexts. A study by Daewoo (1996) affirms gender differences in leadership along tasks and relations themes for decision-making. Rosenthal (2000) also argues for gender differences in conditions of conflict-solution styles driven by socialization.

Gender differences in leadership can be explained through a variety of rationale. From interpersonal relationships to social role expectations to differences in perception and styles, men and women may so lead differently additionally to being 'followed' differently. The successful establishment of the future will not only realize leadership in terms of gender but also its share to manpower and organizational effectiveness.

CHALLENGES FACED BY LEADERS

Organizations now-a-days place multiple demands on leaders, expecting them to impart vision, initiate change, and make difficult decisions. To handle these demands, leaders must be flexible and adaptable.

Transformational leadership blends the behavioural theories with a little dab of trait theories. Transactional leaders, such as those identified in contingency theories, guide followers in the direction of set up aims by clarifying role and task necessities. Nevertheless, transformational leaders, who are charismatic and visionary, can instigate followers to transcend their own self-interest for the good of their organizations. Transformational leaders appeal to followers' ideals and moral values and inspire them to think about problems in new or different ways. These leaders influence followers through vision, framing, and impression management.

Vision is the power of the leader to bind individuals together with an idea. Framing is the process whereby leaders decide the function of their movements in extremely meaningful terms. Impression management is an attempt to control the impressions that others form of a leader by practicing behaviours that make him or his more attractive and appealing to others. A transformational leader instils feelings of confidence, admiration, and commitment in his followers. This type of leader is charismatic, producing a special bond with followers and articulating a vision with which his or his followers key out and for which these followers are willing to work. Each follower is coached, advised, and delegated some authority. The transformational leader stimulates followers intellectually, arousing them to develop new ways to think about problems. This leader uses contingent rewards to positively reinforce performances that are consistent with his or his wishes. Management is by exclusion. Transformational leaders take first step only when problems occur and aren't actively involved when things are going well. He or he commits individuals to actions and converts followers into leaders. Research indicates that transformational, as equated to transactional, leadership is more powerfully correlated with lower turnover rates, higher productivity, and higher employee gratification.

Transformational leaders are applicable to present day's workplace because they are flexible and innovative. Though it is significant to have leaders with the appropriate orientation determining tasks and managing interrelationships, it is even more important to have leaders who can bring organizations into futures they have not yet imagined. Transformational leadership is the kernel of producing and confirming competitive advantage.

Note: Leaders are crucial to present day's workplace because they are flexible and innovative. It is significant to have leaders who can bring organizations into futures they have not yet imagined. We can take the example of Richard Branson, Founder of Virgin Group. For detailed information on him, reader can visit his site: http://www.virgin.com/AboutVirgin/RichardBranson/WhosRichardBranson.aspx

14

Human Resource Management

Human resource management (HRM) is the most precious and coherent approach to the management of any establishment's most valued assets - the individuals working there who individually and jointly lead to the achievement of the objectives of the business. The terms "human resource management" and "human resources" (HR) have largely substituted the term "personnel management" as a description of the processes needed in managing individuals in organizations. Human Resource management is evolving rapidly. Human resource management is both an academic theory and a business practice that addresses the theoretical and practical techniques of managing manpower.

Its features include:

- Personnel administration
- Personnel management
- Manpower management
- Industrial management

But these conventional expressions are becoming rarer for the theoretical discipline. Occasionally even industrial relations and employee relations are confusingly listed as synonyms, though these typically refer to the relationship between management and workers and the behaviour of workers in the establishment. The theoretical discipline is based mainly on the assumption that employees are individuals with varying aims and needs, and therefore ought to not be thought of as fundamental business resources, such as trucks and filing cabinets. The field takes a positive view of workers, assuming that almost all wish to add to the enterprise productively, and that the main obstacles to their endeavours are want of knowledge, insufficient training, and failures of process.

Human Resource Management is seen by practitioners in the field as a modern view of workplace management than the conventional approach.

Its proficiencies force the managers of an enterprise to express their aims with specificity in order that they can be understood and undertaken by the work-force, and to provide the resources demanded for them to successfully attain their assignments. Therefore, Human Resource Management techniques, when the right way practiced, are expressive of the aims and operating practices of the enterprise overall. Human Resource Management is also seen by many to have a key role in risk reduction inside organizations.

Synonyms such as personnel management are frequently used in a more qualified sense to describe activities that are necessary in the recruiting of manpower, providing its members with payroll and gains, and administrating their work-life needs.

STAFFING AS A MANAGEMENT FUNCTION

After an establishment's structural design is in place, it necessitates individuals with the right skills, knowledge, and abilities to fill in that structure. Individuals are an establishment's most significant resource, because individuals either produce or undermine an establishment's reputation for quality in both products and service. Additionally, an establishment must respond to change effectively in order to remain competitive. The right staff can carry an establishment through a period of change and ensure its future success. Because of the implication of employing and maintaining a committed and competent staff, effectual human resource management is essential to the success of all organizations.

Human resource management (HRM), or staffing, is the management function devoted to gaining, training, appraising, and compensating employees. In effect, all managers are human resource managers, though human resource specialists may perform some of these activities in large organizations. Solid Human Resource Management practices can mould a company's manpower into a prompted and committed team capable of managing change effectively and accomplishing the organizational objectives.

Realizing the fundamental principles of Human Resource Management can help any manager lead more effectively. Every manager ought to realize the following three principles:

- All managers are human resource managers.
- Employees are much more significant assets than buildings or equipments good employees give a company the competitive edge.

- Human resource management is a coping with process; it must match the needs of the establishment with the needs of the employee.

HR MANAGEMENT: LAWS AND REGULATIONS

Laws and regulations at the federal, state, and local levels regulate how organizations carry on staffing. Many laws were established, which banished most discriminatory employing practices. Three sensitive areas of legal concern that managers must abide by with are equal opportunity, affirmative action, and sexual harassment, described in the following sections. These fields, as well as other laws, impact all human resource practices.

Equal Employment Opportunity

Individuals are saved from illegal discrimination, which occurs when individuals who share a certain characteristic, such as race, age, or gender, are discriminated against because of that characteristic. Individuals who have the assigned characteristics are called the protected class. Laws have keyed out the following characteristics for protection:

- Age (people over 40)
- Gender (women, comprising those who are pregnant)
- People with disabilities (physical and mental)
- Military experience
- Caste
- Religion (special beliefs and practices)

The main goal of the laws is to ensure that everyone has an equal opportunity of getting a task or being promoted at work.

The Industrial Employment (Standing Orders) Act, 1946

Classification ought to be made as per the Standing Orders. Where there are no Standing Orders or service rules applicable to employees, then classification can be made either based on trade tests or any other test which is reasonable and in accordance with the Model Standing Orders. In general, the workers are classified as:

- Apprentice/trainee;
- Casual;
- Temporary;

- Badli/substitute;
- Probationer;
- Permanent; and
- Fixed period employees

Factories Act of 1948

The main aim of the Factories Act is:

- To regulate working conditions in factories.
- To ensure that fundamental minimum necessities for the safety, health and welfare of the factory workers are provided.
- To regulate of working hours, leave, holidays, overtime and employment of children, women and young persons.

This act applies to all factories letting in Government factories. A "factory" as defined in the Act means any premises admitting the precincts:

- Where ten or more workers are employed on any day of the preceding 12 months and a manufacturing process is carried on with the aid of electric power; and
- Where 20 or more workers are employed on any day of the preceding 12 months and a manufacturing process is conducted without the aid of electric power.

The obligations of the employers are, basically speaking, the rights of the employees to claim the minimal health and safety measures and welfare amenities as provided for in the Act, observance of working hours, holidays, overtime, annual leave and special protection against risky processes and dangerous contents, to obtain data relating to workers' health and safety at work from the occupier, to get trained by or through the occupier, in respect of workers' health and safety, to represent to the Inspector directly or although a representative in the matter of inadequate provision for protection of health or safety in the factory, not to pay any fee or charge for the facilities or appliances rendered by the employer and to claim wages for or in lieu of allowable leave under the provisions of the Payment of Wages Act.

Payment of Wages Act, 1936

Under the Payment of Wages Act, 1936 the following are the common responsibilities of the employer:

- Every employer is mainly accountable for payment of wages to employees. The employer ought to fix the wage period (which may be per day, per week or per month) but in no case it ought to exceed one month;

- Every employer ought to make well-timed payment of wages. If the employment of any person is being terminated, those wages ought to be paid within two days of the date of termination; and
- The employer ought to pay the wages in cash, i.e., in current coins or currency notes. Nevertheless wages may also be paid either by cheque or by crediting in employee's bank account after obtaining written consent.

Minimum Wages Act, 1948

The employer is bound to pay to every employee employed by him wages at a rate not less than the minimum rates of wages fixed for that class of employees without making any deduction (except as permitted under the Payment of Wages Act). The employees are entitled to the minimum wages at all times and under all considerations.

Workmen's Compensation Act, 1923

The employer must pay compensation for an accident suffered by an employee during the course of employment and in accordance with the Act. The employer must submit a statement to the Commissioner (within 30 days of receiving the notice) giving the considerations attending the death of a worker as result of an accident and indicating whether the employer is liable to deposit any compensation for the same. It ought to also submit an accident report to the Commissioner within seven days of the accident.

Employees Provident Funds and Miscellaneous Provisions Act, 1952

The employer must pay its and the employees' contributions and administrative charges as required under the Act and schemes. Financial difficulty is no excuse for non-payment. The contribution has to be made regardless of the fact whether wages are paid to the employee due to lockout, strike, or other related reason. Employer must furnish the requirement returns to the Provident Funds Commissioner.

DETERMINING HUMAN RESOURCE NEEDS

Staffing is an ongoing process that commences with finding the right individuals through proper planning, recruiting, and selecting. But staffing does not end once employees are hired; management must keep and foster its individuals via training, appraising, compensating, and implementing employment decisions that decide such things as promotions, transfers, and layoffs.

Selecting the Best Person for the Job

The first step in the staffing process demands human resource planning. Human resource planning begins with a task analysis in which descriptions of all jobs (tasks) and the qualifications demanded for each position are developed. A task description is a written statement of what a jobholder does, how it is done, and why it is done. It normally impersonates task content, environment, and conditions of employment. The task specification states the minimum satisfactory qualifications an incumbent must possess to execute a given task successfully. It identifies the knowledge, skills, and powers demanded to do the task effectively.

Task analysis is then complied by a human resource inventory, which catalogues qualifications and interests. Next, a human resource guess is developed to predict the establishment's future needs for jobs and individuals based on its strategic plans and normal attrition. The forecast is then equated to the inventory to determine whether the establishment's staffing needs will be met with being personnel or whether managers will have to recruit new employees or terminate existent ones.

Having the right individuals on staff is essential to the success of an establishment. Numerous selection devices help employers predict which applicants will be successful if hired. These devices aim to be not only valid, but also reliable. Validity is proof that the relationship between the selection device and some relevant task criterion exists. Reliability is an indicant that the device measures the same thing consistently.

For instance, it would be appropriate to give a keyboarding test to a candidate applying for a task as an administrative assistant. Nonetheless, it would not be valid to give a keyboarding test to a candidate for a task as a physical education teacher. If a keyboarding test is given to the same individual on two distinguish occasions, the results ought to be similar. To be effectual predictors, a selection device must have an acceptable level of consistency.

Recruiting Strategies

Recruitment makes up all the activities an establishment may use to attract a pool of viable candidates. Effectual recruiting is more and more important today for numerous reasons:

- The employment rate has in general declined each year through the 1990s. Experts refer to the current enrolling position as one of "evaporated employee resources."
- Many experts believe that today's Generation X employees (those born between 1963 and 1981) are less inclined to build long-term employment relationships than were their predecessors. Therefore, finding the right motivators for attracting, employing, and retaining qualified personnel may be more complicated than in former years.

Keep in mind that recruiting strategies differ among organizations. Though one may instantly think of campus recruiting as a typical recruiting activity, many organizations use internal recruiting, or promote-from-within policies, to fill their high-level positions. Open positions are posted, and current employees are given preferences when these positions become available. Internal recruitment is less costly than an external search. It also gives higher employee commitment, development, and satisfaction because it offers chances for career progress to employees rather than outsiders.

If internal sources don't create an acceptable candidate, many external recruiting strategies are uncommitted, comprising the following:

- Employee referrals
- Employment agencies (private, public, or temporary agencies)
- Executive recruiters (occasionally called head-hunters)
- Internet employment sites
- Internship programs
- Newspaper advertising
- Unions

But there's more to entering than just attracting employees; managers need to be able to weed out the top candidates. Once a manger has a consortium of applicants, the selection process can start out.

STEPS IN SELECTION PROCESS

Application Forms

For almost all employers, the application form is the first step in the selection process. Application forms provide a record of salient information about applicants for positions, and also furnish data for personnel research. Interviewers may use replies from the application for follow-up questions during an interview. These forms range from requests for fundamental information, such as names, addresses, and telephone numbers, to comprehensive personal history profiles detailing applicants' education, task experience skills, and achievements.

For example, employers ought to not ask whether an applicant rents or owns his or his own home, because an applicant's response may adversely affect his or his chances at the task. Minorities and women may be less likely to own a home, and home ownership is probably unrelated to task performance. Alternatively, asking about the CPA exam for an accounting position is set aside, even if only one-half of all female or minority applicants have taken the exam versus nine-tenths of male appliers.

A quick test for disparate affect suggested by the Uniform Selection Guidelines is the four-fifths rules. In general, a disparate impact is presumed when the proportions of protected class applicants who are actually hired is less that 80 percent (four-fifths) of the proportion of the majority group applicants selected. For instance, assume that an employer has 100 white male applicants for an entry-level task and hires one-half of them, for a selection ratio of 1:2, or 50 percent (50/100). The four-fifths rule doesn't mean that the employers must hire four-fifths, or 40 protected class members. Rather, the rule means that the employer's selection ratio of protected class-applicants ought to be at least four-fifths of that of the absolute majority groups.

Testing

Testing is some other method of selecting competent future employees. Though testing use has ebbed and flowed during the past two decades, current studies reveal that more than 80 percent of employers use testing as part of their selection process. Again, these tests must be valid and reliable, or serious EEO questions may be raised about the use of them. As a result, a manager necessitates to make sure that the test measures only task-relevant dimensions of applicants.

Most tests focus on specific task-related abilities and skills, such as math or motor skills. Typical types of exams constitute the following:

- Integrity tests measurement elements such as dependability, carefulness, responsibility, and honesty. These tests are used to learn about the attitudes of applicants toward a variety of task-related subjects. Since the passage of the Employee Polygraph Protection Act in 1988, polygraph (lie detector) tests have been effectively banned in employment situations. In their place, attitude tests are being used to evaluate attitudes about honesty and, presumably, on-the-task behaviours.

- Personality tests measurement personality or temperament. These tests are among the least reliable. Personality tests are debatable and not very valid, because little or no relationship exists between personality and performance.
- Knowledge tests are more authentic than personality tests because they measure an applicant's comprehension or knowledge of a subject. A math test for an accountant and a weather test for a pilot are examples. Human relations specialists must be able to demonstrate that the test reflects the knowledge needed to perform the task. For example, a teacher hired to teach math ought to not be given a keyboarding test.
- Performance simulation tests are altering in popularity. Based on task analysis data, they more easily meet the requirement of task relatedness than written tests. Performance simulation tests are made up of real task behaviours. The best-known performance simulation test is known as work sampling, and other credible simulation processes are performed at judgment centres.
- An assessment is a selection skill that examines candidates' dealing of simulated task situations and evaluates a candidate's potentiality by observing his or his performance in experiential activities designed to assume daily work.
- Assessment centres, where work sampling is frequently completed, utilize line executives, supervisors, or trained psychologists to assess candidates as they go through exercises that simulate real problems that these candidates would confront on their jobs. Activities may constitute interviews, problem-solving exercises, group discussions, and business-decision games. Assessment centres have consistently demonstrated results that accurately predict later task performance in managerial places.
- Work sampling is an effort to produce a illumination replica of a task, giving applicants the chance to demonstrate that they possess the essential talents by actually doing the tasks.

Interviews

Another widely used selection proficiency is the interview, a formal, in-depth conversation conducted to evaluate an applicant's acceptability. In general, the interviewer seeks to answer three broad questions:

1. Can the applicant do the task?
2. Will the applicant do the task?
3. How does the applicant compare with others who are being considered for the task?

Interviews are famous because of their flexibility. They can be adapted to unskilled, skilled, managerial, and staff employees. They also allow a two-way exchange of information where interviewers can learn about the applicant and the applicant can learn about the employer. Interviews do have some shortcomings, nevertheless. The most noticeable flaws are in the areas of reliability and validity. Good reliability means that the interpretation of the interview results doesn't vary from interviewer to interviewer. Reliability is meliorated when identical questions are asked. The validity of interviews is frequently questionable because few departments use standardized interviews.

Managers can boost the dependability and robustness of selection interviews by planning the interviews, establishing rapport, closing the interview with time for questions, and reviewing the interview as soon as possible after its decision.

Other Selection Techniques

Reference checking and health exams are two other significant selection techniques that help in the staffing decision.

- Reference checking allows employers to verify information rendered by the candidate. Nonetheless, obtaining information about potential candidates is frequently difficult because of privacy laws and employer business concern about defamation lawsuits.
- Health exams key out health problems that increase absenteeism and accidents, as well as discovering diseases that may be unknown to the applicant.

ORIENTATION AND TRAINING PROGRAMS

Once employees are selected, they must be ready to do their jobs, which is when orientation and training come in. Orientation means allowing for new employees with fundamental information about the employer. Training programs are used to ensure that the new employee has the fundamental knowledge required to perform the task satisfactorily. Orientation and training programs are significant elements in the processes of developing committed and flexible high-potential manpower and socializing new employees. Additionally, these programs can save employers money, providing big returns to an establishment, because an establishment that invests money to train its employees results in both the employees and the establishment relishing the dividends.

Orientation

Orientation programs not only amend the rate at which employees are able to perform their jobs but also help employees satisfy their personal desires to feel they are part of the establishment's social fabric. The HR department generally orients newcomers to broad organizational issues and fringe benefits. Supervisors complete the orientation process by introducing new employees to co-workers and others involved in the task. A buddy or wise man (mentor) may be assigned to uphold the process.

Training Needs

Merely employing and placing employees in jobs doesn't assure their success. In fact, even tenured employees may need training, because of changes in the business environment. Here are some changes that may indicate that current employees need training:

- Introduction of new equipment or processes
- A change in the employee's task responsibilities
- A drop in an employee's productivity or in the quality of output
- An increase in safety violations or accidents
- An increased number of questions
- Complaints by customers or co-workers

Once managers decide that their employees need training, these managers necessitate to develop clear training aims that outline anticipated results. These managers must also be able to distinctly communicate these aims to employees. Keep in mind that training is only one response to a performance problem. If the problem is want of motivation, a poorly designed task, or an extraneous condition (such as a family problem), training isn't likely to offer much help.

Types of Training

After particular training aims have been demonstrated, training sessions ought to be scheduled to provide the employee an opportunity to meet his or his aims. The following are typical training programs provided by employers:

- Basic literacy training: Organizations more and more necessitate to provide fundamental literacy training in the areas of reading and math skills to their employees.
- Technical training: New technology and structural designs have increased the demand to upgrade and improve employees' technical skills in both white-collar and blue-collar jobs.
- Interpersonal skills training: To the highest degree employees belong to a work team, and their work performance depends on their abilities to in effect interact with their co-workers. Interpersonal skills training help employees build communication skills.
- Problem-solving training: Today's employees frequently work as members of self-managed teams who are accountable for solving their own problems. Problem-solving training has become a fundamental part of almost every organizational effort to introduce self-managed teams or implement Total Quality Management (TQM).
- Diversity training: As one of the fastest growing areas of training, diversity training increases awareness and builds cultural sensitivity skills. Awareness training tries to produce a discernment of the need for, and meaning of, managing and evaluating diversity. Skill-building training educates employees about specific cultural conflicts in the workplace.

Training Methods

Most training takes place on the task due to the simplicity and lower cost of on-the-task training method acting. Two popular types of on-the-task training constitute the following:

- Task rotation: By allotting individuals to dissimilar jobs or tasks to different individuals on an irregular basis, leaders can add variety and expose individuals to the dependence that one task has on others. Task rotation can help stimulate individuals to higher levels of contributions, renew individual's interest and enthusiasm, and promote them to work more as a team.

- Mentoring programs: A fresh employee frequently learns his or his task under the direction of a seasoned old hand. In the trades, this type of training generally is called an apprenticeship. In white-collar jobs, it is called a coaching or mentoring relationship. In each, the new employee works under the observation of an experienced worker.

Occasionally, training aims cannot be conformed to through on-the-task training; the employer needs to look to other resources. Off-the-task training can rely on outside consultants, local college faculty, or in-house personnel. The more popular off-the-task training methods are classroom lectures, videos, and simulation exercises. Thanks to new technologies, employers can now facilitate some training, such as tutorials, on the employees' own computers, reducing the overall costs. Irrespective of the method selected, effectual training ought to be individualized. Some individuals absorb selective information better when they read about it, others learn best by observation, and still others learn better when they hear the information. These different learning styles aren't contradictory. When training is designed around the preferred learning style of an employee, the benefits of training are maximized because employees are able to hold more of what they learn.

Additionally to training, employers ought to extend development plans, which include a series of steps that can help employees acquire skills to reach long-term aims, such as a task promotion. Training, alternatively, is quick and specific to a present task.

EVALUATING EMPLOYEE PERFORMANCE

Employee performance ought to be assessed regularly. Employees want feedback-they want to know what their supervisors think about their work. Regular performance evaluations not only provide feedback to employees, but also provide employees with a chance to correct deficiencies. Evaluations or reviews also help in making key personnel decisions, such as the following:

- Justifying promotions, transfers, and terminations
- Identifying training needs
- Providing feedback to employees on their performance
- Determining necessary pay adjustments

Most organizations employ employee evaluation systems; one such system is known as a performance appraisal. A performance appraisal is a formal, structured system designed to evaluate the real task performance of an employee against designated performance standards. Though performance appraisals systems vary by organizations, all employee evaluations ought to have the following three components:

- Specific, task-related criteria against which performance can be equated
- A rating scale that lets employees know how well they're meeting the criteria
- Objective methods, forms, and processes to determine the rating

Customarily, an employee's immediate boss conducts his or his performance appraisal. Notwithstanding, some organizations use other devices, such as peer evaluations, self-appraisals, and even customer evaluations, for conducting this significant task. The latest approach to performance evaluation is the use of 360-degree feedback. The 360-degree feedback appraisal provides performance feedback from the full circle of daily contacts that an employee may have. This method acting of performance appraisal fits well into organizations that have introduced teams, employee involvement, and Total Quality Management programs.

MAKING EMPLOYMENT DECISIONS

Employment decisions go outside determining which employees are due for raises. Through regular, objective performance appraisals, managers assume information to make and implement decisions about promotions, transfers, demotions, separations, and compensation. In most organizations, outstanding employees are acknowledged for their hard work and outstanding performances, and offered promotions. A promotion broadly speaking means rewarding an employee's efforts by moving that person to a task with increased authority and responsibility.

Downsizing has led numerous firms to rely on lateral moves or transfers instead of promoting employees. A lateral move can act as an opportunity for future vertical advancement because it can broaden an employee's experiences and add skills. Alternatively, occasionally employees' performances signal that they are not adapting well to their jobs and may need fewer duties. One option is a demotion, or reassignment to a lower rank or less prestigious position. Demotions aren't a popular skill because of the stigma accompanied this move. A thought is that demotions ought to be used as punishment for inefficient performance.

The departure of an employee from an establishment is denoted as separation. Separation may be voluntary or involuntary. Resignations and retirements are voluntary separations. Involuntary separations are layoffs and/or firings. Recently, the rash of downsizing all through the country has resulted in many layoffs.

Occasionally, nonetheless, an employee must be terminated because of poor performance. Dismissal or firing of employees ought to occur only on the basis of just cause and only after all sensible steps to rehabilitate the employee have failed. In some cases, such as gross insubordination or theft, immediate discharge is necessitated.

COMPENSATING EMPLOYEES

Employee compensation concerns to all work-related payments, comprising wages, commissions, insurance, and time off. Wages and salaries are the most obvious forms of compensation and are based on task evaluations that determine the relative values of jobs to the establishment. Under the hourly wage system, employees are paid a determined amount for each hour they work. The system is in general used for lower skilled occupations. Salaried employees receive a fixed sum per week or month, irrespective how many hours they work. Most professional positions are salaried; the reality is that these employees normally work in excessiveness of a "minimum" 40-hour workweek.

Some businesses are compensated through incentive pay programs. Salespeople normally receive commissions based upon the quantities of goods they sell. Some sales compensation plans contain elements of both a salary and commission. A production worker's pay may be based upon some combination of an hourly wage and an incentive for each "piece" he or he makes. Some employees are offered merit awards as an honour for sustained superior performance.

Employee benefits are adds on to wages or pay. Some benefits, such as unemployment and worker's compensation, are legally mandated. Other benefits are optional and help build employee loyalty to an establishment, comprising the following:

- Bonuses (incentive money paid to employees additionally to their regular compensation)
- Employee discounts
- Health insurance
- Pension plans
- Profit-sharing (money from a portion of the company profits used to supplement regular compensation)

- Stock options (a plan that permits employees to buy shares of stock in the employee's firm at or below the present market value)
- Vacation, sick, and personal days

A top management executive is given benefits unequalled to his or her status. Additional executive benefits are termed perquisites (perks).

RELATIONS WITH OUTSIDE FACTORS

The Employment Relations Act was brought in the year 2000 to provide the framework for regulating relationships between employers and employees. The Act recognises "that employment relationships must be built on good faith behaviour" (Section 3(a)(i)) and the "inherent inequality of bargaining power in employment relationships" (Section 3(a)(ii)).

The Department of Labour has carried on research into the operation of the personal grievance provisions of the Act, including a long term and short term series of projects.

Long Term Research Programme

- A survey of businesses, with 852 respondents, of which 130 had experienced challenges during the previous 12 months;
- A survey of public sector organizations, with 130 respondents of which 40 had experienced quarrels during the previous 12 months;
- Case studies of 15 challenges

Short Term Research Programme

- A survey of mediations carried out over a one month period,
- A review of Employment Relations Authority determinations over the same period
- A series of focus groups

Consequences from the long term research programme provided the basic source for the findings presented in this report, with additional information from the short term research programme used where pertinent. Nevertheless, a formal, external solution pathway can be started by either party. Once an employee or employer applied for mediation or an Employment Relations Authority hearing, there was little chance for the problem solution to go forward down an informal path.

In the case studies, pure misconduct cases tended to follow a more certain path - an internal disciplinary meeting, attended by the employee with a representative, followed by a warning, dismissal, or resignation. In contrast, performance and relationship issues (in particular) tended to be more complex. Employers seemed to be less clear about how to resolve these issues. As a result, the problem frequently continued for a longer time. This was aggravated where employers or employees went "fishing" for additional issues, which increased the level of tension and made the trouble more difficult to resolve.

For both employers and employees, the interests involved impacted on their choices regarding the path of the employment relationship problem. For employees, the stakes included whether the employee had found a new task, the impact on their families, or the hope to clear their name. For employers, the stakes included their assessment of the costs of the solution pathway, the effect of publicity on their reputation, or whether the problem would produce a case law within their organization.

Employers frequently assert that process is more important than substance. Nevertheless, in hearings on employment disputes, matters of substance and process aren't always easy (or appropriate) to disentangle. For example, if an employee "wins" because the Authority finds that the employer failed to investigate alleged misconduct, the employer is likely to see this as "process trumping substance" while the employee may conceive that their claim on the substance would have prevailed had an investigation taken place.

Though the Act doesn't explicitly discern between substantive and procedural unfairness, the Authority can and does modify awards as per its assessment of the merits. For instance, the review of Authority determinations found two examples where the Authority found that discharges were unacceptable in process terms, but awarded nothing to the employees because of their contributory behaviour. In around one quarter of all cases examined the Authority reduced or rejected awards on the base of contributory conduct.

WELFARE AND SECURITY MEASURES

Welfare constitutes anything that is done for the comfort and improvement of employees and is provided over and above the wages. Welfare helps in keeping the morale and motivation of the employees high so as to retain the employees for longer duration. The welfare measures need not be in monetary terms only but in any kind/forms.

Employee welfare lets in monitoring of working conditions, creation of industrial harmony through infrastructure for health, industrial relations and insurance against disease, accident and unemployment for the workers and their families.

Employee welfare means all those activities of employer which are directed towards providing the employees with certain facilities and services additionally to wages or salaries.

Employee welfare has the following objectives:

1. To render better life and health to the workers.
2. To make the workers happy and satisfied.
3. To relieve workers from industrial fatigue and to improve intellectual, cultural and material conditions of living of the workers.

The fundamental features of employee welfare measures are as follows:

1. Employee welfare comprises numerous facilities, services and amenities provided to workers for improving their health, efficiency, economic improvement and social status.
2. Welfare measures are additionally to regular wages and other economic gains available to workers due to legal provisions and collective bargaining.
3. Employee welfare schemes are flexible and invariably changing. New welfare measures are added to the existing ones from time to time.
4. Welfare measures may be introduced by the employers, government, employees or by any social or charitable agency.
5. The purpose of employee welfare is to bring about the growth of the whole personality of the workers to make a better manpower.

The very logic behind providing welfare schemes is to produce efficient, healthy, loyal and satisfied labour force for the establishment. The intention of providing such facilities is to make their work life better and also to raise their standard of living. The important benefits of welfare measures can be summarized as follows:

- They provide better physical and mental health to workers and therefore promote a healthy work environment.

- Facilities like housing schemes, medical benefits, and education and recreation facilities for workers' families help in raising their standards of living. This makes workers to pay more attention towards work and therefore increases their productivity.
- Employers get stable labour force by providing welfare facilities. Workers take active interest in their jobs and work with a feeling of involvement and participation.
- Employee welfare measures increase the productivity of establishment and promote healthy industrial relations thereby maintaining industrial peace.
- The social evils prevalent among the labours such as substance abuse, etc are reduced to a greater extent by the welfare policies.

Note: The aim of human resource management is to help an establishment to meet strategic aims by attracting, and maintaining employees and also to manage them effectively. Take the example of Microsoft. It is dedicated to a corporate culture that inspires and rewards its employees. Benefits, Information Solutions and Compensation play an important role in demonstrating the high value Microsoft places on all its employees, both personally and professionally. For more detailed information, reader can visit their site: http://members.microsoft.com/careers/mslife/benefits/default.mspx

15

Organizational Behaviour

Organizational behaviour is the systematic study and careful application of knowledge about how people, as individuals and as groups, act within organization.

Whenever people interact in organizations, many factors come into play. Modern organizational studies attempt to understand and model these factors. Like all modernist social sciences, organizational studies seek to control, predict, and explain. There is some controversy over the ethics of controlling workers' behaviour. As such, organizational behaviour or OB has at times been accused of being the scientific tool of the powerful. Those accusations notwithstanding, OB can play a major role in organizational development and success.

DEFINITION

Organizational behaviour is the study and application of knowledge more or less concerning how individuals as people and as groups act within organizations. It can be defined as the understanding, prediction and management of human behaviour in organizations. Organizational Behaviour is related to other disciplines like Organizations Theory, Establishment Development and Personnel/Human Resources Management. The classification of Organizational Behaviour given by Henry Mintzberg says that the roles depending on the extent of interpersonal relationships, the transfer of information and decision-making involved in the task.

An overall model of organizational behaviour can be formulated on the basis of three theoretical frameworks. They are the cognitive, behaviouristic and social learning frameworks. The cognitive approach gives more credit to individuals than the other approaches and is based on the expectancy, demand and incentive concepts. Edward Tolman has made significant contributions to this approach.

Behaviouristic framework centres on observable behaviours. Ivan Pavlov and John B.Watson were the pioneers of the behaviouristic theory. They explained human behaviour on the basis of the association between stimulus and response. The social learning approach incorporates the concepts and principles of both the cognitive and behaviouristic frameworks. In this approach, behaviour is explained as a continuous reciprocal interaction between cognitive, behavioural and environmental determinants. The establishment behaviour model (S, O, B, C) has comprised the best expressions from the three frameworks of human behaviour. In this model, the letters S, O, B, C represent situation, organizm, behaviour and consequences, respectively.

IMPORTANCE

In contemporary world, managers confront many challenges and opportunities. The greatest challenges among all of them are the result of environmental changes occurring due to globalization, information technology, total quality, and diversity and ethics. OB models help managers to face these challenges and take set aside actions. The four models of OB are the autocratic model, the custodial model, the supportive model and the collegial model. The autocratic model is based on power. It works well particularly in times of an organizational crisis. Organizations are collections of interacting and inter related human and non-human resources working toward a common end or set of aims within the framework of integrated relationships.

Organizational behaviour is concerned with all aspects of how organizations determine the behaviour of individuals and how individuals in turn influence organizations. Organizational behaviour is an inter-disciplinary field that draws freely from a number of the behavioural sciences, constituting anthropology, psychology, sociology, and many others. The unique mission of organizational behaviour is to apply the concepts of behavioural sciences to the pressing problems of management, and, more in general, to administrative theory and practice. In approaching the problems of organizational behaviour, there are a number of available strategies we can utilize. Historically, the study of management and organizations took a closed-systems view. The preoccupation of this view is to maximize the efficiency of internal operations. In doing so, the uncertainty of uncontrollable and external environmental factors frequently were assumed away or denied. This conventional closed-systems perspective of organizations made significant shares to the theory of organizational design.

At the same time, for analytical reasons, organizations came to be deemed precise and complicated machines. In this framework, human beings were reduced to components of the organizational machine. More recently, the study of organizations and the behaviour of human beings within them have accepted a more open-systems perspective. Factors such as human sentiments and attitudes, as well as technological and sociological forces developing outside the organizations, have assumed greater importance in analyzing organizational behaviour. This discussion adopts the open perspective, as this is a contemporary and more meaningful way to view organizations and human behaviour within them. After some preliminary issues, we shall examine the individual. We shall move from the person to the small group, to the complicated establishment, and eventually to some environmental factors significant to the process of organizational change.

HISTORICAL BACKGROUND

English philosophers adopted fundamentally the same view but placed more emphasis on the interests of the state (or establishment) and less stress on the personal aspirations of the people in power. Weber avoided moralistic assumptions about the inherent good or evil of human nature and chose to view individuals as irrational and emotional. Taylor looked upon human beings as lazy and inspired by self-interest. Reasoning from any of these assumptions, one comes to the conclusion that control of human behaviour is necessary, as evidenced by the concern for authority in early administrative and political thought. With Mayo and the Hawthorne Studies, nevertheless, we see the assumption of the cooperative social human being. Therefore, it isn't surprising that the emphasis proceeded away from the control philosophy.

Behavioural scientists today presume that human beings are neither good nor evil. For this reason, there has been more stress placed on describing behaviour as it exists under different conditions. The result has been no clear-cut prescription for any specific type of authority orientation that can be applied to all cases. With regard to the methods employed in understanding in behaviour, Machiavelli relied on historical analogy and observation. The English philosophers advocated inductive logic, while Weber approached the subject deductively. Taylor was exceedingly experimental and scientific; Mayo mixed experiments with philosophy. Behavioural scientists today are almost completely experimental in their orientation. Machiavelli sought a practical theory of power, while the philosophers sought order, Weber's quest was for rationality, and Taylor defended justice. Mayo's engrossment was with the mental and emotional health of workers.

Today's behavioural scientists are related primarily with understanding behaviour for its own sake. The person in power, or aspiring to be in power, would be the benefactor of Machiavellianism, while society with a stable system of government would gain from the guidelines proposed by the English philosophers. Weber's bureaucracy was designed to add rationality to decision making. Both managers and workers conceivably could gain from the systems proposed by Taylor and Mayo, though the benefits derived would be different. Modern science would be served best by the actions of contemporary behavioural scientists, as would workers and managers through the application of scientific knowledge. Finally, Machiavelli's practical-objective approach to reality establishes his appeal.

The philosophers are appealing as of their ideal of order. Weber and Taylor find support from business individuals because their ideas contain a promise of rationality and economic efficiency. Mayo is attractive because he enhances our image as unique beings unlike all others. Behavioural science today is compelling because of its objectivity and systematic structure.

In this discussion numerous things have been acknowledged. First, the fundamental interest in human behaviour in organizations can be traced to distant origins. The interest goes back even further than we have noted, perhaps even to Biblical times. Secondly, the contributions have come from a variety of sources. Political and moral philosophy made their contributions along with economics, psychology, engineering, and sociology. Systematic administrative thought, where the business concern is for practical matters relating to the management of organizations, is properly viewed as a product of the twentieth century. From the mechanistic views of Weber, Fayol, and Taylor came the humanistic interest of Mayo and others in the 1920s and 1930s. This human relations perspective has been refined even more by modern behavioural scientists.

FUNDAMENTAL CONCEPTS OF ORGANIZATIONAL BEHAVIOUR

In this discussion a detailed look has been accepted as the alternative methods available for generating valid knowledge in organizational behaviour. Main emphasis has been placed on the requirements for an acceptable deductive argument and the elements necessary for accurate empirical analysis. The problems of behavioural measurement are also examined. We will conclude with an examination of the functional explanation, which is frequently encountered in the biological and behavioural sciences. Rather than reiterating here the arguments developed, the need for devoting a chapter to the discussion of selected philosophical problems of the approximate sciences is reviewed. The goal isn't abstractedness for the sake of abstraction.

Sir Roy Harrod, the grand British economic expert, once said that, "the barrenness of methodological conclusions is frequently a fitting compliment to the weariness entailed in the process of reaching them." Such discussions do so occasionally seem remarkably boring and tiresome. Nevertheless, in the area of organizational behaviour, methodological issues are especially pressing.

Whenever a systematic understanding of the concepts of organizational behaviour is to be developed, then the methods applied in formulating them has to be appreciated. Therefore, it is hoped that this chapter has provided a brief introduction to the methodology of the behavioural sciences. Of special importance is the recognition that though organizational behaviour is scientific in character, it deals with human beings. Human beings are different from inanimate objects and organizational behaviour is an empirical discipline. The application of the strict and unmodified inductive method, nevertheless, fails to account for many unique qualities of humans. The goal is to be as scientific as possible, while rest open to the realities of human behaviour.

PERSONALITY DEVELOPMENT AND ATTITUDES

In this discussion there are numerous things of special importance that have been considered. First, personality is in short traced and attention given to the contributions and limitations of psychological theory, trait-factor theory, and the need theories of Maslow and McClelland. All of these significant formulations provide some useful information about the behaviour of individuals in organizations. Next, a systems view of human behaviour was proposed to illustrate how cognitive processes and needs act upon environmentally induced stimuli. This interaction results in actions that are once again subjected to the determination of environmental forces. In this section, attention is given to the composite problem of how heredity (nature) and experience (nurture) interact in determining human behaviour.

The conclusion drawn is that most important aspects of behaviour are neither genetic nor environmental decided. Instead they result from the influence of the two. An attempt has also been made to examine the relationship between culture and behaviour. Since culture comprises all learned behaviour, the discussion is restricted to the influence of generational values and the specific implication of value differences among social classes and work groups. The final major topic of discussion related to attitudes and attitude change. A deliberate analysis is made of attitude formation and the controversial relationship between attitudes and behaviour. Though some studies question any casual association between attitudes and behaviour, most of the discrepancies can be explained on methodological grounds. With regard to attitude change, it is noted that congruent changes (changes in scale rather than in direction) are easier to effect than incongruent changes. Behaviourally, factors such as communicator credibility and attractiveness are significant determinants of the ease alteration.

THE COGNITIVE BASIS OF INDIVIDUAL BEHAVIOUR

This discussion has examined the gist of cognitive processes and has illustrated their importance to organizational demeanour. In the first place, it looks at perception and specifies three characteristics of the perceptual process. Perception was first characterized as a selective activity. Individuals cannot perceive all the stimuli confronting them from the surrounding environment. Therefore, it is safe to say that managerial action generally takes place on the basis of imperfect or incomplete information. The stimuli that are selected are in general those that reinforce the attitudes of the perceiver. Perception is further characterized by closure. Even although individuals selectively screen environmental stimuli, they fill in gaps and complete the perceptual picture as if they had complete information. Finally, perception takes place within a perspective. The perspective helps individuals to orient themselves to reality. In practical terms, the perceptual process is significant to management because this process determines the quantity and quality of selective information upon which decisions are made.

Learning is talked about as a cognitive operation and a distinction is made between classic and conditioning, in classical conditioning a stimulant is presented prior to or concurrently with a response. In instrumental conditioning a response occurs in anticipation of some consequence. In current years some of the most significant implications of learning theory for management have been in the area of motivation. The cognitive process of human problem solving has been examined. It is noted that few real-world situations, present individuals with one, and only one, course of action. Usually, one must make a choice among alternatives and engage in problem solving. Applications of problem solving were shown to be apparent in the managerial activity of decision making. Two approaches to decision making have been examined. Normative decision theory tells us how decisions ought to be made if maximizing behaviour is to be achieved. Behavioural decision theory tells us how decisions are really made and doesn't attempt to prescribe normative guidelines. The objective of core cognitive operation has set the stage for discussion of modern motivation theory and practice.

INDIVIDUAL DETERMINANTS OF ORGANIZATION

In this discussion, an endeavour has been made to review selected topics in motivation. The format was methodological primarily to illustrate that significant controversy exists in the area, even although motivation has consumed much of the energy of writers in the behavioural sciences and management. The significant point to distinguish is that the generality and pragmatic usefulness of a particular approach to motivation is closely related to the manner in which that approach is developed. Rational-deductive theories such as the Barnard-Simon model (exchange theory) and expectancy theory are based on certain prior assumptions about rational human being choice.

Accordingly, they are highly global, in a scientific sense, because they can be applied to a wide range of situations and circumstances. Herzberg's two-factor theory and operant conditioning are more inductive and empirical. Therefore, they are more specific and less ubiquitously adaptable. Given the present sate of motivation theory, the best strategy for a prospective manager is to become as familiar as possible with all of the theories currently available.

The truth is that thee is something new and something true in all of them. The manager's problem is to carefully choose those new things that are true, and to sceptically decide which true matters are really new. This, of course, isn't an easy dilemma for the manager to resolve. Even behavioural scientists who devote most of their time studying motivational problems find the issue complicated and frustrating. Once the essential foundations of motivation theory and practice are understood, one is able to confront the more philosophical questions of how behavioural science knowledge ought to be used in the managerial perspective. Issues of this quality immediately converge on such questions as the ethics of behaviour modification. This issue cannot be avoided by any managers because of very real forces from society, constituting legal intervention into motivational practices and the protection of individual rights on and off the task.

SMALL GROUP BEHAVIOUR

This chapter has discussed the concept of the small group and has illustrated the importance of the small group within the broader topic of organizational behaviour. Small group has been defined as a collection of interacting individuals who have common aims, similar values, and a structure of relationships. Groups come in a variety of forms, depending on the classification schema utilized.

The problem of defining the size of a small group is particularly troublesome. Because of their uniqueness, dyads and triads are considered special cases. Consequently, the main body of small- group theory that we discussed was related to groups of four or more, up to some theoretical limit where personal interaction is no more possible. One of the more important characteristics discussed is the nature of normative behaviour in groups.

A highly complicated relationship exists among such factors as group norms, conformity, cohesiveness, and group performance. Since performance is a manager's basic concern, care has been taken to examine this interrelationship in detail and specific examples given of ways in which knowledge of this process has been used by the managers of organizations. No discussion of small group behaviour is complete without an analysis of the structures that inevitably develop in the group perspective. For this reason, role relations have been examined, including clarity, ambiguity, and conflict, along with the highly relevant topic of position. In all cases, care has been taken to report the hard research data that have developed with respect to these topics.

One is too familiar with the fact that the role expectations and status hierarchies exist in all kinds of groups. A careful reading of the research ought to help to understand why this is true and even necessary for proper group functioning. Current attention has been given to other topics involving group interaction. One of the important areas has to do with the effectiveness of groups as problem solvers. After the discussion the pros and cons of individual versus group problem solving, guidelines were offered for effectively using a combined interacting-nominal group process. Remarks on sociometry and interaction process analysis were comprised as methods of understanding group behaviour.

There are other methods of analyzing interpersonal behaviour. Particular methods were selected primarily for intentions of illustration - to show that there are indeed systematic techniques for gaining insights into small-group phenomena.

MODELS OF ORGANIZATIONAL BEHAVIOUR

There are four major models or frameworks that organizations operate out of:

- Autocratic - The basis of this model is power with a managerial orientation of authority. The employees successively are oriented towards obedience and dependence on the boss. The employee need that is met is subsistence. The performance outcome is minimal.
- Custodial - The basis of this model is economic resources with a managerial orientation of money. The employees successively are oriented towards security and benefits and dependence on the establishment. The employee want that is met is security. The performance result is peaceful cooperation.
- Supportive - The basis of this model is leadership with a managerial orientation of support. The employees successively are oriented towards task performance and participation. The employee need that is met is status and recognition. The performance result is awakened drives.
- Collegial - The cornerstone of this model is partnership with a managerial orientation of teamwork. The employees in turn are oriented towards accountable behaviour and self-discipline. The employee demand that is met is self-actualization. The performance result is moderate enthusiasm.

Although there are four separate models, almost no establishment functions exclusively in one. There will typically be a predominate one, with one or more areas over-lapping in the other models.

The first model, autocratic, has its origin in the industrial revolution. The managers of this type of establishment operate out of McGregor's Theory X. The next three models begin to build on McGregor's Theory Y. They have each developed over a period of time and there is no one "best" model. The collegial model ought to not be thought as the last or best model, but the commencing of a new model or paradigm.

ORGANIZATIONAL CULTURE AND CLIMATE

The specifics of the complicated linkage between environmental externalities, establishment and individual behaviour are very important. In sociotechnical systems, social relationships in work groups can be associated with the technological demands of their tasks. In spite of the enthusiasm of the proponents of the sociotechnical view, important controversies exist with respect to the nature of the effect of environmental factors on organizational structures and consequently on behaviour.

These sources range from exceedingly personal things such as charisma to structural or positional influences. The use of power is really a question of leadership styles. The power one holds over another is associated with dependency. When one person is determined by another for something he or he values, the former is more easily influenced by the latter. Complicated interrelationship between organizational aims and the political process known as coalition formation is discussed. No matter of whether one accepts the natural systems view or the individual view of organizational aims, one must explain how the desires of several interest groups and/or individuals are translated into objectives of organizations. This is where theory of political coalition becomes an important issue. Viewing power and aim formation as political processes adds a classifiable behavioural tone to the processes evident in organizations of every type. Human beings are in fact political animals and it is significant to recognize this look of organizational behaviour.

Note: Procter & Gamble establishment is the role model in Organizational culture. Reader can go to their site for detailed in-depth knowledge on their in Organizational culture: http://www.pg.com/content/pdf/01_about_pg/01_about_pg_homepage/about_pg_toolbar/download_report/values_policies0708.pdf

16

Organizational Design

It is general assumption that a few things bear long term without being altered. Even well-known brand names, familiar slogans, and classic songs face updates in today's changing culture. Organizations are no unlike, and must respond to changes in their environments as well. Whether it is technology upgrades to meet client demands or policy updates to adapt employee growth, managers must be both willing to deal with the challenges of change. An establishment's structure is defined by its configuration and interrelationships of positions and departments.

ORGANIZATIONAL DESIGN DEFINED

Organizational design is the creation or change of an establishment's structure. The organizational design of a company ponders its efforts to respond to changes, incorporate new elements, insure collaboration, and allow flexibility.

Organizing a business is somewhat difficult. Once an establishment has a plan, the next step is to make it encounter. The major features of organizational structure are, in many ways, like the significant parts of a jigsaw puzzle-you pick them out, one by one. In particular, the two fundamental forms of organizational structure are mechanical and organic.

ORGANIZATIONAL STRUCTURES AND THEIR EFFECTS ON HUMAN BEHAVIOUR

Till a few decades back, organizations were usually structured as bureaucracies. A bureaucracy is a form of establishment based on logic, order, and the legitimate use of formal authority. Bureaucracies are intended to be orderly, fair, and extremely efficient. Their features include a clear-cut division of labour, strict hierarchy of authority, formal rules and processes, and promotion based on competency. Now-a-days, many individuals view bureaucracies negatively and recognize that bureaucracies have their limits. If organizations trust too much on rules and processes, they become gawky and too rigid-making them slow to respond to altering environments and more likely to die in the long run.

But management theory does not consider all bureaucratic structures as inevitably blemished. Instead, they ask these critical questions:

- When is a bureaucracy a good choice for an establishment?
- What alternatives survive when a bureaucracy isn't a good choice?

A research, conducted in England by Tom Burns and George Stalker in the early 1960s, undertook to answer these questions. Burns and Stalker studied industrial firms to determine how the nature of each firm's environment affected the way the firm was organized and managed. They believed a stable, stable environment demanded a different type of establishment than a rapidly changing one. Though a stable environment worked well under a bureaucracy, managers in constantly changing, innovative environments necessitated an organizational structure that allowed them to be responsive and creative. As a result, two distinguishable frameworks, the mechanistic and organic structures, were keyed out.

The Mechanistic Structure

The mechanistic structure, many a times used synonymously with bureaucratic structure, is a management system based on a formal framework of authority that is carefully outlined and precisely followed. An establishment that uses a mechanistic structure is likely to have the following characteristics:

- Clearly defined line and staff positions with formal relationships between the two
- Clearly specified tasks
- Precise definitions of the rights and responsibilities of members
- Tendency toward formal communication all through the organizational structure

Possibly the best example of a mechanistic structure is found in a college or university. Consider the very rigid and formal college entrance and registration processes. The reason for such processes is to insure that the establishment is able to deal with a large number of individuals in an equitable and fair manner. Though many individuals don't like them, regulations and standard operating processes pretty much guarantee undifferentiated treatment. But those same rules and processes, with their time-consuming communication and decision-making processes, incline to bog down organizations. Mechanistic organizations are appropriate when the external environment is reasonably stable. The biggest retreat to the mechanistic structure is its want of flexibility, which may induce an establishment to have trouble adjusting to change and coping with the unexpected.

The Organic Structure

The organic structure inclines to work better in dynamic environments where managers need to react quickly to change. An organic structure is a management system founded on cooperation and knowledge-based authority. It is much less conventional than a mechanistic establishment, and much more flexible. Organic structures are characterized by

- Decentralized control.
- Fast decision making.
- Informal patterns of both delegation and communication.
- Little reliance on formal authority.
- Roles that aren't extremely defined.
- Tasks that are continually redefined.

Because the atmosphere is intimate and the lines of authority may shift depending on the situation, the organic structure requires more cooperation among employees than does a bureaucracy. One instance of an organic structure is the Salvation Army. Though branches are located all through the nation, the establishment doesn't have a complicated structure; it promotes different units to take on new challenges.

The Salvation Army doesn't rely heavily on written rules and processes. Hence, this establishment can produce the processes that work best as different positions arise. The Salvation Army's power to take on new tasks and to fulfil its mission irrespective of the considerations it faces is one reason why it is a hallmark of organic organizations.

FACTORS AFFECTING ORGANIZATIONAL DESIGN

Though many factors can affect the choice of an appropriate structure for an establishment, the following five factors are the most general: size, life cycle, strategy, environment, and technology.

Organizational Size

The larger an establishment turns, the more complicated its structure. When an establishment is small - such as a single retail store, a two-person consulting firm, or a restaurant - its structure can be simple. In reality, if the establishment is very small, it may not even have a formal structure. Instead of following an organizational chart or specified task functions, individuals merely perform tasks based on their likes, dislikes, ability, and/or need. Rules and guidelines aren't prevalent and may exist only to provide the parameters within which organizational members can make decisions. Small organizations are very often organic systems.

As an establishment develops, nevertheless, it becomes more and more difficult to manage without more formal work assignments and some delegation of authority. Hence, large organizations develop formal structures. Tasks are extremely specialized and detailed rules and guidelines dictate work processes. Interorganizational communication flow rate primarily from superior to subordinate, and hierarchical relationships serve as the foundation for authority, responsibility, and control. The type of structure that develops will be one that provides the establishment with the power to operate effectively. That's one reason larger organizations are often mechanistic-mechanistic systems are in general designed to maximize specialization and amend efficiency.

Establishment Life Cycle

Organizations, like humans, incline to progress through levels known as a life cycle. Like humans, most organizations go through the following four stages: birth, youth, midlife, and maturity. Each phase has characteristics that have implications for the structure of the firm.

- Birth: In the birth state, a firm is just commencement. An establishment in the birth stage doesn't yet have a formal structure. In a young establishment, there isn't much delegation of authority. The founder generally "calls the shots."
- Youth: In this phase, the establishment is trying to develop. The emphasis in this stage is on becoming larger. The company shifts its attention from the wishes of the founder to the wishes of the customer. The establishment turns more organic in structure during this phase. It is during this phase that the formal structure is designed, and some delegation of authority occurs.
- Midlife: This phase occurs when the establishment has achieved a high level of success. An establishment in midlife is larger,

with a more complicated and more and more formal structure. More levels appear in the chain of command, and the founder may have trouble remaining in control. As the establishment becomes older, it may also become more mechanical in structure.

- Maturity: Once a firm has reached the maturity phase, it tends to become less innòvative, less interested in expanding, and more interested in maintaining itself in a stable, secure environment. The emphasis is on improving skilfulness and profitability. Nevertheless, in an attempt to improve efficiency and profitability, the firm frequently tends to become less innovative. Stale products result in sales declines and reduced profitability. Organizations in this stage are slowly dying. Nevertheless, maturity isn't an inevitable stage. Firms experiencing the decline of maturity may institute the changes requirement to revitalize.

Though an establishment may proceed consecutive through all four stages, it doesn't have to. An establishment may skip a phase, or it may cycle back to an earlier phase. An establishment may even try to change its perspective in the life cycle by changing its structure.

As the life-cycle concept involves, a relationship exists between an establishment's size and age. As organizations age, they tend to get larger; therefore, the structural changes a firm experiences as it gets larger and the changes it experiences as it advances through the life cycle are parallel. Hence, the older the establishment and the larger the establishment, the greater its demand for more structure, more specialization of tasks, and more rules. As a result, the older and larger the establishment becomes, the greater the likelihood that it will move from a physical structure of establishment to a mechanistic structure.

Strategy

How an establishment is attending position itself in the market in terms of its product is considered its strategy. A company may decide to be always the first on the market with the latest and most beneficial product (differentiation strategy), or it may decide that it will create a product already on the market more efficiently and more cost effectively (cost-leadership strategy). Each of these strategies demands a structure that helps the establishment reach its objectives. In other words, the structure must fit the strategy.

Companies that want to be the first on the market with the latest and best product probably are organic, because organic structures permit organizations to respond quickly to changes. Organizations that elect to create the same products more efficiently and effectively will likely be mechanistic.

Environment

The environment is the world in which the establishment functions, and comprises conditions that determine the establishment such as economic, social-cultural, legal-political, technological, and natural environment conditions. Environments are frequently described as either unchanging or dynamic.

- In a stable environment, the customers' hopes are well understood and probably will remain consistent for a relatively long time. Examples of organizations that face relatively stable environments constitute manufacturers of staple items such as detergent, cleaning supplies, and paper products.
- In a dynamic environment, the customers' desires are endlessly changing-the opposite of a stable environment. This condition is frequently thought of as turbulent. Additionally, the technology that a company uses while in this environment may need to be endlessly improved and updated. An example of an industry functioning in a dynamic environment is electronics. Technology changes produce competitive pressures for all electronics industries, since as technology changes, so do the desires of consumers.

In the main, organizations that operate in stable external environments find mechanistic structures to be good. This system provides a level of skilfulness that enhances the long-term performances of organizations that enjoy relatively stable operating environments. In contrast, organizations that operate in fickle and often changing environments are more likely to find that an organic structure provides the greatest gains. This structure allows the establishment to answer to environment change more proactively.

Technology

Advances in technology are the most usual cause of change in organizations since they generally result in greater efficiency and lower costs for the firm. Technology is the way tasks are carried out using tools, equipment, techniques, and human ability.

In the early 1960s, Joan Woodward discovered that the right combination of structure and technology were vital to organizational success. He conducted a study of technology and structure in more than 100 English manufacturing firms, which he classified into three categories of core-manufacturing technology:

- Small-batch production: Small-batch production is used to manufacture a form of custom, made-to-order goods. Each item is made somewhat differently to meet a customer's specifications. A print shop is an example of a business that employs small-batch production.
- Mass production: Mass production is used to create a large number of uniform goods in an assembly-line system. Workers are extremely dependent on one another, as the product passes from stage to stage until completion. Equipment may be sophisticated, and workers frequently follow detailed instructions while performing modified jobs. A company that bottles soda pop is an instance of an establishment that utilizes mass production.
- Continuous-process production: Organizations using continuous-process production produce goods by ceaselessly feeding raw materials, such as liquid, solids, and gases, through an extremely automated system. Such systems are equipment intensive, but can frequently be operated by a relatively small labour force. Classic examples are automatized chemical plants and oil refineries.

Woodward came upon that small-batch and continuous processes had more pliable structures, and the best mass-production operations were more rigid structures. Over again, organizational design depends on the type of business. The small-batch and uninterrupted processes work well in organic structures and mass production operations work best in mechanistic structures.

APPROACHES TO ORGANIZATIONAL DESIGN

Managers must make selections about how to group individuals together to perform their work. Five common approaches - functional, divisional, matrix, team, and networking-help managers determine departmental groupings (grouping of positions into departments). The five structures are introductory organizational structures, which are then adapted to an establishment's needs. All five approaches combine varying elements of mechanistic and organic structures. For instance, the organizational design trend today integrates a minimum of bureaucratic features and displays more features of the organic design with a decentralized authority structure, fewer rules and processes, and so forth.

Functional Structure

The functional structure groups positions into work units established on like activities, skills, expertise, and resources. Production, marketing, finance, and human resources are usual groupings within a functional structure. As the most uncomplicated approach, a functional structure features clear channels of communication and authority/responsibility relationships. Not only can this structure improve productivity by minimizing duplication of personnel and equipment, but it also makes employees comfortable and changes training as well.

But the functional structure has numerous downsides that may make it incompatible for some organizations. Here are a few examples:

- The functional structure can result in narrowed down perspectives because of the separateness of different department work groups. Managers may have a hard time relating to marketing, for instance, which is frequently in an entirely different grouping. As a result, anticipating or reacting to changing consumer needs may be difficult. Additionally, reduced cooperation and communication may take place.
- Decisions and communication are slow to take place since of the many layers of hierarchy. Authority is more centralized.
- The functional structure gives managers experience in only one field-their own. Managers don't have the opportunity to see how all the firm's departments work together and understand their interrelationships and interdependence. In the long run, this specialization ensues in executives with narrow grounds and little training handling top management duties.

Divisional Structure

Because managers in large organizations may have difficulty keeping track of all their company's products and activities, specialized departments may develop. These departments are divided as per their organizational outputs. Examples include departments created to distinguish among production, customer service, and geographical categories. This grouping of departments is called divisional structure. These departments allow managers to better focus their resources and results. Divisional structure also makes performance easier to monitor. As a result, this structure is flexible and reactive to change.

Notwithstanding, divisional structure does have its drawbacks. Because managers are so specialized, they may waste time duplicating each other's activities and resources. Additionally, competition between divisions may develop due to limited resources.

Matrix Structure

The matrix structure compounds functional specialization with the focus of divisional structure. This structure uses permanent cross-functional teams to integrate operational expertise with a divisional focus.

In a matrix structure employees belong to at least two formal groups at the same time-a functional group and a product, program, or project team. They also report to two bosses-one within the functional group and the other within the team.

This structure not only step-ups employee motivation, but it also allows technical and general management training across functional areas as well. Potential merits include

- Better cooperation and problem solving.
- Better customer service.
- Better performance accountability.
- Improved strategic management.
- Increased flexibility.

Predictably, the matrix structure also has potential faults. Here are a few of this structure's pulls away:

- Adding the team leaders, a crucial component, to a matrix structure can result in increased costs.
- Members of the matrix may suffer task confusion when taking orders from more than one boss.
- Teams may develop strong team loyalties that cause a loss of focus on larger establishment aims.
- The two-boss system is susceptible to power struggles, as functional supervisors and team leaders vie with one another to exercise authority.

Team Structure

Team structure organizes classify functions into a group based on one overall objective. These cross-functional teams are composed of members from different departments who work together as required to solve problems and explore opportunities. The intention is to break down functional barriers among departments and create a more effectual relationship for solving ongoing problems.

The team structure has many potential merits, constituting the following:

- Administrative costs are lowered.
- Decision-making and response times speed up.
- Employees are inspired.
- Intradepartmental barriers break down.
- Levels of managers are eliminated.

The drawbacks include:

- Conflicting loyalties among team members.
- Increased time spent in meetings.
- Time-management issues.

Managers must be aware that how well team members work together frequently depends upon the quality of interpersonal relations, group dynamics, and their team direction abilities.

Network Structure

The network structure depends on other organizations to perform critical functions on a contractual basis. In other words, managers can contract out specific work to specialists. This approach provides flexibility and reduces overhead because the size of staff and operations can be reduced. Alternatively, the network structure may result in capriciousness of supply and want of control because managers are relying on contractual workers to perform significant work.

There are numerous approaches to organizational architecture comprising:

- (1986, 1991, 2004) - Kenneth D. Mackenzie
- (1992, 1993) - David Nadler & Michael Tushman.
- Organizational Architecture by David Nadler, Marc C. Gerstein and Robert B. Shaw.
- (1993, 1995) - Designing organizations using the Star Model as developed by Jay Galbraith

- Benjamin's Layered Model of organizations.
- The Organizational Adaption Model by Raymond E. Miles and Charles C. Snow.
- (1995) - Richard M. Burton & Borge Obel
- (2004) - Richard K. Daft
- (2001) - Ralph Kilmann
- (2005) - The Tricord Model - Designing organizations from a Whole Systems Perspective

Irrespective of how obvious this statement may seem, many organizations fall short in taking the necessary actions to build the probability of success in their favour. In the late have witnessed the fantasy of the dot-com bubble and the foolish alchemy of amateur financial engineering at entities like Enron, both events driven possibly by greed and delusion, as well as the common rash of less than value-adding amalgamations and acquisitions.

Following this, likely as a consequence, we have had bear markets and pension crises. The requirement of the times suggests the need for leaders who can inspire their individuals and shape the perspective in which their individuals work to facilitate achievement. Such leaders will be individuals who have an interest in leadership itself, an interest in individuals and the human spirit's wish for fulfilment and power to use power for the benefit of the whole organization and its stakeholders. They are unlikely to be those who can only have a sparkle in their eye when in avocation of the next deal.

Clearly, it is all significant to establish a robust sense of intention and direction and a business strategy that will enable the realisation of such intention. Nevertheless, the formulation of strategy is less likely to be the cause of failure than its inadequate implementation. The centre attention now needs to be on the generation of profitability through individuals' innovation and development of new ideas. In many sectors, the scope for further performance improvements from cost reduction now risks cutting beyond the fat into the muscle of businesses capableness to deliver customer satisfaction.

If individuals are to be the source of new ideas, it will be vital for them to be adjusted to the function and direction of the business. But this requires more than a strategy and a willing manpower. It also necessitates the organization structure, the operating processes and systems and the culture to be aligned with the individuals to realise intention and direction.

Effectiveness, the power to maximise ensues the competitive external environment, arises when all these organizational fields are in alignment.

In leading an organization to realise its ambitions, it is critical for the leadership to relate current reality to the vision of the future. This is both an inspirational activity and a task of reason. Individuals need to believe that the ambitions for the future are possible if not probable. For managers to be efficient as leaders they must engage their individuals in both the shaping of the vision of the future and an analysis of the organization's current reality.

Of course, some of the analysis is classical stuff. Many organizations have invested in studying the external environment. Environmental scanning, market research and the analysis of the forces and pressures that mould the external circumstance in which the organization has to operate are among a number of techniques.

In order to nurture the development of individuals' commitment to the vision, the analysis of current reality needs to examine the organization itself as well as the external environment. It is significant that the organization's capability to deliver satisfaction to its customers and build competitive merit is comprehensively examined.

Nelson Consulting advocates the use of its Model for Organizational Integration as a framework for analysis. This Model treats the organization as an open system, which interacts with external forces and pressures: competitors, legal necessities and social trends among others. Inside the organization, the major domains of organization structure, processes and systems, culture and individuals need to be assessed in terms of their alignment to business intention and direction. Executives, managers and at least a sample of employees can be involved in the analysis of current world in relation to the business's required competitive position. This position will be enunciated by any stated vision of the future, strategic aims and business strategy.

Typical actions may necessitate developing a Strategic and Cultural Framework to integrate vision, strategic aims, performance measures, guiding principles and competencies. The organizational structure may also need some refinement, simplifying reporting lines and clarifying accountabilities with respect to the new business imperatives. How to deliver information to enable speedy and quality decisions at the sharp-end for the customer will be an important focus of process/system improvement.

This work will need to be increased by ensuring that managers have an updated performance management process as a vehicle to implement the new business strategy in a consistent way and within agreed budgeted resources all through the whole organization. Communication, both briefing and seeking feedback about understanding is also crucial to building commitment. Education and training are likely to be high priorities in engrafting an understanding of the current reality and how capability will be developed to realise the vision of the future. New knowledge, skills, behaviours and attitudes can be developed to ensure that the guidance to meet the strategic aspirations of the business is followed and success is achieved.

ORGANIZATIONAL CLIMATE

In the organizational behaviour research literature, the impression of organizational climate is defined mainly in terms of shared perceptions of organizational policies, practices and processes. Therefore organizational climate comprises employee perceptions and evaluations of leadership practices, decision-making processes, working relationships among employees, appraisal and recognition, as well as roles and aims. Organizational climate reflects the way things are done in a special work environment. Organizational climate perceptions are viewed as a vital determinant of individual behaviour in organizations, mediating the relationship between objective characteristics of the work environment and individual employee responses.

Whilst all researchers agree on the implication of the climate construct, there is no consensus as yet on the core dimensions of climate. Therefore, Campbell and colleagues (1970) proposed four basic climate dimensions: individual autonomy, the degree of structure imposed on positions, reward orientation, and consideration, warmth and support. Other researchers have proposed different taxonomies of climate dimensions. The organizational health model incorporates 10 core dimensions of organizational climate: supportive leadership, role clarity, participative decision-making, co-worker interaction, appraisal and feedback, employee development, aim alignment, work demands, workgroup esprit de corps and workgroup distress.

The climate construct has also lately been expanded to include a focus on more specific domains such as the climate for customer service and the climate for safety. What about the difference between climate and culture? From an organizational behaviour position, climate is viewed as the surface or face of culture. Climate can be measured and changed in organizational development programs, whereas culture is highly difficult to directly measurement and change in a required direction.

Whilst there is as yet no global agreement on core climate dimensions, there is however consensus that climate influences individual level outcomes through its impact on employee cognitive and affective states (i.e., job satisfaction, morale, commitment, motivation etc.). In other words, levels of employee satisfaction etc. mediate the determination of climate on individuals-performance-related outcomes.

Numerous studies have examined how climate impacts on a broad range of outcomes constituting psychological wellbeing, workers compensation claims, absenteeism and turnover, harassment and violence, safety behaviours, learner academic effects in schools, and company financial performance. A current meta-analytic review (i.e., where different studies are adjusted with statistical processes in order that they can be added together) of 51 climate studies conducted over past 20 years found that organizational climate exerts full-bodied effects over a range of individuals performance-related outcomes, all through a wide range of work environments.

The most effectual and efficient way to improve organizational climate is to: (a) use a good quality measurement system to diagnose how several elements of climate are operating, and then to (b) implement a process that engages employees in reviewing the diagnostic data and contributing to the design of interventions. In relation to measurement issues, some managers seem to be able to identify problem areas through experience and intuition, but this is a very 'hit and miss' approach. Other qualitative approaches such as interviews and focus groups may aid in diagnosing deficits in organizational climate, but these are also variable and can yield treacherous information.

There is an altering trend for organizations to use employee opinion survey technology to assess organizational climate. There are a wide range of survey products and processes available. Like any industry sector, there are top end measurement systems that accurately measure core climate dimensions, as well as surveys that are no more exact or reliable than guess work, and a host of products in between.

Organizational health research has discovered that work teams where these four elements are operating optimally show the lowest risk for employee withdrawal behaviours.

ORGANIZATIONAL EFFECTIVENESS

Organizational effectiveness is the conception of how effectual an establishment is in achieving the outcomes the establishment intends to create. The idea of organizational effectiveness is especially important for non-profit organizations as most individuals who donate money to non-profit organizations and charities are interested in knowing whether the establishment is efficient in attaining its aims.

An establishment's effectiveness is also depending on its communicative competence and ethics. The relationships between these three are simultaneous. Ethics is a discovered within organizational effectiveness. An establishment must exemplify respect, honesty, integrity and equity to allow communicative competency with the participating members. Along with ethics and communicative competence, members in that particular group can finally attain their intended aims.

Foundations and other sources of grants and other types of funds are interested in organizational potency of those individuals who seek funds from the foundations. Foundations always have more requests for funds or funding proposals and treat funding as an investment using the same care as a venture capitalist would in picking a company in which to invest.

Organizational effectiveness is an abstract concept and is essentially impossible to measure. Instead of measuring organizational effectiveness, the establishment determines proxy measures which will be used to represent effectiveness. Proxy measures used may include such things as number of individuals served, types and sizes of population sections served, and the demand within those segments for the services the establishment supplies.

For example, a non-profit establishment which supplies meals to house bound individuals may gather statistics such as the number of meals cooked and served, the number of volunteers delivering meals, the turnover and retention rates of volunteers, the demographics of the individuals served, the turnover and retention of consumers, the number of requests for meals turned down due to want of capacity (amount of food, capacity of meal preparation facilities, and number of delivery volunteers), and amount of wastage. Since the establishment has as its aim the formulation of meals and the delivery of those meals to house bound individuals, it measurements its organizational effectiveness by trying to determine what real activities the individuals in the establishment do in order to give the outcomes the establishment wants to produce.

Activities such as fundraising or volunteer training are most important because they provide the support needed for the establishment to deliver its services but they aren't the outcomes per se. These other activities are overhead activities which assist the establishment in achieving its required outcomes. The term Organizational Effectiveness is frequently used interchangeably with Establishment Development, especially when used as the name of a department or a part of the Human Resources operate within an establishment.

THEORIES OF ORGANIZATIONAL STRUCTURE

An establishment is a collection of individuals working together under a defined structure for the intention of achieving predetermined consequences through the use of financial, human, and material resources. There are numerous approaches to the structure and management of organizations.

Classical or Scientific Theory

The most former theory of management has a focus on efficiency and production. Evolved into classical organizational theory with the principals of chain of command, unity of command, span of control, specialization, and the function of a scalar chain or vertical levels of authority. The organizational design is bureaucracy.

Humanistic Theory

- Less formal, less control. More participation in decision making with decision authority at the point of service.
- Results in a flat structure developed along horizontal lines with fewer levels of management.
- Communication is enhanced, but managers can be overburdened.

Neoclassical Theory

- Seeks to validate aspects of human behaviour in organizations through research; the Hawthorne study.
- Views managers as coaches, not as authority figures.
- Concerned with employee motivation, satisfaction, creativity.
- Authority works with willing participants.

Systems Theory

- A system is a set of interrelated parts arranged in a unified whole.

- Productivity is viewed as a function of the interplay among individuals, structure, and the environment.
- The establishment is a complicated social and technical open system that requires human, financial, and material resources.

Contingency Theory

- The establishment's structure must be matched to its environment to enhance performance.
- The optimal form of an establishment is contingent on the considerations faced by that establishment comprising patients, third-party payers, regulators, and personnel.

Chaos Theory

- Based upon the belief in the uncertainty and capriciousness of the environment, chaos theory asserts that organizations are living, self-organizing systems that are complicated and self-adaptive.
- The system moves among order and chaos and is only stable temporarily.

ORGANIZATIONAL PROCESS

Inter-organizational Relationships

- Horizontal integration refers to arrangements between or among organizations that provide similar services.
- Vertical integration refers to an arrangement between or among unlike but related organizations to provide a continuum of services.

Diversification

- Diversification is the expansion of an establishment into different arenas either by complementing existing services or by getting in areas that differ from the original product or service.
- Multi-organizational Arrangements
- Mergers-organizations combining assets to ensure profits and survival.
- Acquisitions-buy out in general of a smaller facility.
- Consolidated systems-large regional or national multi-hospital entities.

Future Trends

- The growth of multi-hospital systems has took exception of many principles of management and establishment.
- Decentralization is the trend and a challenge to nursing services.
- Nursing must be able to contribute to corporate profits while meeting market demands.

Organizational Structure

- Functional structures-employees are grouped in departments by specialty with all nursing tasks under nursing service and centralized decision making as the norm.
- Hybrid structure-both self-contained and functional units are organized in an attempt to provide functional co-ordination across service or product structures.
- Parallel structure-the medical staff is separate and autonomous from the establishment producing two lines of authority.
- Service integrated structure-all functions needed to create a product or service are grouped together.

Matrix Structure

- Matrix designs have a duel authority structure with both a functional manager and a project manager.
- Other designs include project management, collegial management, and the corporate model which has led to mergers, buyouts, etc.
- Participatory Management allows participation in decision making but the power over the final decision remains with the top executive.
- Product and functional structures are integrated and results in a dual organizational focus.
- Professional practice or self-governance allows staff to govern themselves using specific councils with decision authority.
- Shared governance, based on participatory management uses a committee structure whereby staff makes either managerial or clinical decisions.

Key Concepts of Organizing

Strategic and Operational Planning: Strategic planning extends 3 to 5 years into the future and involves an analysis of the internal and external environment so as to determine the direction of the establishment. Operational planning is short range and concerned with daily activities.

COMPONENTS OF ORGANIZATIONS

Organizational Charts are the visual internal representation or blue print of an organizational structure showing how resources, departments, and personnel are grouped horizontally and vertically into lines of authority, communication, delegation, and decisions.

Charts

- The chart designates areas of responsibility and areas of specialization
- Charts show only formal relationships, the framework in which the management process takes place. The informal structure, personal and social relationships, isn't depicted on the chart.

Chain of Command

The chain of command is the formal line of authority and communication. In bureaucratic structures or hierarchies, authority and communication flow from the top downward.

Centrality

Centrality indicates the location of a position in an establishment where frequent communication occurs. It is determined by organizational distance as depicted by the chart.

Unity of Command

Unity of command represents the managerial dictum of "one person, one boss". It is represented by the vertical solid line between positions on the organizational chart.

Span of Control

Span of control or span of management is the number of individuals the manager directs. The optimal span of management is extremely variable. Generally, managers in bureaucratic structures have a narrow span of control while those in flat structures have a broader span.

CENTRALIZED VERSUS DECENTRALIZED

Centralization refers to the area where decisions are made. In autocratic structures decisions are made at the top and flow downward. There is a small span of control resulting in many layers of management and a tall structure. Decentralized structures are flat and decisions are made at the level where they occur.

In a broader sense it can be said, Establishment Design is a formal, guided process for integrating the individuals, information and technology of an establishment. It is used to match the form of the establishment as intimately as possible to the purpose(s) the establishment seeks to attain. Through the design process, organizations act to improve the probability that the collective efforts of members will be successful. Normally, design is approached as an internal change under the guidance of an external facilitator. Managers and members work together to define the needs of the establishment then produce systems to meet those needs most effectively. The facilitator assures that a systematic process is followed and encourages creative thinking.

Note: A sterling example in Organizational Designing is the company "General Motors". Today, General Motors Corporation is the world's largest automaker; it has been the annual global industry sales leader for 77 years. Founded in 1908, GM today employs about 270,000 individuals around the world. For detailed information, reader can visit their site http://www.gm.com/corporate/responsibility/reports/06/

17

Organizational Culture

Organizational culture is an idea in the field of Organizational studies and management which describes the attitudes, experiences, beliefs and values of an organization. It has been defined as "the specific collection of values and norms that are shared by people and groups in an organization and that control the way they interact with each other and with stakeholders outside the organization."

This definition continues to explain organizational values also known as "beliefs and ideas about what kinds of goals members of an organization should pursue and ideas about the appropriate kinds or standards of behaviour organizational members should use to achieve these goals. From organizational values develop organizational norms, guidelines or expectations that prescribe appropriate kinds of behaviour by employees in particular situations and control the behaviour of organizational members towards one another."

Organizational culture is not the same as corporate culture. It is wider and deeper concepts, something that an organization 'is' rather than what it 'has' (according to Buchanan and Huczynski). Senior management may try to determine a corporate culture. They may wish to impose corporate values and standards of behaviour that specifically reflect the objectives of the organization. In addition, there will also be an extant internal culture within the workforce. Work-groups within the organization have their own behavioural quirks and interactions which, to an extent, affect the whole system. Roger Harrison's four-culture typology, and adapted by Charles Handy, suggests that unlike organizational culture, corporate culture can be 'imported'. For example, computer technicians will have expertise, language and behaviours gained independently of the organization, but their presence can influence the culture of the organization as a whole.

DEFINING ORGANIZATIONAL CULTURE

There is no individual definition for organizational culture. The topic has been studied from a variety of perspectives ranging from disciplines such as anthropology and sociology, to the applied disciplines of organizational behaviour, management science, and organizational communication. Some of the definitions are listed below:

A set of common understandings around which action is organized, finding expression in language whose nuances are peculiar to the group (Becker and Geer 1960).

A set of understandings or meanings shared by a group of individuals that are largely tacit among members and are clearly relevant and distinctive to the particular group which are also passed on to new members (Louis 1980).

A system of knowledge, of standards for perceiving, believing, evaluating and acting that serve to relate human communities to their environmental settings (Allaire and Firsirotu 1984).

The deeper level of fundamental assumptions and beliefs that are: learned responses to the group's problems of survival in its external environment and its problems of internal integration; are shared by members of an establishment; that operate unconsciously; and that define in a fundamental "taken -for-granted" fashion in an establishment's view of itself and its environment.

Any social system arising from a network of shared ideologies consisting of two components: substance-the networks of meaning associated with ideologies, norms, and values; and forms-the practices whereby the meanings are expressed, affirmed, and communicated to members.

This sampling of definitions represents the two major camps that subsist in the study of organizational culture and its "application strategies." The first camp views culture as implicit in social life. Culture is what naturally emerges as individuals transform themselves into social groups as tribes, communities, and ultimately, nations. The second camp constitutes the view that culture is an explicit social product arising from social interaction either as an intentional or unintentional consequence of behaviour. In other words, culture is comprised of distinct observable forms (e.g., language, use of symbols, ceremonies, customs, methods of problem solving, use of tools or technology, and design of work settings) that groups of individuals produce through social interaction and use to confront the broader social environment. This second view of culture is most applicable to the analysis and evaluation of organizational culture and to cultural change strategies that leaders can employ to improve organizational performance.

One of the main responsibilities of strategic leaders is to produce and maintain the organizational characteristics that reward and encourage collective effort. Possibly the most fundamental of these is organizational culture. But what do we really mean by organizational culture? What influence does it have on an establishment? How does one go about building, influencing or changing an establishment's culture?

IMPORTANCE OF ORGANIZATIONAL CULTURE

Why is culture so significant to an establishment? Edgar Schein, an MIT Professor of Management and author of "Organizational Culture and Leadership: A Dynamic View", suggests that an establishment's culture develops to help it cope with its environment. Today, organizational leaders are faced up with many complicated issues during their attempts to generate organizational achievement in VUCA environments. A leader's success will depend, to a great extent, upon understanding organizational culture.

Schein argues that many of the problems confronting leaders can be traced to their inability to analyze and evaluate organizational cultures. Many leaders, when trying to enforce new strategies or a strategic plan leading to a new vision, will discover that their strategies will fail if they are discrepant with the establishment's culture. A CEO, SES, political appointee, or flag officer who comes into an establishment prepared to "shake the place up" and institute sweeping changes, frequently experiences resistance to changes and failure. Difficulties with organizational transformations come up from failures to analyze an establishment's existing culture.

We can also characterize culture as comprising of three levels (Schein 1988). The most visible level is behaviour and artefacts. This is the observable level of culture, and consists of behaviour patterns and outward manifestations of culture: perquisites provided to executives, dress codes, level of technology utilized (and where it is utilized), and the physical set up of work spaces. All may be visible indicators of culture, but difficult to interpret. Artefacts and behaviour also may tell us what a group is doing, but not why. One cartoon which captures this aspect shows two executives sitting at their desks in an office. Both have large billed black and white checked hats. One is reading to the other, "I do not know how it started, either. All I know is that it is part of our corporate culture."

To really understand culture, we have to get to the most mysterious level, the level of assumptions and beliefs. Schein contends that underlying assumptions grow out of values, until they become taken for granted and drop out of awareness.

To understand culture, we must understand all three levels, a difficult task. One additional aspect complicates the study of culture: the group or cultural unit which "owns" the culture. An establishment may have many unlike cultures or subcultures, or even no discernible dominant culture at the organizational level. Recognizing the cultural unit is of the essence to identifying and understanding the culture.

Organizational cultures are created, maintained, or metamorphosed by individuals. An establishment's culture is, in part, also created and maintained by the establishment's leadership. Leaders at the executive level are the principle source for the generation and re-infusion of an establishment's ideology, articulation of core values and specification of norms. Organizational values express preferences for certain behaviours or certain outcomes. Organizational norms express behaviours accepted by others. They are culturally acceptable ways of pursuing aims. Leaders also establish the parameters for formal lines of communication and message content-the formal interaction rules for the establishment. Values and norms, once transmitted through the establishment, establish the permanency of the establishment's culture.

Productive cultural change will occur if leaders aptly analyze the establishment's existing culture, and evaluate it against the cultural attributes needed to attain strategic objectives. Accordingly, leaders must first possess a clear understanding of the strategic objectives for their establishment and identify the actions needed to reach those objectives. These two tasks by themselves are difficult, in particular for the federal agencies that are experiencing volatile rates of change and reorientation. However, without these specifications, any cultural transformation is a blind exercise.

Next conduct an analysis of the organizations living ideologies, values and norms. Two critical questions that leaders ought to ask are: (1) Are existing explanations of cause and effect relationships, and acceptable beliefs and behaviours applicable to the establishment's achievement of strategic objectives? (2) Are organizational members facing equivocalnesses about the external environment and internal work processes that can only be clarified by organizational leadership?

Strategic leadership necessitates to be transformational if it is to serve the establishment. Transformational leaders must operate from a foundation of high morality and ethical practices and have a central understanding of the extremely complicated factors that support and make possible collective effort in an establishment. They must personally act in accord with productive values and beliefs, and they must teach others to do the same. They must promulgate the culture. The key method strategy leaders ought to follow to transform cultures is to teach symbolically. This type of strategy demands the artful crafting of new stories, new symbols, new traditions, and even new humour in order that the ambiguities surrounding organizational life can be productively managed by all members of the establishment. Without collective understanding-shared networks of revised meaning- the new ways of acting and conceiving cannot be internalized by organizational members.

That is what organizations are undertaking when they propose tightening up admissions standards to screen out undesirables. This strategy is reproducible with the belief that the problems experienced by the establishment result from a few "bad apples" and don't reflect systemic problems. Nevertheless, if a strong culture bias exists, it may be too firm to be changed by selection alone.

An understanding of culture, and how to transform it, is a crucial skill for leaders trying to attain strategic results. Strategic leaders have the best perspective, because of their position in the establishment, to see the dynamics of the culture, what ought to remain, and what needs transformation. This is the essence of strategical success.

As an employee in any type of establishment can manifest, organizational culture is as prevalent and as varied as individuals themselves. Organizational culture is enduring and complex, and may have both a positive and a negative effect on the staff and the workplace. In many ways culture will determine the survival of an establishment over the long term, especially in volatile industries. Cultures that can be a liability to an establishment include those that produce barriers to change, produce barriers to diversity or barriers to mergers and acquisitions. Understanding the organizational culture can help you to understand why change doesn't take place, or why a project fails. It will also help you to determine where to strain to make changes to the culture.

As managers and library leaders, why do we motive to get a sense of the established organizational culture? It is essential to understand the organizational culture if you want to make changes to how work is done, what type of work is being done, or at the broadest level, to impress the establishment's standing in its industry. Understanding the culture and, as required, changing it, can mean the difference between attracting and holding good employees and driving away the best employees with an environment that does not encourage, challenge, or reward them.

Organizational culture is basically a system of shared beliefs that members of the establishment have. This determines how members in an establishment act when confronted with decision-making responsibilities. In every establishment, you will notice that there are systems or patterns of values that are constantly evolving. These shared values will also affect how the employees will deal with issues and concerns within and outside the establishment.

Every single person comes from different backgrounds and modus vivendi but in an organizational culture, each one of them perceive the organizational culture in the same way, therefore, this perception is one of the shared aspects of an organizational culture. There are seven dimensions of an organizational culture, namely, attention to detail, invention and risk taking, outcome orientation, stability, individual's orientation, aggressiveness, and team orientation. Each of these aspects has its own role in defining what the organizational acculturation will be.

Organizational change is proven to be difficult to attain since the organizational culture is already the accepted norm of the way to do things. Individuals inside the establishment regard culture change with fear, anxiety, and suspicious. That is why effectual communication is essential when undergoing culture change. This is especially true in merger and skills because you need to integrate two unlike cultures in one establishment.

Another thing that makes two culture clashes in a merger is the perceptual experience of being a "winner" or a "loser." Obviously, the winner in this case is the bigger company but everyone from both organizations needs to let go of this perception because it comes in the way of an effectual and efficient workplace. This will also make the employees from the smaller establishment bitter and suspicious of their counterparts.

CLASSIFICATION OF ORGANIZATIONAL CULTURE

Several methods have been used to classify organizational culture. Some are described below:

Geert Hofstede

Geert Hofstede demonstrated that there are national and regional cultural groupings that affect the behaviour of organizations.

Hofstede looked for national differences between over 100,000 of IBM's employees in different parts of the world, in an attempt to find aspects of culture that might influence business behaviour. Hofstede identified five dimensions of culture in his study of national influences:

- Power distance: The degree to which a society expects there to be differences in the levels of power. A high score suggests that there is an expectation that some individuals wield larger amounts of power than others. A low score reflects the view that all people should have equal rights.
- Uncertainty avoidance: Reflects the extent to which a society accepts uncertainty and risk.
- Individualism vs. collectivism: Individualism is contrasted with collectivism, and refers to the extent to which people are expected to stand up for themselves, or alternatively act predominantly as a member of the group or organization. However, recent researches have shown that high individualism may not necessarily mean low collectivism, and vice versa. Research indicates that the two concepts are actually unrelated. Some people and cultures might have both high individualism and high collectivism, for example. Someone who highly values duty to his or her group does not necessarily give a low priority to personal freedom and self-sufficiency
- Masculinity vs. femininity: Refers to the value placed on traditionally male or female values. Male values for example include competitiveness, assertiveness, ambition, and the accumulation of wealth and material possessions.
- Long vs. short term orientation: Describes a society's "time horizon," or the importance attached to the future versus the past and present. In long term oriented societies, thrift and perseverance are valued more; in short term oriented societies, respect for tradition and reciprocation of gifts and favours are valued more. Eastern nations tend to score especially high here, with Western nations scoring low and the less developed nations very low; China scored highest and Pakistan lowest.

Deal and Kennedy

Deal and Kennedy defined organizational culture as the way things get done around here. They measured organizations in respect of:

- Feedback: Quick feedback means an instant response. This could be in monetary terms, but could also be seen in other ways, such as the impact of a great save in a soccer match.
- Risk: Represents the degree of uncertainty in the organization's activities.

Using these parameters, they were able to suggest four classifications of organizational culture:

- The Tough-Guy Macho Culture. Feedback is quick and the rewards are high. This often applies to fast moving financial activities such as brokerage, but could also apply to a police force, or athletes competing in team sports. This can be a very stressful culture in which to operate.
- The Work Hard/Play Hard Culture is characterized by few risks being taken, all with rapid feedback. This is typical in large organizations, which strive for high quality customer service. It is often characterized by team meetings, jargon and buzzwords.
- The Bet your Company Culture, where big stakes decisions are taken, but it may be years before the results are known. Typically, these might involve development or exploration projects, which take years to come to fruition, such as oil prospecting or military aviation.
- The Process Culture occurs in organizations where there is little or no feedback. People become bogged down with how things are done not with what is to be achieved. This is often associated with bureaucracies. While it is easy to criticize these cultures for being overly cautious or bogged down in red tape, they do produce consistent results, which are ideal in, for example, public services.

Charles Handy

Charles Handy (1985) popularized the 1972 work of Roger Harrison of looking at culture which some scholars have used to link organizational structure to Organizational Culture. He describes Harrison's four types thus:

- A Power Culture which concentrates power among a few. Control radiates from the centre like a web. Power Cultures have few rules and little bureaucracy; swift decisions can ensue.
- In a Role Culture, people have clearly delegated authorities within a highly defined structure. Typically, these organizations form hierarchical bureaucracies. Power derives from a person's position and little scope exists for expert power.
- By contrast, in a Task Culture, teams are formed to solve particular problems. Power derives from expertise as long as a team requires expertise. These cultures often feature the multiple reporting lines of a matrix structure.
- A Person Culture exists where all individuals believe themselves superior to the organization. Survival can become difficult for such organizations, since the concept of an organization suggests that a group of like-minded individuals pursue the organizational goals. Some professional partnerships can operate as person cultures, because each partner brings a particular expertise and clientele to the firm.

Edgar Schein

Edgar Schein, an MIT Sloan School of Management professor, defines organizational culture as:

"A pattern of shared basic assumptions that the group learned as it solved its problems of external adaptation and internal integration, that has worked well enough to be considered valid and, therefore, to be taught to new members as the correct way you perceive, think, and feel in relation to those problems".

According to Schein, culture is the most difficult organizational attribute to change, outlasting organizational products, services, founders and leadership and all other physical attributes of the organization. His organizational model illuminates culture from the standpoint of the observer, described by three cognitive levels of organizational culture.

At the first and most cursory level of Schein's model is organizational attributes that can be seen, felt and heard by the uninitiated observer. Included are the facilities, offices, furnishings, visible awards and recognition, the way that its members dress, and how each person visibly interacts with each other and with organizational outsiders.

The next level deals with the professed culture of an organization's members. At this level, company slogans, mission statements and other operational creeds are often expressed, and local and personal values are widely expressed within the organization. Organizational behaviour at this level usually can be studied by interviewing the organization's membership and using questionnaires to gather attitudes about organizational membership.

At the third and deepest level, the organization's tacit assumptions are found. These are the elements of culture that are unseen and not cognitively identified in everyday interactions between organizational members. Additionally, these are the elements of culture which are often taboo to discuss inside the organization.

Many of these 'unspoken rules' exist without the conscious knowledge of the membership. Those with sufficient experience to understand this deepest level of organizational culture usually become acclimatized to its attributes over time, thus reinforcing the invisibility of their existence. Surveys and casual interviews with organizational members cannot draw out these attributes--rather much more in-depth means is required to first identify then understand organizational culture at this level. Notably, culture at this level is the underlying and driving element often missed by organizational behaviourists.

Using Schein's model, understanding paradoxical organizational behaviours becomes more apparent. For instance, an organization can profess highly aesthetic and moral standards at the second level of Schein's model while simultaneously displaying curiously opposing behaviour at the third and deepest level of culture.

Superficially, organizational rewards can imply one organizational norm but at the deepest level imply something completely different. This insight offers an understanding of the difficulty that organizational newcomers have in assimilating organizational culture and why it takes time to become acclimatized.

It also explains why organizational change agents usually fail to achieve their goals: underlying tacit cultural norms are generally not understood before would-be change agents begin their actions. Merely understanding culture at the deepest level may be insufficient to institute cultural change because the dynamics of interpersonal relationships (often under threatening conditions) are added to the dynamics of organizational culture while attempts are made to institute desired change.

Arthur F. Carmazzi

The Blame culture: This culture cultivates distrust and fear, people blame each other to avoid being reprimanded or put down, this results in no new ideas or personal initiative because people don't want to risk being wrong.

Multi-directional culture: This culture cultivates minimized cross-department communication and cooperation. Loyalty is only to specific groups (departments). Each department becomes a clique and is often critical of other departments which in turn create lots of gossip. The lack of cooperation and Multi-Direction is manifested in the organization's inefficiency.

Live and let live culture: This culture is Complacency; it manifests Mental Stagnation and Low Creativity. People here have little future vision and have given up their passion. There is Average cooperation and communication and things do work, but they do not grow. People have developed their personal relationships and decided who to stay away from, there is not much left to learn.

Brand congruent culture: People in this culture believe in the product or service of the organization, they feel good about what their company is trying to achieve and cooperate to achieve it. People here are passionate and seem to have similar goals in the organization. They use personal resources to actively solve problems and while they don't always accept the actions of management or others around them, they see their job as important. Most everyone in this culture is operating at the level of Group.

Leadership enriched culture: People view the organization as an extension of themselves; they feel good about what they personally achieve through the organization and have exceptional Cooperation. Individual goals are aligned with the goals of the organization and people will do what it takes to make things happen. As a group, the organization is more like family providing personal fulfilment which often transcends ego so people are consistently bringing out the best in each other. In this culture, Leaders do not develop followers, but develop other leaders. Most everyone in this culture is operating at the level of Organization.

Carmazzi's model requires application of his Directive Communication psychology to evolve the culture. While the idea of having a Leadership Enriched organization is inspirational, it would require substantial Leadership resources to develop. The concept of Evolving the culture assumes that "Every Individual in the organization wants to do a good job", and the behaviours that result in poor performance are manifestations of psychology the group or organization has created through policies, leadership and poor communication.

Note: Procter & Gamble establishment is the role model in Organizational culture. Reader can go to their site for detailed in-depth knowledge on their in Organizational culture: http://www.pg.com/content/pdf/01_about_pg/01_about_pg_homepage/about_pg_toolbar/download_report/values_policies0708.pdf

18

Management of Change

This is a time of unexampled change in our society. The changes one experiences are happening at faster and faster rates. As examples, the telephone, radio, TV, and microwave weren't even in use decades ago, and today these gadgets are commonplace, along with the computer, Internet, and fax machine. In just a few months, the technology that an establishment uses on an everyday cornerstone may be outdated and replaced. That means an establishment inevitably to be responsive to advances in the technological environment; its employees' work skills must evolve as technology develops. Organizations that refuse to adapt are likely to be the ones that won't be around in a few short years. If an establishment wants to survive and prosper, its managers must continually innovate and adapt to new situations.

Every establishment goes through periods of transmutation that can cause stress and uncertainty. To be successful, organizations must embrace many types of change. Businesses must develop improved production technologies, produce new products required in the marketplace, implement new administrative systems, and advance employees' skills. Organizations that adapt successfully are both productive and admired.

Managers must compete with all factors that affect their organizations. The following lists internal and external environmental factors that can encourage organizational changes:

- The external environment is affected by political, social, technological, and economic stimuli outside of the establishment that induce changes.
- The internal environment is affected by the establishment's management policies and styles, systems, and processes, as well as employee positions.

CAUSES OF ORGANIZATIONAL CHANGE

Companies are required to modify productive processes or strategic goals and aims in response to an external influence, change in consumer behaviour or a shift in the industry landscape. This necessitates a reorientation of capital, resources, employees and corporate systems. Below are some of the common causes of organizational change:

Exit Strategy at the End of the product Life Cycle: As the market for a company's product reaches maturity, market growth and profits begin to diminish. Despite the fact that cost cutting occurs and marketing budgets are reduced, when the opportunity cost of deploying capital and resources to another more favourable opportunity presents, companies either sell off existing operations or cease production altogether. This can be in response to a new superior product release, a change in consumer purchasing habits or the introduction of a new technology. Irrespective of the cause, capital and labour are redeployed to new more promising business activities. The exit strategy is a common cause of organizational change.

Change in Government: Employees that work for government departments can find existing initiatives get discontinued when a change in government takes place. The subsequent refocus of priorities that takes place as a result of the new governments mandate can create redundancies or a radical change in the way the department conducts its affairs.

Mergers and Acquisitions: When two competitors merge the existing business operations of both companies get centralized and streamlined. This can result in the merging of departments and processes, cost cutting and a redeployment of existing resources. Mergers and acquisitions are one of the most frequent causes of organizational change.

Strategic Refocus: When the company changes its business processes to adopt a new paradigm organizational change ensues. Consider the plight of a company that shifts its focus form a product centric to a customer-centric platform. New manufacturing specifications, new marketing and a change in logistical operations create a change reaction for change throughout the organization.

Structural Change: When new administrative processes get introduced, organizational change results. Consider the ramifications of centralizing an archiving process using computer technology. Old redundant processes get replaced by new software and hardware and staff members are required to retrain to operate the new systems.

Process Oriented: When a company redefines its manufacturing operations by changing its manufacturing process to a JIT operation, infrastructure, warehousing and logistical operations are required to be redesigned and deployed. This structural shift in the way a product is created has a domino effect on organizational change.

IMPORTANCE OF ORGANIZATIONAL CHANGE

Normally, the concept of organizational change is used to describe establishment-wide change, as opposed to smaller changes such as adding a new person, modifying a program, and so forth. Instances of establishment-wide change might include a change in mission, reconstituting operations (for instance, restructuring to self-managed teams or due to layoffs), new technologies, mergers, or new programs such as Total Quality Management, re-engineering, and so forth. Managers ought to note that all changes ought to be implemented as part of a strategy to attain an overall aim; these transformations ought to not take place just for the sake of change.

TYPES OF ORGANIZATIONAL CHANGE

The major areas of changes in a company's internal environment constitute:

Strategic: Occasionally in the course of normal business process it is necessary for management to adjust the firm's strategy to attain the aims of the company, or even to change the mission statement of the establishment in response to demands of the external environments. Adjusting a company's strategy may involve changing its fundamental approach to doing business: the markets it will target, the kinds of products it will sell, plans for how they will be sold, its overall strategic orientation, the level of universal activity, and its several partnerships and other joint-business arrangements.

Structural: Organizations frequently find it required to redesign the structure of the company due to influences from the external environment. Structural changes involve the hierarchy of authority, aims, structural characteristics, administrative processes, and management systems. Almost all change in how an establishment is handled falls under the category of structural change. A structural change may be as simple as implementing a no-smoking policy, or as involved as restructuring the company to meet the customer demands more effectively.

Process-oriented: Organizations may need to reengineer processes to attain optimum workflow and productivity. Process-oriented change is frequently related to an establishment's production process or how the establishment assembles products or delivers services. The acceptance of robotics in a manufacturing plant or of laser-scanning checkout systems at supermarkets are examples of process-oriented changes.

Individuals-centred: This type of change alters the attitudes, behaviours, skills, or performance of employees in the company. Changing individuals-centred processes involves communicating, motivating, leading, and acting within groups. This focus may entail changing how problems are solved, the way employees learn new skills, and even the very nature of how employees comprehend themselves, their jobs, and the establishment.

Some individuals-centred changes may necessitate only incremental changes or small improvements in a process. For example, many organizations undergo leadership training that teaches managers how to communicate more openly with employees. Other programs may concentrate on team processes by teaching both managers and employees to work unitedly more effectively to solve problems.

Remember that strategic, structural, process-oriented, and individuals-centred changes occur ceaselessly in dynamic businesses. Frequently, changes in one of these areas impact changes in the other areas. Many employees believe that a change is frequently reactive and nothing more than a quick fix; then they brace themselves for more changes in the future. Management involves to realize that serious underlying problems in organizations must be addressed with long-term effects in mind. Therefore, when management implements changes, careful thought must be given to ensure that the new processes are for the long-term good of the company.

CHALLENGES OF ORGANIZATIONAL CHANGE

Planning and managing change, both cultural and technological, is one of the most challenging components of a manager's task. Obviously, the more a manager can plan in anticipation of a change, the better he serves his subordinates and the establishment. Diagnosing the causes of change and structuring a program to promote a smooth transition to the new process, structure, and so forth, is vital to a manager's success.

Managers need to be aware that organizations change in numerous dimensions that frequently relate to one another. These dimensions include:

Extent of planning: Though experts differ about how much change can be planned, managers still need to take steps to set up conditions that allow and even encourage change to occur.

Degree of change: Changes may be incremental (relatively small, involving fine-tuning processes and behaviours within just one system or level of the establishment) or quantum (important change altering how a company operates).

Degree of learning: This dimension relates to the degree to which organizational members are actively involved in learning how to plan and implement change while helping solve an existing problem.

Target of change: Organizational change programs can change with respect to the hierarchical level or functional area of which the change is targeted. Some changes are designed to determine top management and assist them in becoming stronger leaders. Other change programs may involve fundamental discovering, such as customer services techniques for lower level employees.

Establishment's structure: Is it very stiff and bureaucratic? Is there a need for emphasis on policies, processes, and rules? Some organizations are very stiff and bureaucratic and may need to "loosen up." Other organizations may suffer from want of establishment structure. They may necessitate to emphasize policies, processes, and rules.

DIAGNOSING THE NEED FOR CHANGE

To plan change, managers must anticipate and diagnose the need for change. An organizational development theory developed by Larry E. Greiner is helpful in change management. Greiner's model shows an establishment as it evolves through the five stages of growth, and the end of each of these stages is branded by a crisis that calls for a change. The five stages of growth are as follows:

Creativity: The founders of the establishment prevail this stage, and the emphasis is on producing both a product and a market. But as the establishment grows, management problems occur that cannot be handled by informal communication. The founders find themselves burdened with unwanted management responsibilities, and conflicts between the employees and management grow. It is at this point that the crisis of leadership occurs, and the first revolutionary period begins.

Direction: During this period, a strong manager, who is acceptable to the founder and who can pull the establishment together, is appointed.

During this phase the new manager and key staff take most of the responsibility for instituting direction, while lower level supervisors are treated more as functional specialists than autonomous decision-making managers. Lower level managers begin to demand more autonomy, and the next revolutionary period commences.

Delegation: This stage frequently poses problems for top managers who have been successful at being directive: They may find giving up responsibility hard. Furthermore, lower level managers in general aren't accustomed to making decisions for themselves. As a result, numerous organizations flounder during this revolutionary period, adhering to centralized methods, while lower level employees grow disillusioned and leave the establishment.

When an establishment gets to the growth stage of delegation, it generally begins to develop a decentralized establishment structure, which heightens motivation at the lower levels. Finally, the next crisis begins to evolve as the top managers sense that they are missing control over a extremely diversified operation. The crisis of control results in a return to centralization, which is now incompatible and creates resentment and hostility among those who had been given freedom.

Control: This stage is characterized by the use of formal systems for accomplishing greater co-ordination, with top management as the watchdog. It results in the next revolutionary period, the crisis of red tape. This crisis most often occurs when the establishment has become too large and complex, and is managed through formal programs and rigid systems. If the crisis of red tape is to be defeated, the establishment must move to the next evolutionary phase.

Collaboration: The last of Greiner's phases emphasizes greater spontaneity in management action through teams and the skilful confrontation of interpersonal differences. Social control and self-discipline take over from formal action. Greiner's model shows uncertainty about what the next revolution of change will be, but anticipates that it will centre on the psychological saturation of employees who grow emotionally and physically exhausted by the intensity level of teamwork and the heavy pressure for innovative solutions.

To plan change, managers must predict and diagnose the demand for change. Greiner's model of organizational growth and change can help managers understand how the need for change relates to the organizational cycles.

STEPS IN PLANNED CHANGE

Once managers and an establishment devote to planned change, they need to produce a logical step-by step approach in order to attain the objectives. Planned change requires managers to follow a process for successful implementations, which is illustrated in Figure below:

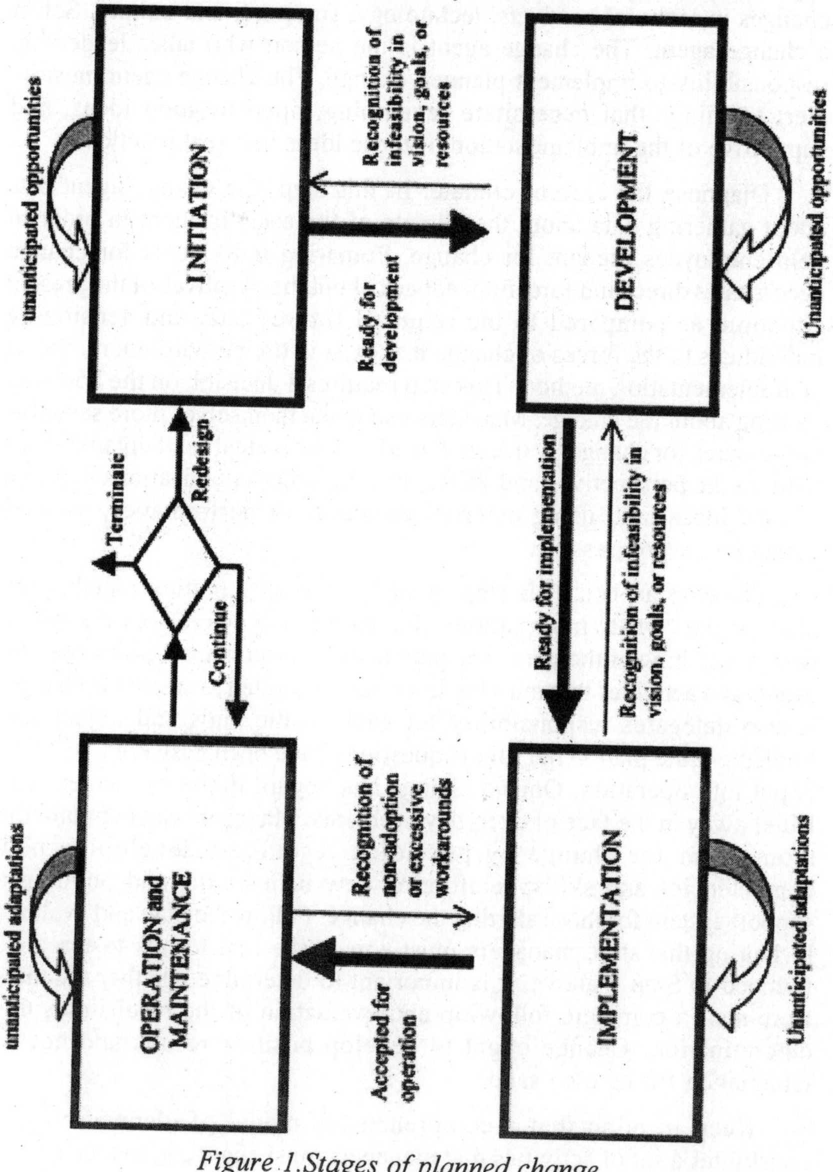

Figure 1.Stages of planned change.

Recognize the need for change. Recognition of the need for change may occur at the top management level or in peripheral parts of the establishment. The change may be due to either internal or external forces.

Develop the aims of the change. Before any action is taken, it is necessary to determine why the change is necessary. Both problems and opportunities must be evaluated. Then it is significant to define the needed changes in terms of products, technology, structure, and culture. Select a change agent. The change agent is the person who takes leadership responsibility to implement planned change. The change agent must be alert to things that necessitate revamping, open to good ideas, and supportive of the implementation of those ideas into real practice.

Diagnose the current climate. In this step, the change agent sets about gathering data about the climate of the establishment in order to help employees prepare for change. Preparing individuals for change necessitates direct and forceful feedback about the negatives of the present situation, as compared to the required future state, and sensitizing individuals to the forces of change that exist in their environment. Select an implementation method. This step requires a decision on the best way to bring about the change. Managers can make themselves more sensitive to pressures for change by using networks of individuals and organizations with unlike perspectives and views, visiting other organizations exposed to new ideas, and using external standards of performance, such as competitor's progress.

Develop a plan. This step involves in reality putting together the plan, or the "what" information. This phase also determines the when, where, and how of the plan. The plan is like a road map. It notes specific events and activities that must be timed and integrated to create the change. It also delegates responsibility for each of the aims and objectives. Implement the plan. After all the questions have been answered, the plan is put into operation. Once a change has begun, initial excitement can fritter away in the face of everyday problems. Managers can maintain the momentum for change by providing resources, developing new competencies and skills, reinforcing new behaviours, and building a support system for those starting the change. Follow the plan and evaluate it. During this step, managers must equate the real results to the aims founded in Step 4 above. It is important to determine whether the aims were met; a complete follow-up and evaluation of the results aids this determination. Change ought to develop positive results and not be undertaken for its own sake.

Keep in mind that a comprehensive model of planned change constitutes a set of activities that managers must engage in to manage the change process effectively. They must recognize the need for alteration, motivate change, produce a vision, develop political support, manage the transition, and sustain momentum all through the change.

OPPOSITION TO ORGANIZATIONAL CHANGES

A manager designs his change effort, and then confronts the toughest step: the inevitable opposition. History shows that workers have resisted some of the best-laid plans. A few may openly fight it. Many more may dismiss or try to sabotage a manager's plan. In the corporate world, most individuals, most of the time, resist change. Why? These individuals believe that change has very little upside for them-in other words, that change is seldom for the better.

One kind of resistance demands employees who have been with a company for a few years, and have seen flavour-of-the-month change programs come and go: Management launches some kind of change effort to great fanfare. Managers talk up the gains and explain why this program will be good for both the company and its employees. They make forebodes, but at the end of the day, they fail to deliver. Nothing really happens, and the whole effort seems like a waste of time. Well, it makes sense to protest things that are a pure waste of time.

A number of consultants analyze a corporate department comprising of 100 individuals, and they conclude that the company requires just 48 of these individuals to complete the same amount of work. When an employee in this department learns of the consultants' commendation, he or he fears being fired or working longer hours. These kinds of dismal scenarios give employees the impression that change isn't good. And employees have no ground to believe that it is attending be better in the future.

Here are some of the most common reasons employees hold out change:

- Cynicism and want of trust
- Perceptual differences and want of understanding
- Reaction against the way change is presented
- Threats to vested interests
- Uncertainty and insecurity

To get over resistance, managers can regard workers in the change process by communicating clearly about changes, providing advance notice of an upcoming change, exercising sensitivity to workers' concerns, and reassuring workers that change will not affect their security. Additionally, managers are more likely to implement changes successfully if they avoid common drawbacks that cause changes to fail. Some of these pitfalls are as follows:

- A culture resistant to change
- Faulty thinking
- Inadequate change process
- Insufficient resources
- Want of commitment to change
- Poor timing

Overcoming Resistance to Change

To implement planned change effectively, managers must understand how to get over resistance to change, why change efforts fail, and what techniques they can use to modify behaviour. Managers can use two approaches to change positions and behaviours at the individual level: the three-step approach and force-field analysis.

The cognitive process of change has been characterized as having three fundamental stages: unfreezing, changing, and refreezing.

1. Unfreezing. This step necessitates developing an initial awareness of the need for change and the forces supporting and resisting change. Because most individuals and organizations prefer stability and the perpetuation of the status quo, a successful change process must get over the status quo by unfreezing old behaviours, processes, or structure. This approach constitutes the use of one-on-one discussions, presentations to groups, memos, reports, company newsletters, training programs, and demonstrations to educate employees about an imminent change and help them see the logic of the decision. Deficiencies in the current situation are keyed out and the benefits of the replacement are stressed.
2. Changing. This step centres on learning new behaviours. Change results from individuals being uncomfortable with the identified negative behaviours and being presented with new behaviours, role models, and support. In this phase, something new takes place in a system, and change is actually implemented. This is the point at which managers initiate change

in such organizational targets as tasks, individuals, culture, technology, and structure. When managers implement change, individuals must be ready.

3. Refreezing. Refreezing centres on reinforcing new behaviours, generally by positive results, feelings of accomplishment, or rewards. After management has implemented changes in organizational aims, products, processes, structures, or individuals, they cannot sit back and expect the change to be maintained over time. Behaviours that are positively reinforced tend to be repeated. In designing change, attention must be paid to how the new behaviours will be strengthened and rewarded.

Force-field Analysis

One of the most former and most fundamental models of change, the Force-Field Analytic Problem-Solving Model, was developed by Behavioural scientist Kurt Lewin in the 1940s. Since that time, this model has been widely used as a skill for encouraging groups of individuals to tackle organizational issues that antecedently seemed too complicated or too deeply rooted to approach.

Force-field analysis depicts the change process as one that must get the better of a person's or establishment's status quo or existing state of equilibrium-the equilibrium between forces for change and forces that resist change. In any problem situation, the existing condition (status quo) has been reached because of a number of opposing forces.

The change forces are known as drivers. (Drivers push toward a solution to the problem.) Other forces are known as resisters. (Resisters inhibit improvement or solution of the problem.) When the strength of the device driver is approximately equal to the strength of the resisters, an equilibrium or status quo is apparent. Until the relative strength of the forces is changed, the problem will continue to persist.

When a change is introduced, some forces drive it and other forces dissent it. To implement a change, management ought to analyze the change forces. By selectively removing forces that resist change, the driving forces will be strong enough to enable implementation. As resistant forces are reduced or removed, behaviour will shift to incorporate the wanted changes.

To apply the model to a problem, a manager ought to follow these steps:

1. Carefully and fully specify the problem (status quo). A problem may be defined as the difference between what presently exists and what ought to exist.
2. Define objectives. A manager must conceive what the situation will be like when it is solved.
3. Brainstorm to determine the driving and protesting forces that contribute to the problem.
4. Analyze these forces more fully and develop a strategy. This strategy ought to be directed at strengthening the driving forces under a manager's control and weakening the resisting forces that a manager can realistically do something about.
5. Compare strategy against company or departmental objectives. A manager must conceive whether his or his problem-solving strategy will promote a change in the status quo.

ORGANIZATIONAL DEVELOPMENT AS TOOL FOR INTRODUCTION OF CHANGE

Earlier research has highlighted the sensitive ethnical dimension of the Organizational Development process when employed in Asian organizations. Subsequent research in East Asian organizations, particularly in Greater China, and the developments in Organizational Development practices in India, Singapore, and the Philippines, suggest that wisely applied Organizational Development processes, and a befittingly adapted Organizational Development philosophy may not only benefit specific enterprises, but may also impact on the future function of the establishment economically transitionally, such as China and Vietnam. This study reports on a pilot project conducted in Vietnam to evaluate the state of Organizational Development. The determinations of the study, though of a preliminary nature, clearly indicate that Organizational Development is underdeveloped as a vocation, that Organizational Development processes are utilized to a limited extent in enterprises, and that there is a limited awareness of the vocation and Organizational Development as a management tool.

Note: Wipro Company is exemplary role model for studying management of change, Wipro started as a vegetable oil company in 1947and now it is a big multi business and multi location corporate entity. Wipro was ranked 4th on the 'Top Companies for Leaders' in India, 5th in Asia Pacific region and 20th globally" in a study conducted by Hewitt Associates in collaboration with Fortune and the RBL Group. For in-depth study, Reader can visit their site: http://www.wipro.com

19

Control Systems

Control is a fundamental organizational function and results out of decentralization efforts. It is the means by which activities and resources are co-ordinated and directed towards the accomplishment of an organization's aim and implies a degree of monitoring and feedback. Salaman et al. argue that "Control means that members of the organization have their actions, determined, or influenced, by membership of the organization." It is impossible to conceive organizational control without considering the nature of power within organizations, how it is disseminated and how it originates. Bedford depicted administrative controls as "Administrative controls relate to the structural composition of the organization and the formal policies and processes within the firm. Structure is in general defined as relationship patterns within the organization, and comprises the configuration of business units, conventional lines of authority and accountability, patterns of communication and information flows, and systems of corporate governance.

Policies and processes conventionally relate to antecedently delineated concepts of personnel and behavioural control mechanisms, and include processes such as standard operating processes, human resources management, management supervision and codes of conduct". Self controls emphasize behaviours and actions that are promoting the use of intuition through playfulness. It facilitates error detection and error correction instead of compliance and adherence with rules. Self-control focuses on the development of a large response to suggest not only alternative solutions, but also unlike approaches for executing those solutions. Social controls have been defined by Alvesson et al. as "efforts to persuade individuals to adapt to certain values, norms and ideas about what is good, important, praiseworthy, etc in terms of work and organizational life."

These systems are in particular important in large organizations where communication of organizational intention becomes more and more difficult. Typical examples of belief or value systems include mission statements, statements of intention, and corporate visions. Nevertheless, the focus of the project is on administrative controls, which may be defined as "Those mechanisms, techniques and processes that have been consciously and purposefully designed in order to try to control the organizational behaviour(s) of other people, groups and organizations."

Two means by which administrative control may be achieved are through output control and rules and processes. Rules and processes are the most explicit form of administrative control. One specific perspective in which such rules become inherently apparent is in the analysis and definition of business processes, ordinarily referred to as workflows. Here tasks can be broken down and be ultimately captured in the form of rules and processes constraining the range of members' behaviour; increasing the foregone conclusion of their actions; and increasing the probability that perceived organizational necessities dominate that behaviour. Specifically with the current trend to establish (partially) automated workflows such as credit applications, insurance claims, material ordering etc., this form of control has gained in implication. Alternatively when it isn't possible or feasible to define rules because of the complexity and unpredictability of the tasks that are performed, then output controls need to be founded. The everyday achievement of tasks is left to the members' judgment and discretion. This requires the power to define and measure these outputs, as well as taking appropriate corrective or adjusting actions.

Generally, organizational control is defined a priori. Therefore, the underlying organizational aims have been predefined and there exists predefined procedural guidelines that need to be adopted by the employees for attaining the company's aims. Systems are designed to impose these guidelines. Nalder argued that these designed guidelines could result into locked-in behaviour patterns resulting in a reduced organizational performance. Organizational control is considered as inhibiting creativity and initiative by enforcing task definition, measurement, and control. A control system based on such measurements is considered to be rewarding maladaptive behaviour leading to a decline of organizational performance. A contradicted control model emphasizes the self-control principle. This principle is build upon the argument of changing environments and therefore organizations have to behave experimentally and dynamically. Therefore, organizational access control has to support experimentation and be easy to re-arrange and adapt with the changing business environment.

Experts describe a productive implementation of organizational control systems as driven by the concurrently processes of ongoing learning, examination of assumptions behind best practices and reinterpretation of this information. They stated that the simultaneous processes are needed for assuring the optimization based on the current best practices. Therefore, the design of an organizational control system involves to take into consideration ambiguity, inconsistency, multiple perspectives, and impermanency of existing information. This section shows the shifting from an administrative controls model towards a mixture of administrative control and self-control.

ORGANIZATIONAL CONTROL OBJECTIVES

Plainly put, organizational control is the process of assigning, evaluating, and regulating resources on an ongoing basis to attain an establishment's aims. To successfully control an establishment, managers need to not only know what the performance standards are, but also solve how to share that information with employees.

Control can be defined narrowly as the process a manager takes to ensure that real performance conforms to the establishment's plan, or more broadly as anything that regulates the process or activity of an establishment. The following message follows the general interpretation by defining managerial control as monitoring performance against a plan and then making adjustments either in the plan or in processes as essential.

The six major aims of controls are as follows:

- Controls make the plans efficient: Managers require to measure progress, offer feedback, and direct their teams if they want to succeed.
- Controls make a point that organizational actions are logical: Policies and processes help ensure that efforts are integrated.
- Controls make organizations efficient: Organizations need controls in place if they want to attain and attain their objectives.
- Controls make organizations effectual: Efficiency probably depends more on controls than any other management function.
- Controls allow for feedback on project position: Not only do they measure progress, but controls also provide feedback to

participants as well. Feedback influences behaviour and is a necessary ingredient in the control process.

- Controls aid in deciding: The ultimate intention of controls is to help managers make better decisions. Controls make managers aware of problems and give them information that is essential for decision making.

Many individuals put forward that as the nature of organizations has altered, so must the nature of management controls. New forms of organizations, such as self-organizing organizations, self-managed teams, and network organizations, allow organizations to be more responsive and adaptable in today's quickly changing world. These forms also cultivate empowerment among employees, much more so than the hierarchical organizations of the past.

Some individuals even claim that management shouldn't exercise any form of control whatsoever, and ought to only support employee attempts to be fully productive members of organizations and communities. Along those same lines, some experts even use the word "co-ordinating" in place of "controlling" to avoid sounding coercive. Nevertheless, some forms of controls must exist for an establishment to exist. For an establishment to exist, it needs some aim or intention, or it is not an establishment at all. Individual behaviours, group behaviours, and all organizational functioning must be in line with the strategic focus of the establishment.

The control process involves carefully gathering information about a system, process, person, or group of individuals in order to make necessary decisions about each. Managers set up control systems that include four key steps:

1. Lay down standards to evaluate functioning: Within an establishment's overall strategic plan, managers define aims for organizational departments in specific, operational terms that constitute standards of performance to compare with organizational activities.

2. Calculate factual operation: Most organizations prepare formal reports of performance measurements that manager's critical review on a regular basis. These measurements ought to be related to the standards set in the first step of the control process. For example, if sales growth is a target, the establishment ought to have a means of gathering and reporting sales data.

3. Equate operation with the measures: This step compares real activities to performance standards. When managers read computer reports or rehearse their plants, they identify whether real performance meets, exceeds, or falls short of standards. Normally, performance reports simplify such comparison by placing the performance standards for the reporting period alongside the real performance for the same period and by computing the variance-that is, the deviation between each real amount and the associated standard.
4. Take restorative actions: When performance deviates from standards, managers must determine what changes, if any, are necessary and how to apply them. In the productivity and quality-centred environment, workers and managers are frequently empowered to evaluate their own work. After the evaluator determines the cause or causes of difference, he or he can take the fourth step-corrective action. The most effectual course may be prescribed by policies or may be best left up to employees' judgment and initiative.

These steps must be repeated sporadically until the organizational aim is attained.

TYPES OF ORGANIZATIONAL CONTROLS

Control can centre on events before, during, or after a process. For example, a local automobile dealer can focus on activities before, during, or after sales of new cars. Careful inspection of new cars and cautious selection of sales employees are ways to insure high quality or profitable sales even before those sales take place. Monitoring how salespeople act with customers is a control during the sales task. Counting the number of new cars sold during the month and telephoning buyers about their satisfaction with sales proceedings are controls after sales have occurred. These types of controls are formally called feeding, concurrent, and feedback, respectively.

- Feed forward controls, also called prelim or pre-emptive controls, seek to identify and keep differences in the standards before they occur. Feed forward controls focus on human, material, and financial resources within the establishment. These controls are evident in the selection and employing of new employees. For instance, organizations attempt to meliorate the likelihood that employees will perform up to standards by identifying the necessary task skills and by using tests and other screening devices to hire individuals with those skills.

- Concurrent controls supervise ongoing employee action to ensure consistency with quality criteria. These controls rely on performance standards, rules, and regulations for guiding employee projects and behaviours. Their intention is to ensure that work activities create the required results. As an example, many manufacturing operations include devices that measure whether the items being produced meet quality standards. Employees monitor the measurements; if they see that standards aren't being conformed to in some area, they make a correction themselves or let a manager know that a problem is occurring.
- Feedback controls call for reviewing data to determine whether functioning meets based standards. For example, suppose that an establishment establishes an aim of increasing its profit by twelve percent next year. To ensure that this aim is reached, the establishment must supervise its profit on a monthly basis. After three months, if profit has increased by three percent, management might put on that plans are going as per schedule.

EFFECTIVE ORGANIZATIONAL CONTROL SYSTEMS

The management of any establishment must develop a control system made-to-order to its establishment's aims and resources. Effectual control systems share numerous common characteristics. These characteristics are as follows:

- A focus on critical points: For example, controls are applied where failure cannot be tolerated or where costs cannot exceed a certain amount. The critical points include all the areas of an establishment's operations that directly affect the success of its fundamental operations.
- Integrating into instituted processes: Controls must function harmoniously within these processes and ought to not constriction operations.
- Acceptation by employees: Employee involvement in the design of controls can increase acceptance.
- Accessibility of information when wanted: Deadlines, time needed to complete the project, costs associated with the project, and priority demands are apparent in these criteria. Costs are often attributed to time shortcomings or failures.

- Economic feasibleness: Effectual control systems answer questions such as, "How much does it cost?" "What will it save?" or "What are the returns on the investment?" In short, equivalence of the costs to the benefits ensures that the benefits of controls outweigh the costs.
- Accuracy: Effectual control systems provide factual information that's useful, reliable, valid, and consistent.
- Understandability: Controls must be simple and easy to understand.

CONTROL TECHNIQUES

Control techniques furnish managers with the type and amount of information they need to measure and monitor performance. The information from numerous controls must be sewed to a specific management level, department, unit, or operation. To ensure complete and consistent information, organizations frequently use standardized documents such as financial, status, and project reports. Each area within an establishment, however, uses its own specific control techniques, described in the following sections.

Financial Controls

After the establishment has strategies in place to reach its ends, funds are set aside for the necessary resources and labour. As money is spent, statements are updated to reflect how much was spent, how it was spent, and what it received. Managers use these financial statements, such as an income statement or balance sheet, to monitor the progress of programs and plans. Financial statements furnish management with information to monitor financial resources and activities. The income statement shows the results of the establishment's operations over a period of time, such as revenues, expenses, and gain or loss. The balance sheet shows what the establishment is worth (assets) at a single point in time, and the extent to which those assets were financed by debt (liabilities) or owner's investment (equity).

Financial audits, or formal investigations, are regularly conducted to ensure that financial management practices follow in general accepted processes, policies, laws, and ethical guidelines. Audits may be conducted internally or externally. Financial ratio analysis analyses the relationship between specific figures on the financial statements and helps explain the importance of those figures:

- Liquidity ratios measure an establishment's power to generate cash.
- Profitability ratios measure an establishment's power to generate profits.
- Debt ratios measure an establishment's power to pay its debts.
- Activity ratios measure an establishment's efficiency in operations and use of assets.

Additionally, financial responsibility centres necessitate managers to account for a unit's progress toward financial aims within the scope of their influences. A manager's aims and responsibilities may focus on unit profits, costs, revenues, or investments.

Budget Controls

A budget shows how much an organization expects to spend (expenses) and earn (revenues) over a period of time. Amounts are categorized as per the type of business activity or account, such as telephone costs or sales of catalogues. Budgets not only help managers plan their finances, but also help them keep track of their overall spending. A budget, actually, is both a planning tool and a control mechanism. Budget development processes vary among organizations as per who does the budgeting and how the financial resources are allocated. Some budget development methods acting are as follows:

- Top-down budgeting: Managers prepare the budget and send it to subordinates.
- Bottom-up budgeting: Figures come from the lower levels and are adjusted and interconnected as they move up the hierarchy.
- Zero-based budgeting: Managers develop each new budget by warranting the projected allocation against its contribution to departmental or organizational aims.
- Flexible budgeting: Any budget exercise can integrate flexible budgets, which set "meet or beat" standards that can be compared to expenditures.

Marketing Controls

Marketing controls assist monitor advance toward ends for client satisfaction with productions and services, costs, and delivery. The following are illustrations of controls used to evaluate an establishment's marketing functions:

- Market research gathers data to assess customer needs-information critical to an establishment's success. Ongoing market research reflects how well an establishment is conforming to customers' expectations and helps anticipate customer needs. It also helps identify competitors.
- Test marketing is small-scale product marketing to assess customer acceptance. Using surveys and focus groups test marketing goes outside identifying general demands and looks at what (or who) actually influences buying decisions.
- Marketing statistics measure performance by collecting data and analyzing results. In most cases, competency with a computer spreadsheet program is all a manager needs. Managers look at marketing ratios, which measure profitability, activity, and market shares, as well as sales quotas, which measure progress toward sales aims and aid with inventory controls.

Regrettably, scheduling a regular evaluation of an establishment's marketing program is easier to propose than to execute. Ordinarily, only a crisis, such as increased competition or a sales drop, forces a company to take a closer look at its marketing program. Nevertheless, more regular evaluations aid minimizes the number of marketing problems.

Human Resource Controls

Human resource controls aid managers regulate the quality of newly hired personnel, as well as monitor current employees' developments and daily performances.

On a daily basis, managers can go a long way in helping to control workers' behaviours in organizations. They can help direct workers' performances toward aims by making sure that ends are clearly set and understood. Managers can also institute policies and processes to help guide workers' actions. Finally, they can consider past experiences when developing future strategies, objectives, policies, and processes.

Common control types constitute performance appraisals, disciplinary programs, observations, and training and development assessments. Because the quality of a firm's personnel, to a large degree, decides the firm's overall effectiveness, controlling this area is very crucial.

Computers and Information Controls

Almost all organizations have secret and sensitive information that they do not want to become general knowledge. Controlling access to computer databases is the key to this area. More and more, computers are being used to collect and store information for control intentions. Many organizations privately monitor each employee's computer usage to measure employee performance, among other things. Some individuals question the rightness of computer monitoring. Managers must carefully weigh the benefits against the costs-both human and financial-before investing in and carrying out computerized control techniques.

Though computers and information systems provide tremendous benefits, such as improved productivity and information management, organizations ought to remember the following limitations of the use of information technology:

- Operation restrictions: Though management information systems have the potential to increase overall performance, replacing long-time organizational employees with information systems technology may result in the loss of expert cognition that these individuals hold. Additionally, computerized information systems are expensive and difficult to develop. After the system has been purchased, co-ordinating it-possibly with existing equipment-may be more difficult than expected. Accordingly, a company may cut corners or install the system carelessly to the detriment of the system's performance and utility. And like other sophisticated electronic equipment, data system doesn't work all the time, resulting in costly downtime.
- Behaviour restrictions: Information technology appropriates managers to access more information than ever before. But too much information can overwhelm employees, cause stress, and even slow decision making. Therefore, managing the quality and amount of information available to avoid information overload is significant.
- Health dangers: Potentially serious health-related issues associated with the use of computers and other information technology has been aroused in current years. An example is carpal tunnel syndrome, a painful disorder in the hands and wrists caused by repetitious movements.

Note: An effectual system determines whether employees and several parts of an establishment are on target in achieving organizational aims. Take the example of Pepsico. It is a living role model in employing the best control systems in in its working; Reader can go their site for more detailed information. http://www.pepsico.com/Purpose/Sustainability/Performance-with-Purpose.aspx

20

Conflict Management

Conflict management can be defined in words as "a battle, contest of opposing forces, discord, antagonism existing between primitive desires, instincts and moral, religious, or ethical ideals." Conflict takes place when two or more individuals or organizations differ because their needs, wants, aims, or values are different. Hurt feelings, anger, bruised egos, and poor communication are all the precursors to conflict. Nevertheless, conflict isn't the end of the world, or your team or group. Some tools have been extremely-developed that will help us all recognize conflict and conduct with it in order that our group or team can move on, stronger than earlier.

TRADITIONAL VIEW OF CONFLICT

One of the most remarkable characteristics of twenty-first century organizations is continuous change. Unstable economic conditions, speedily changing technologies, universal competition, manpower diversity, and new organizational structures are only a few of the factors contributing to an age of discontinuity. Moreover, exponential change-whether in society, the family, or the firm-in general creates significant chaos. Where there is chaos, there is frequently stress, and stress often becomes the progenitor of conflict. Therefore, in this era of radical change and significant chaos, high levels of anxiety and interpersonal conflict pervade the workplace.

Conflict, of course, has always existed-even in less complex times. Where two or more individuals are gathered together, there is a potential for conflict. As human beings interact within organizations, differing aims, values, styles, and situations produce tension. Additionally to these interpersonal and behavioural factors, conventional organizational structures promote conflict. Functional silos and a plethora of several skill sets and technical specialties lead to communication challenges that frequently result in conflict. These factors, along with numerous others, make conflict an organizational reality.

This discussion purports that interpersonal conflict isn't only inescapable, it is necessary for individual and organizational evolution. Each conflict situation extends organizations, and the people they include, opportunities for transformation. Conflict challenges the status quo, providing a breeding ground for innovation. Managers who try to do away with conflict are operating under an outdated paradigm. If organizations are to thrive in the twenty-first century, a new way of thinking about conflict is required. The mental models-assumptions and beliefs-that permeate twenty-first century organizations are mainly conflict adverse. As these mental models shift, new and more conflict-appreciative behaviours and feelings will ad libitum emerge. Individuals experience world as per their beliefs.

The conventional view of conflict in real is negative. It has normally been seen as non-adaptive, destructive, irrational, and time-consuming-something to be eliminated or at least suppressed. From this perspective, conflict occurs as a result of malfunctioning people or organizations. Hence, in order to resolve conflict, problems must be identified, causes must be examined, and those individuals or situations contributing to the conflict must be "fixed". This mechanistic view approaches conflict resolution as a logical, linear process. Robbins comments: "Though research studies now provide strong evidence to dispute that this approach to conflict reduction results in high group performance, many still evaluate conflict situations utilizing this outmoded standard."

In the 1950s the rising human relations view of conflict started out to replace the earlier conventional view. The human relations position suggests that conflict is a natural phenomenon in groups and organizations. Therefore, since it is inevitable, it must be accepted and managed. During this era, the management literature introduced the term conflict management; and, by the 1970s, the field of establishment development, with its tool-kit of team-building treatments, began to go mainstream, therefore providing organizations with new resources for carrying on with conflict.

MODERN VIEW OF CONFLICT

More recently, a third conflict school of thought has come out, mentioned as the interactionist view. This perspective moves beyond accepting conflict to really encouraging conflict. Proponents purport that "a harmonious, peaceful, tranquil, and cooperative group is prone to becoming static, apathetic, and unresponsive to needs for change and innovation" (Robbins). Although this view is now widely accepted by management theorists and establishment development practitioners, most individuals in most organizations still disfavour (and frequently try to avoid) conflict. They continue to view conflict through the length of the three-hundred-year-old scientific paradigm that emerged from Newton's mechanistic laws of classical physics. Harmonising to this paradigm, conflict is to be avoided because conflict leads to chaos and chaos triggers entropy (the second law of thermodynamics). Therefore, conflict is the enemy of rational, scientifically managed organizations.

The trouble with such a paradigm is that it fails to cope with current reality. Avoiding conflict is impossible and managing it is a task that all too frequently leads to frustration and fatigue. Furthermore, when conflict is tightly managed, opportunities for transformation are blocked. In fact, contemporary scientific theories (e.g., quantum mechanics and chaos theory) demonstrate that high levels of disorder are requirement for system evolution. Without chaos, living systems stagnate and entropy ensures. Newton's second law of thermodynamics represents a partial truth relevant only to closed or static systems. In open or dynamic systems- e.g. human organizations-chaos catapults the system to higher levels of complicated operating through a process of self-establishment.

The tension of conflict can give significant new action options. However, if chaos is prematurely suppressed, participants all too frequently retreat back to a state of apparent peace while passive chaos continues to suppurate just below the surface. In such a position, no paradigm shifts occur. No breakthrough insights emerge. Consequently, old behaviours finally resurface and the conflict resumes, requiring yet another conflict management intervention.

Research proposes that although most managers spend about 20% of their time dealing with conflict, they dislike it and would prefer to avoid it. In fact, conflict is often cited as one of the least pleasurable aspects of the leadership role. The need for a new way of thinking about conflict is pressing. An updated paradigm is sorely needed-one in which conflict is viewed as a catalyst for personal and organizational transformation. It has been almost 100 years since Taylor (1911) challenged organizations to assume a more scientifically based approach to management. Remarkable new discoveries have occurred and radical scientific theories have been formulated. It is time to employ these new insights to twenty-first century organizational challenges.

SCIENTIFIC MANAGEMENT

Many business authors have suggested that it is time for a new scientific theory of management-one based on all that has been learned since Newton developed his seventeenth-century principles of classical physics. One place to look for more present-day management metaphors is in the twentieth-century scientific theories of chaos and quantum mechanics. These two "new science" theories have much in common. They both raise questions about the truth of the reductionistic, mechanistic, and deterministic worldview that came forth from seventeenth-century classical physics. These new theories characterize the universe as a dynamic, unpredictable, subjective, self-organizing system rather than as a static, predictable, documentary machine. Embedded within these theories is the assumption that change is the catalyst for development and the fundamental operating principle of all living systems.

Furthermore, these new science theories demonstrate that change, even in non-biological systems, normally involves conflict. For example, the very existence of matter is a result of subatomic particles colliding together. Out of these collisions, matter is birthed. This is a wonderful metaphor for looking at conflict from a new science perspective. From this vantage point, conflict isn't only requirement; it gives all involved an opportunity to incorporate their beliefs with others who have very different ones and out of these collisions, a higher level of personal and organizational functioning emerges.

Each of these new science theories also recognizes that there is inherent order in the universe. This is demonstrated at the physical level by the previously described chemical clock experiments. At the biological level we observe the orderliness of the evolutionary process and the ordering of the seasons. At the organizational level the power of a system to use chaos to manifest higher levels of order and effectiveness is clearly demonstrated by Greiner's (1991) research on organizational evolution and revolution. Why then do most managers and leaders have such strong needs to control chaos? Why it is that conflict is still so frequently avoided and/or so rigorously monitored and controlled? The authors purport that the answers to these questions are based on the fact that most managers hold limiting mental models regarding conflict. Our present-day organizational challenges necessitate a new paradigm and new management skills-skills that are more appropriate for workplaces where change is constant and conflict is pervasive.

While Taylor was promoting scientific management in the United States, Fayol, writing in Europe, developed a set of management skills that are congruous with Taylor's mechanistic worldview. Fayol referred to these skills as planning, organizing, directing, and controlling (Robbins, 2001). Despite the fact that Minzberg challenged the adequacy of these fundamental management skills over 30 years ago, twenty-first century business books proceed to discuss them and managers continue to rely on them. Nevertheless, in a complicated world of continuous change, these skills are rapidly becoming obsolete. They were formulated for life in simpler times when organizations were viewed as stable entities that functioned in a logical, linear, predictable manner. Today's fast-paced, invariably changing, intricately inter-connected world is neither stable nor predictable. In such a world, a manager's power to plan, organize, direct, and control is more and more settled.

The new sciences furnish the conceptual foundation for a new management skill set-a set of skills that can change managers not only to view conflict from a new perspective, but also to respond to conflict in new ways. These skills are called Quantum Skills, not solely because they are derived from key principles of the new sciences but, more importantly, because they require a quantum leap into a new management paradigm. They aren't intended to replace the conventional Newtonian management skills, but instead to complement them. They provide managers with a more whole-brained approach to managing individuals and conflict.

The Quantum Skills are defined as follows:

1. Quantum Seeing: The power to see intentionally.
2. Quantum Thinking: The power to think paradoxically.
3. Quantum Feeling: The power to feel vitally alive.
4. Quantum Knowing: The power to know intuitively.
5. Quantum Acting: The power to act responsibly.
6. Quantum Trusting: The power to trust life's process.
7. Quantum Being: The power to be in relationship.

The first skill, Quantum seeing (the power to see intentionally), is based on the premise that reality is inherently subjective-it shows up consorting to the expectations and beliefs (intentions) of the observer. Research in quantum mechanics, human perception, and social constructionism all support the premise that the majority of what is seen in the external world is a part of internal assumptions and beliefs. Zukav explains:

Reality is what we regard as true. What we take to be true is what we believe. What we believe is based upon our perceptions. What we perceive depends on what we look for. What we look for depends on what we think. What we think depends, on what we perceive. What we perceive determines what we believe. What we believe determines what we take to be true. What we look upon true is our reality.

Hence, beliefs reinforce perceptions and perceptions reinforce beliefs. Accordingly, most individuals stay stuck in an on-going cycle of repetitiveness, seeing the world as they have always seen it and living their lives amongst a very narrow band of hypothesis, not because life is limited, but because perceptions always are.

Csikszentmihalyi (1990) believes that purpose is the psychological process through which reality is constructed. Intentions direct attention to certain stimuli causing embarrassment of other perceptual possibilities to be ignored. The skill of Quantum seeing enables managers to consciously select their intentions. For instance, when conflict occurs the quantum response would be for those involved to willingly explore their own assumptions and beliefs about the other(s), searching for the underlying intentions that are producing conflict. Not only would each party fully distinguish the relationship between internal cognitive processes and external perceptions, each would also set clear intentions for the situation-visualizing and confirming a positive solution.

A manager who is capable in the skill of Quantum seeing, models the power to identify and test assumptions and beliefs. Such a manager might use processes such as Argyris' (1993) "two-column" skill, therefore receiving those individuals involved in conflict to track their conversations-writing what they say in the right column and what they think in the left. Or, the manager might introduce Senge's (1990) "ladder of assumptions" as a process that participants can use to name the underlying assumptions and beliefs that are activating conflict. These quantum managers would also be careful to state all their observations of the conflict as subjective perceptions, rather than as recognized facts. In so doing, the manager contributes those involved in the conflict the right to have differing perceptions. This doesn't mean there is no "right" action; it simply shows that the manager doesn't presume to perceive reality more accurately than others who are also involved. "Ultimately, no world will succeed in which the behaviour of some hurts others, or in which the behaviour of all hurts that larger process of increasing, ordered coherence in the universe at large."

At first sight, this skill may sound similar to other popular conflict solution methodologies. Nevertheless, it is distinctly different. While these earlier models offer practical skills for answering to conflict more collaboratively, and while they recognize that there is value in each party's needs, they don't recognize the totally subjective nature of reality that is implied in almost one hundred years of "new science" research and developed in the twentieth-century philosophical theory of social constructionism.

CONSTRUCTIVE AND DESTRUCTIVE CONFLICT

To better conduct with intractable conflicts, we have been formulating an approach which we call constructive confrontation. This approach is based on the assumption that intense, long-term confrontations over important and difficult issues are inevitable. What isn't inevitable, nevertheless, is the destructiveness commonly associated with these conflicts. To limit such destructiveness, we suggest that the parties and intermediaries involved in intractable conflicts ought to move away from the unrealistic end of solution, and focus, instead, on how these conflicts can be carried on more constructively.

The constructive confrontation approach follows a medical model in which destructive conflict marches (but not conflicts themselves) are likened to diseases-pathological processes that adversely affect individuals, organizations, and societies as a whole. Occasionally these "diseases" can be entirely cured; at other times, we can only limit the most troublesome symptoms. As in medicine, prevention frequently works better than a cure. For that reason constructive confrontation advocates utilizing positive strategies at the start of a conflict, not just at the end when the situation is grim. Also like medicine, constructive confrontation takes an incremental approach. Instead than looking at conflict as a single problem and asking how can it be totally "fixed" or resolved, constructive confrontation looks at each aspect of the conflict process and asks whether or not that part is effectual and constructive, and if not, how it might be ameliorated.

Constructive Confrontation Steps

As in practice of medicine, the first step in constructive confrontation is diagnosis. This process starts with preparation of a conflict map. Such a map ought to comprise the identification of active and potential adversary groups and intermediaries, along with their interests and positions. It ought to also place the immediate dispute into the perspective of the long-term, underlying conflict. The next part of the diagnosis regards differentiating the core aspects of the conflict from what we call complicating factors. These are problems in the conflict process that get "laid over" the core, making the core issues harder to see and address. Instances comprise the categories examined in this training program: escalation and polarization, misunderstandings, fact-finding problems, procedural problems, and framing troubles.

After diagnosing complicating factors, problems in the core confrontation process must also be named. These admit the inadequate identification of power options, the inadequate assessment of the costs and gains of several options, overlooking ripe moments, and reliance on bitter end power struggles.

Identification, Selection, and Implementation of Treatment Options

After destructive conflict dynamics are diagnosed, the next step in constructive confrontation is the identification and implementation of realistic, incremental steps for reducing as many of the complicating factors as possible. In some cases these remedies involve easy "do not do its"-pitfalls which are easy to avoid once you see them. Other steps necessitate either the acquisition of new skills, outside assistance from conflict professionals, or the making of hard choices for which there are no clear responses (deciding whether to pursue a short-term victory even although it is likely to provoke a damaging, long-term backlash, for example.)

While some remedies can be carried out unilaterally, others require the joint efforts of adversaries, intermediaries, or both. Once specific options are selected and implemented, results ought to be monitored and adjustments made when needed as the conflict continues and changes over time.

The Constructive Confrontation Cycle

Conventional problem-solving intermediation is linear. It goes through a predetermined series of steps, in a dictated order. Though different mediators list different steps, most represent rather closely to those set out by Chris Moore. First, the parties are contacted, background information is collected, a strategy is developed, and the parties' agreement to participate is obtained. Then the mediation session starts out--opening statements are made, issues are defined, interests are elicited, alternatives for settlement are developed and assessed, and agreement is reached. A settlement document is drawn up and signed, the mediation is over, and the parties go home.

Constructive confrontation is really different. There is no recognized commencing point, and usually no end. Rather, parties begin when and where they want to, usually when they have decided (or acknowledged) that the conflict they are involved in is more destructive than constructive, and that they necessitate to develop a more effectual way of managing it. To do this, they do begin with a diagnosis process (this is necessary), but then they can choose any of many different approach to treating the pathologies they discover. They can try to tackle all the problems at once, or they can take them one at a time. They can deal with misunderstandings first, and then procedural troubles, or they can go the other way around. They can start down one path, and switch to another path as the pauperism develops. Constructive confrontation is very flexible and adaptable to the trouble at hand.

Constructive confrontation is also cyclical, after treatments are taken on, results are monitored, and strategies adjusted if the treatments didn't work. It is expected that the underlying conflict will go forward, so in order to keep that conflict productive, parties must continue to monitor the changes in core issues and the development of complicating problems over time. Things that were "fixed" a few months or years ago may spring up again and need further attention. So constructive confrontation is an on-going process, not a one-time event plopped in the middle (or at the end) of a protracted conflict.

Conflict is negative or Destructive when it...

- Damages the spirit of the team or an individual
- Divides individuals and groups, and constructs cooperation difficult
- Leads to harmful behaviour, like fighting or name-calling
- Makes individuals or group focus on their differences
- Takes attention off from other activities

But it can be positive or constructive when it...

- Brings about solutions to problems
- Causes real communication
- Clears up important problems or issues
- Develops understanding and skills
- Gets everyone needed in solving issues

- Helps individuals learn more about each other and cooperate
- Release emotion, anxiety, and stress in a positive way

While the definition of conflict and our feelings about it tend to be negative, conflict itself doesn't need to be negative. How we manage our conflict can persuade the consequence, our feelings about the way it was handled, and the individuals called for conflict.

CONFLICT PROCESS

Each and every establishment carries on with internal conflict creates its own culture when dealing with conflict and seeks to minimize costs while doing so.

Can an establishment change or shift its internal or external conflict culture? Can organizations control conflicts' side affects? Can the use of mediation skills help do so? In order to examine the potential use of mediation one requires to define the scope of the term: mediation has been defined as a process which assists challenging parties reach solution of their conflict in a consensual manner while the mediator lacks all authority in deciding or ruling its outcome.

Ready for the mediator to be effectual he or she must dwell upon mediation skills which primarily include of an innovative yet simple strategy: process thinking and designing - marking between process and content as two distinctive elements on the way to resolving disputes.

In house mediation between employees, employees and their mangers, different divisions within the establishment etc., can be in particular beneficial as mediation inherently focuses on relationship (long and short-term) issues.

The basic role of the mediator revolves around his or her ability to transform the party's discussion - helping them shift from position rhetoric to interest based negotiations. Frequently, the "Art and Science" of listening may prove to be one of the most indispensable tools on the path towards dispute solution.

The mediator helping the disputants in their negotiation efforts can in certain cases, educate them as to how negotiations can be conducted in the most effectual manner. The win/win doctrine presented by Ury and Fischer can be amazingly easy to adapt to, if all employees within the establishment get the opportunity to learn these skills, prior to the happening or outburst of conflict.

Who ought to mediate in house conflicts? Frequently, in big organizations Human Resources personal resume the role of in-house mediators. This may produce a trouble such as the parties' unwillingness to disclose confidential information pertaining their interests - fearing it will used against them or exposed in such a way which could be harmful to them.

Evidently, not all conflicts within the establishment can afford non-in-house mediators. The in-house mediator will only succeed if he or she projects trust and enjoys a high level of believability within the establishment. The professional manner in which a system is designed within an establishment can determine the level and intensity of internal conflict. Additionally, when an establishment engages in the initial process of system design a lot can be learned. For example producing a monitored bank of knowledge concerning the organizations' use of different styles when dealing with both internal and external conflict, can help reduce unnecessary costs, as well as produce a useful pattern assisting those practicing dispute resolution do so more expeditiously.

Dealing with internal conflict, in a preventative manner, focusing on relationship issues while practicing mediation and basic negotiation skills, can create a far more positive atmosphere within the establishment, heighten productivity, minimize costs incurred by internal turbulence and litigation and above all produce a sense of world-wide well being. When we resolve issues, we need to focus on the things we need or want as a group, and not things needed or wanted by people. This encourages working with each other instead of against each other. There are some proven schemes that you can use to help resolve conflicts within your groups.

STRATEGIES FOR ENCOURAGING CONSTRUCTIVE CONFLICT

Does constructive conflict live in your establishment, your department, on your team, in your silo or in your group? Or, do you lead, manage or supervise in an environment where were one big, happy family, where all are in agreement, ever smiling and saying yes? If you're not experiencing constructive conflict in your workplace, you're most likely not making high-quality decisions, nor are you encouraging your colleagues to be devoted to carrying out the decisions you are making.

There's no question that many a leaders, managers, supervisors and employees are frequently conflict-averse. They shy away from conflict, feel nervous about going against the grain, rocking the boat, or being perceived as a trouble-maker or not being a team player.

Much of one's resistance to conflict has to do with folks who, when maturating, were subject to uniform loud arguments, disagreements and fights between their parents, basic care-givers, relatives or friends, and as a result grew to become fearful, scared, threatened or unsafe around folks who raised their voices in argument, dissent, disagreement and communicative abuse. Now, as adults, many of these folks resist conflict as, frequently unconsciously, their childhood fear and terror leak out in workplace positions where conflict develops.

Therefore, in the workplace, and elsewhere in life, they do what they can to avoid or deny conflict. They defer, become quiet, accommodate others, or systematically nod in agreement. They go along to get along, and opt to be silent when facing real or comprehended conflict. They see conflict as bad and threatening to their personal or professional feel of safety, security and well-being. Therefore, two things need to be said:

That was then and this is now. When faced with conflict, its important to be conscious and aware of the dynamic that is playing out and know that fear around conflict at work is most likely old stuff that is coming up. Working to deal with and move through one's fear and resistance with a qualified coach or counsellor can bring one to "metabolize" their childhood fear, realize what it is and choose to engage in conflict without fear of reprisal, being "bad" or "wrong", or constituting physically or verbally hurt in some way, shape or form.

Constructive conflict not only is a necessity for optimizing the decision-making process, but as leaders, managers and supervisors, you have a responsibility to foster dissent in your establishment, on your team or in your department. There are those who aren't conflicted by conflict. But, how do you generate dissent or disagreement, and generate engagement, when some folks prefer to annul conflicts at all costs?

Engaging Individuals who are Resistant

One strategy to require resistant folks in constructive conflict is to appoint (and allow) them to be "contrarian." You can ask, encourage and permit them to take an opposite point of view, to play devils advocate and speak to an issue from a different perspective. Manager can ask folks to play the role of your competition and demonstrate a conflicting view that his competitors might take.

The Point of Constructive Conflict

It is important not only to comprise all essential players in the decision-making process but to be sure to cover all the decision-making bases even although some folks initially may feel uncomfortable or experience some illness in the process. It is important that folks not be seen, or made to be seen, as bad or wrong but as valuable contributors to the process. It is also critical to produce a safe and trusting environment where folks can open up and say what's on their mind without dreading ostracism, reprisal or unfair personal judgments or criticism.

One intention of fostering constructive conflict is to have everybody put all their cards on the table, dissent, differ, diverge, be ambiguous, be inconsistent with recognized wisdom and be out in the open with their views or perspectives irrespective of ones role, position or place in the hierarchy. In an environment of constructive conflict, ones ideas can be rebutted, disagreed with, countered, etc., but cannot be silenced, cut off or shut down.

In short, constructive conflict:

- Is constructive being open, allowing, consenting and non-judgmental for "the good of the order."
- Focuses on ideas, not personalities.
- allows for disagreement
- Follows ground rules for interacting.
- Is mutually respectful.
- Fosters and promotes divergent and heuristic program and varied perspectives.
- Takes place in a living laboratory where folks are learning how to engage in positive conflict and learning about themselves in the process.
- Is intentional about repairing any discredited relationships that may arise or result from the process.
- Is fair where all are heard and all ideas are conceived.
- Even although not everybody may be satisfied with ultimate decision.
- Is open and transparent.
- Holds individuals accountable for their role in the process.
- Supports the process of relationship building and meaningful dialogue.

The notion fundamental constructive conflict is to produce a safe and trusting environment where all are heard in order to enhance the decision-making process and garner buy-in and commitment from the participants for implementing decisions. Constructive conflict, when carried out properly, furthers commitment and collaboration. Leaders, managers and supervisors would do well to consider constructive conflict as a process to drive change where all parties are drivers, not passengers.

Dealing with Individuals While Managing Conflict

Some individuals are not willing to admit that they may not be the best at conflict management, but that does not mean that they are not occasionally regarded in the management process. You can not change the way that individuals behave or approach conflict, but you can arm yourself with some tools to help you successfully navigate conflict when not everyone is on the same page.

- Sherman Tanks: These in time get "in your face" to argue and state opinions as facts.
  1. Get their attention by using their first name to start a sentence.
  2. Maintain eye contact; give them time to wind down.
  3. Stand up to them without fighting; do not worry about being civilised.
  4. Suggest you sit down to continue discussions.
- Snipers: These individuals take pot-shots in meetings but avoid one-on-one encounters.
  1. Expose the attack; draw them out in public and do not let social pattern stop you.
  2. Get other opinions--do not give in to the sniper's views.
  3. Provide the sniper with options to a direct contest.
- Chronic Complainers: These individuals find faults with everyone-except themselves.
  1. Politely cut off and get control of the situation.
  2. Quickly sum up the facts.
  3. Ask for their complaints in writing.
- Negativists: These individuals know that nothing new will work; they'll disrupt group brainstorming sessions.
  1. Acknowledge their valid points.
  2. Describe past successes.
  3. Avoid "you're wrong, I'm right" arguments.

- Exploders: These individuals throw tantrums that quickly escalate.
    1. Give them time to regain self control.
    2. If they do not, shout an impersonal phrase such as "Stop!"
    3. Take a time-out or have a private meeting with them.

Steps to Analyzing Conflict

How can you manage conflict and disagreements in ways that strengthen instead of harm personal and professional relationships?

Step 1: Analyze the Conflict

Do not be afraid to ask questions of everybody involved. Take in answers from a variety of sources, and gain as much information as you can.

Step 2: Determine your Management Strategy

When you understand the basis of the conflict and everybody implied, you will need to develop a plan to manage the conflict. There are many plans to choose from; therefore you can pick the one that is most appropriate for your situation.

Step 3: Pre-Negotiation

Steps must be taken for discussion to commence. This to think about include:

- Someone has to begin the conversation! If neither party is willing to do so, bring in an outsider who will remain neutral to begin discussions.
- Everyone must be prepared to come to the table, to work together, and resolve the issues.
- The group must agree on rules for the discussion. Some ideas of things to include are: ways we'll communicate and how we'll make the final decision.
- Be Co-ordinated. Location, time, place and materials must all be in order for conflict management to work.
- Everybody at the table must agree on what information is put on the table, relevant to the conflict, and how the group will get answers to questions.

Step 4: Negotiation

Negotiations ought to be discussions that include:

- Reasons, demands, concerns and motivations for differing positions
- Current options
- Rating of all the current options
- Written agreement that documents what everyone realizes

- Everyone must be confident that all parties will follow through with their parts of the agreement. Make sure everyone is on the same page and understands the expectations.

Step 5: Post-Negotiation

Once negotiation is finish, the group ought to take the actions they decided upon.

- People ought to get support from outside parties who may have been demanded in some way. Outsiders must be on board with the terms of the agreements reached during Step 4.
- Communication and working together ought to continue during this process.

STRATEGIES FOR RESOLVING DESTRUCTIVE CONFLICT

The full term "conflict resolution" denotes a range of processes aimed at alleviating or eliminating sources of conflict. The term "conflict resolution" is occasionally used interchangeably with the term dispute resolution or alternative dispute resolution. Processes of conflict resolution generally include negotiation, mediation and diplomacy. The processes of arbitration, litigation, and formal complaint processes such as ombudsman processes, are generally described with the term dispute resolution, though some refer to them as "conflict resolution." Processes of mediation and arbitration are frequently denoted as alternative dispute resolution.

There is significant controversy about definitions and terminology in the area of conflict resolution. This may be partially as the field is multidisciplinary. Academics and practitioners are found within diverse disciplines constituting political science, international relations, law, psychology, public administration, anthropology, business, education, sociology, philosophy, health care and other fields of study or practice. Internationally, a growing number of undergraduate and graduate programs are rising in "conflict resolution," "conflict management," "dispute resolution," "alternative dispute resolution," "conflict transformation "and" peace and conflict studies". In summation, many fields now integrate courses in negotiation, mediation or conflict management. In most jurisdictions, no specific credentials are lawfully required by conflict resolution practitioners, many of whom have no specific academic qualifications.

Many of the definitional relates spring from diverse definitions of the terms "conflict" and "dispute" and "resolution." The term "conflict" has been defined as "intense interpersonal and/or intrapersonal dissonance (tension or antagonism) between two or more parties based on unfitting aims, needs, desires, values, beliefs, and/or attitudes." "Disputes" have been defined as conflicts that have become particularized around a specific issue or issues. Some conflicts may not become evident as articulated disputes. Therefore, "conflict resolution" tends to refer to processes that address the sources of conflict so as to prevent them from escalating or do away with the conflict altogether. The term "dispute resolution" refers to resolution of disputes and complaints, which may or may not address or annihilate the sources of the conflict.

Related definition controversies have come forth over the term "resolution." Some scholars and practitioners have pointed out that many disputes (and conflicts) cannot be resolved in that the sources of the conflicts cannot be eliminated. Therefore, the term "conflict management" has emerged to bring the idea that even if solution is unacceptable, conflicts and disputes can be managed constructively.

There are many tools available to persons in conflict. How and when they are used depends on several factors (such as the specific issues at stake in the conflict and the cultural perspective of the disputants). The list of tools available to practitioners contains negotiation, mediation, community building, advocacy, diplomacy, activism, non-violence, critical pedagogy, meditation, prayer and counselling.

In real world conflict situations, which range in scale from kinder garden bullying to genocide, practitioners will creatively combine numerous of these approaches as required. Additionally, practitioners will frequently specialize in a particular scale (e.g. interpersonal, community or international), or a particular form of conflict (such as environmental, religious or organizational), and repertoires of tools they find most utile.

Note: For any organization to be effectual and efficient in achieving its aims, there is need of recognising and resolving conflict amongst individuals, in order that conflict doesn't become so serious that co-operation is impossible. All members of any organization need to have ways of keeping conflict to a minimum - and of solving problems caused by conflict, before conflict becomes a major obstacle to your work. Taking the case of Novazymes Company, It has established a 'Golden Set' of guidelines, through which conflict resolution can be solved. For in-depth and detailed knowledge, reader can visit their site: http://www.novozymes.com/en/MainStructure/AboutUs/Our+policies/

21

Productivity and Quality Management

For organizations to survive and grow in today's challenging marketplace they need true commitment to meeting customer needs through communication, planning and continuous process improvement activities. Creating this culture change can improve the products and services of your organization as well as improve employee attitudes and enthusiasm. All of these help with the ultimate goal of improved quality, productivity and customer satisfaction which is an important competitive advantage in today's marketplace.

PRODUCTIVITY AND QUALITY

After organizations decide customer needs, they must centre on meeting those needs by yielding high quality products at an efficient rate. Organizations can improve quality and productivity by ensuring the commitments of all three levels of management and employees as follows:

- Top-level management: Carry out sound management practices, use research and development effectively, adopt modern manufacturing techniques, and improve time management.
- Middle management: Plan and co-ordinate quality and productivity attempts.
- Low-level management: Work with employees to improve productivity by acceptance of change, commitment to quality, and continually improving all facets of their work.

Productivity is the relationship between a given amount of output and the amount of input required to create it. Profitability results when money is left over from sales after costs are paid. The expenditures made to ensure that the product or service conforms to quality specifications affect the final or overall cost of the products and/or services necessitated.

Efficiency of costs will be an important consideration in all stages of the market system from manufacturing to consumption. Quality affects productivity. Both affect profitability. The drive for any one of the three must not interfere with the drive for the others. Efforts at improvement demand to be co-ordinated and integrated. The real cost of quality is the cost of avoiding non-conformance and failure. Another cost is the cost of not having quality-of losing customers and wasting resources. As long as organizations continually act with their customers and several partners, and develop learning relationships between all degrees of management and employees, the levels of productivity and quality ought to stay high.

CONFIGURING THE PRODUCTION SYSTEM

Recently-developed methods have improved the performance of production systems many times over. Nevertheless, these techniques aren't yet adequate for uninterrupted problem solving in a dynamically changing environment. To attain adaptive real-time performance in such environments, we use an establishment of distributed production system agents, rather than a single monolithic production system, to solve problems. Establishment self-design is executed to satisfy real-time constraints and to adapt to changing resource requirements. When overloaded, individual agents decompose themselves to increase parallelism, and when the load brightens the agents compose with each other to free hardware resources. Additionally to increased performance, generalizations of our composition/decomposition access provide numerous new directions for establishment self-design, a pressing concern in production system.

SUPPLY CHAIN MANAGEMENT

A supply chain is a network of facilities and distribution alternatives that performs the functions of procurement of materials, transformation of these materials into intermediate and finished products, and the distribution of these completed products to customers. Supply chains exist in both service and manufacturing organizations, though the complexity of the chain may vary greatly from industry to industry and firm to firm. Below is an instance of a very simple supply chain for a single product, where raw material is procured from vendors, transmuted into finished goods in a single step, and then transported to distribution centres, and ultimately, customers. Realistic supply chains have multiple end products with shared components, facilities and capacities. The flow of materials isn't always along an arborescent network, numerous modes of transportation may be considered, and the bill of materials for the end items may be both deep and large.

Supply chain management is classically regarded as to lie among fully vertically integrated firms, where the entire material flow rate is owned by a single business firm, and those where each channel member operates independently. Hence co-ordination between the several players in the chain is key in its effectual management. Cooper and Ellram compare supply chain management to a well-balanced and well-practiced relay team. Such a team is more competitive when for each one player knows how to be positioned for the hand-off. The kinships are the firmest between players who right away pass the baton, but the entire team needs to make a co-ordinated effort to win the race.

Supply Chain Decisions

We classify the conclusions for supply chain management into two broad categories - strategical and operational. As the term entails, strategic decisions are made normally over a longer time horizon. These are closely linked to the corporate strategy, and guide supply chain policies from a design perspective. Alternatively, operational decisions are short term, and focus on activities over a day-to-day basis. The effort in these type of decisions is to effectively and expeditiously manage the product flow in the "strategically" planned supply chain.

There are four main decision areas in supply chain management:

1. Location,
2. production,
3. Inventory, and
4. Transportation (distribution), and there are both strategic and operational components in each of these decision areas.

Location Decisions

The geographical placement of production facilities, stocking points, and sourcing points is the natural first step in producing a supply chain. The location of facilities necessitates a commitment of resources to a long-term plan. Once the size, number, and location of these are determined, so are the possible paths by which the product flows through to the final customer. These decisions are of great implication to a firm since they represent the fundamental strategy for accessing customer markets, and will have a significant affect on revenue, cost, and level of service. These decisions ought to be determined by an optimization routine that considers production costs, taxes, duties and duty drawback, tariffs, local content, distribution costs, production limitations, etc. Though location decisions are mainly strategic, they also have implications on an operational level.

Production Decisions

The strategic decisions admit what products to create, and which plants to create them in, allocation of suppliers to plants, plants to DC's, and DC's to customer markets. As before, these decisions have a big affect on the revenues, costs and customer service levels of the firm. These decisions assume the existence of the facilities, but decide the exact path(s) through which a product flows to and from these facilities. Another critical issue is the capacity of the manufacturing facilities--and this largely counts the degree of vertical integration within the firm. Operational decisions focus on detailed production scheduling. These decisions comprise the construction of the master production schedules, scheduling production on machines, and instrumentation maintenance. Other considerations comprise workload equilibrating, and quality control measures at a production facility.

Inventory Decisions

These refer to means by which armouries are managed. Inventories exist at every stage of the supply chain as either raw materials, semi-completed or finished goods. They can also be in-process between locations. Their basic intention to buffer against any doubt that might exist in the supply chain. Since holding of inventories can cost anywhere between 20 to 40 percent of their value, their efficient management is critical in supply chain operations. It is strategical in the sense that top management sets aims. However, most researchers have approached the management of inventory from an operational perspective. These admit deployment strategies (push versus pull), control policies --- the determination of the optimal levels of order quantities and reorder points, and setting safety stock levels, at each stocking location. These levels are critical, since they are main determinants of customer service levels.

Transportation Decisions

The style choice aspect of these decisions are the more strategic ones. These are closely linked to the inventory decisions, since the best choice of mode is frequently detected by trading-off the cost of using the particular mode of transport with the indirect cost of inventory associated with that mode. While air shipments may be fast, reliable, and warrant lesser safety stocks, they are valuable.

Meanwhile shipping by sea or rail may be much cheaper, but they demand holding relatively large amounts of inventory to buffer against the inherent uncertainty associated with them. Therefore, customer service levels, and geographic location play vital roles in such conclusions. Since transportation is more than 30 percent of the logistics costs, operating efficiently makes good economic sense. Shipment sizes (consolidated bulk shipments versus Lot-for-Lot), routing and scheduling of instrumentation are fundamental in effectual management of the firm's transport strategy.

Supply Chain Modelling Approaches

Clearly, each of the above two levels of decisions demand a different perspective. The strategic decisions are, for the most part, universal or "all encompassing" in that they try to integrate several aspects of the supply chain. Accordingly, the models that describe these decisions are huge, and require a significant amount of data. Frequently due to the enormity of data requirements, and the broad scope of decisions, these models provide approximate solutions to the decisions they describe. The operational decisions, meanwhile, address the day to day operation of the supply chain. Therefore the models that describe them are frequently very specific in nature. Due to their narrow perspective, these models frequently believe great detail and provide very good, if not optimal, solutions to the operational decisions.

To facilitate a concise review of the literature, and at the same time attempting to adapt the above polarity in modelling, we divide the modelling approaches into three areas --- Network Design, "Rough Cut" methods, and simulation based methods. The network design methods, for the most part, provide normative models for the more strategic decisions. These models normally cover the four major decision areas reported earlier, and focus more on the design aspect of the supply chain; the establishment of the network and the associated flows on them. "Rough cut" methods, alternatively, give guiding policies for the operational decisions. These models normally assume a "single site" (i.e., ignore the network) and add supply chain characteristics to it, such as explicitly believing the site's relation to the others in the network. Simulation method is a method by which a comprehensive supply chain model can be examined, considering both strategic and operational components.

TOTAL QUALITY MANAGEMENT

Total Quality Management (TQM) is a philosophy which states that uniform commitment to quality in all areas of an establishment encourages an organizational culture that meets consumers' perceptions of quality.

The concept of TQM rests largely on five principles:

1. Create quality work the first time.
2. Focus on the customer.
3. Have a strategic approach to improvement.
4. Improve continuously.
5. Promote mutual respect and teamwork.

To be efficient in improving quality, TQM must be supported at all levels of a firm, from the highest executive to the lowest-level hourly employee. TQM extends the definition of quality to all functional areas of the establishment, constituting production, marketing, finance, and information systems. The process begins by listening to customers' wants and demands and then delivering goods and services that fulfil these desires. TQM even expands the definition of customer to constitute any person inside or outside the company to whom an employee passes his or his work. In a restaurant, for example, the cooks' customers are the waiters and waitresses. This notion promotes each member of the establishment to stay centred on quality and remain fully aware of his or his contribution to it and responsibility for it.

The TQM philosophy focuses on teamwork, increasing customer satisfaction, and lowering costs. Organizations implement TQM by encouraging managers and employees to cooperate across functions and departments, as well as with customers and suppliers, to identify areas for improvement, no matter how small. Teams of workers are trained and empowered to make decisions that help their establishment accomplish high standards of quality. Organizations shift responsibility for quality control from specialized departments to all employees. Therefore, total quality management means a shift from a bureaucratic to a decentralized approach to control.

An effectual TQM program has many gains. Financial benefits constitute lower costs, higher returns on sales and investment, and the power to charge higher rather than competitive prices. Other benefits constitute improved access to universal markets, higher customer retention levels, less time required to develop new innovations, and a reputation as a quality firm. Only a small number of organizations use TQM because carrying out an effectual program involves much time, effort, money, and patience. However, firms with the requirement resources may gain major competitive merits in their industries by implementing TQM.

Major Contributors to TQM

Total quality management is a much more liberal concept than just controlling the quality of the product itself. Total quality management is the co-ordination of efforts directed at amending customer satisfaction, increasing employee participation, strengthening supplier partnerships, and facilitating an organizational atmosphere of uninterrupted quality improvement. TQM is a way of thinking about organizations and how individuals ought to relate and work in them. TQM isn't merely a skill, but a philosophy grounded in the belief that long-term success depends on a uniform commitment to quality in all sectors of an establishment.

W. Edwards Deming

The concept of quality started in Japan when the country commenced to rebuild after World War II. Amidst the bomb rubble, Japan embraced the ideas of W. Edwards Deming, an American whose methods and theories are credited for Japan's post-war recovery. Ironically enough, Deming's ideas were ab initio scoffed at in the U.S. As a result, TQM settled down in Japan 30 years earlier than in the United States. American organizations took interest in Deming's ideas only when they began having difficulty competing with the Japanese in the 1980s.

Deming's management system was philosophical, based on uninterrupted improvement toward the perfect ideal. He believed that a commitment to quality demands transforming the entire establishment. His philosophy is founded on a system known as the Fourteen Points. These points express the actions an establishment must take in order to attain TQM:

1. Produce constancy of purpose for improvement of product and service. Dr. Deming suggests a radical new definition of a company's role: A better way to make money is to stay in business and allow for jobs through innovation, research, constant improvement, and maintenance.
2. Adopt a new philosophy. For the new economic age, organizations necessitate to change into "learning organizations." Moreover, we demand a new belief in which mistakes and negativism are unacceptable.

3. Cease dependence on mass inspection. Eliminate the demand for mass inspection by building quality into the product.
4. End awarding business on price. Rather, aim at minimum total cost, and move towards single suppliers.
5. Improve the system of production and service constantly. Improvement isn't a one-time effort. Management is compelled to continually look for ways to reduce waste and improve quality.
6. Institute training. Too frequently, workers learn their jobs from other workers who have never been trained properly.
7. Institute leadership. Leading consists of helping individuals to do a better task and to learn by objective method acting.
8. Drive out fear. Many employees are afraid to ask questions or to take a position-even when they don't understand what their task is or what is right or wrong. The economic losses from fear are alarming. To assure better quality and productivity, it is requirement that individuals feel secure.
9. Break down barriers between departments. Frequently, company departments or units compete with each other or have aims that conflict. They don't work as a team; therefore they cannot solve or foresee problems. Even worse, one department's aim may cause trouble for another.
10. Eliminate slogans, exhortations, and numerical targets for the manpower. These never help anybody do a good task. Let workers formulate their own slogans; then they will be committed to the contents.
11. Eliminate numerical quotas or work standards. Quotas take into account only numbers, not quality or methods. They are generally a guarantee of inefficiency and high cost.
12. Remove barriers that prevent workers from taking pride in their workmanship. Too often, misguided supervisors, faulty equipment, and defective materials stand in the way of good performance. These barriers must be got rid of.
13. Institute a vigorous program of education. Both management and the work force will have to be communicated of new knowledge and techniques.
14. Take action to attain the transformation. It will demand a special top management team with a plan of action to carry out the

quality mission. Workers cannot do it on their own, nor can managers. A critical mass of individuals in the company must understand the Fourteen Points.

Deming emphasized surveying customers, consulting production-line workers to help solve character problems, and teamwork. His system was readily accepted in Japan, where workers and management were used to uniformity and allegiance to institutions. Japanese organizations discovered to collect data for the statistical monitoring and measuring of customer satisfaction. The aims of these organizations were to create many of the same consumer goods-better and cheaper-that were developed in the U.S.

Deming saw businesses as fundamental institutions in a society-much like churches and schools organizations attain long-term success only if business leaders make their employees' contributions matter. If organizations use their employees' ideas, they will amend efficiency and productivity.

Most of the applications of Deming's ideas occurred in the 1950s and 1960s in Japan. In the United States, the desperation demanded for executives to eventually try a "radical" plan such as Deming's came from economic rather than wartime get overs. Most notably, in the 1980s, Japanese car manufacturers pushed their market share toward 25 percent, sending fear all through Detroit. Deming's system made such a feeling that he is known at the Father of TQM.

Joseph Juran

Joseph Juran began professionally as an engineer in 1924. In 1951, his first Quality Control Handbook was published and led him to international prominence. The Union of Japanese Scientists and Engineers (JUSE) invited Juran to Japan in the early 1950s. He arrived in 1954 and conducted seminars for top- and middle-level executives. His lectures had a strong managerial flavour and focused on planning, organizational issues, management's responsibility for quality, and the need to set aims and objectives for improvement. He emphasized that quality control ought to be conducted as an integral part of management control.

Intrinsic to Juran's message is the belief that quality doesn't happen by accident; it must be designed. Juran sees quality planning as part of the quality trilogy of quality planning, quality control, and quality advance. The fundamental elements in implementing company-wide strategic quality planning are in turn seen as: identifying customers and their inevitably;

demonstrating optimal quality aims; producing measurements of quality; planning processes capable of meeting quality ends under operating conditions; and creating continuing results in improved market share, premium prices, and a reduction of error rates in the office and factory.

Juran's formula for results is to demonstrate specific aims to be reached, and then to demonstrate plans for reaching those aims; assign clear responsibility for meeting the aims; and base the rewards on results achieved.

Juran believes that the majority of quality problems are the fault of poor management, not poor workmanship, and that long-term training to improve quality ought to begin at the top with senior management.

Philip Crosby

Philip Crosby is another major contributor to the quality movement. In 1979, he left ITT (International Telephone and Telegraph) and wrote his book, Quality is Free, in which he suggests that dollars spent on quality and the attention paid to it always return greater gains than the costs expended on them. Whereas Deming and Juran emphasized the sacrifice required for a quality commitment, Crosby takes a less philosophical and more practical approach, asserting instead that high quality is relatively easy and inexpensive in the long run. Crosby is the only American quality expert without a doctorate. He is accountable for the zero defects program, which emphasizes "doing it right the first time," (DIRFT) with 100 percent satisfactory output. Unlike Deming and Juran, Crosby argues that quality is always cost effectual. Like Deming and Juran, Crosby doesn't place the damned on workers, but on management.

Crosby also developed a 14-point program, which is once again more practical than philosophical. It provides managers with real concepts that can help them manage productivity and quality. His program is built around four Absolutes of Quality Management:

1. Quality must be deemed conformance to specifications. If a product meets design specifications, then it is a high-quality product.
2. Quality ought to be attained through the prevention of defects rather than inspection after the production process is concluded.

   As per Crosby, the conventional quality control approach taken by American firms isn't cost efficient. Instead, production workers ought to be granted the authority and responsibility to ensure that quality goods or services are developed at every step of the process.

3. Managers demand to demonstrate that a higher standard of performance can lead to perfection-to zero defects. Crosby believed that the company aim ought to be zero defects.
4. Quality ought to be measured by the price of non-conformity. Crosby contends that the costs associated with accomplishing quality ought to be part of a company's financial system.

The Implementation of TQM

The implementation of total quality management is alike to that of other decentralized control methods. In developing TQM, organizations need to understand how consumers determine quality in both the goods and services offered. If a company pays more attention to quality in its production process, more a few problems will occur later when the product is in the consumer's hands. One way to measure product performance and quality is through customer surveys, which can help managers name design or manufacturing problems. As per quality consultant Armand V. Feigenbaum, the end user best defines quality, which intends that quality is open to immanent interpretations. Consumer perceptions have to be changed if a company desires to change a product's quality image. Extended service programs and improved warranties can help attain this feat. As examples, Whirlpool Corporation promises that parts for all models will be available for 15 years, and Mercedes-Benz provides technical roadside aid after service hours.

Another means of ensuring a commitment to quality "after the sale" is via a product or service guarantee. Wal-Mart is known for its no-hassles return policy for any product-with or without a receipt. Mail-order house L. L. Bean will substitute a pair of hunting boots purchased ten years earlier with new boots. Saturn automobile retailers provide total refunds for vehicles within 30 days if the customer isn't amply satisfied. Nevertheless, many organizations aren't willing to incur the short-run costs linked with such guarantees.

Benchmarking

To be effectual, the TQM philosophy must commence at the top. From the board of directors to the hourly line employees, TQM must be backed at all levels if the firm is to realize any real improvements in quality. Additionally to commitment from the top, the establishment must meet these requirements if TQM is to succeed:

- A change in corporate culture about the implication of quality
- Forging of internal team partnerships to attain quality, process, and project improvements, and the conception of external partnerships with customers and suppliers
- Audits to assure quality techniques
- Removal of obstacles to successful implementation, such as deficiency of time or money in the short run

Normally, two to ten years are expected to reap the benefits of a successful TQM program.

WORLD CLASS QUALITY: ISO 9000 CERTIFICATION

With the extremely competitive nature of the current business world, customers can prescribe who, what, when, where, why, and how much concerning market commodities and services. In other words, quality has never counted more. As a result, management and organizations must heed these calls and specifically provide to the ever-changing expectations of their international clientele.

Globally, customers anticipate quality whether they are buying a consumer product or receiving a service. As a result, many countries have adopted the quality standards set by the International Standards Establishment (ISO) in Geneva, Switzerland. Businesses that want to compete as world-class organizations are more and more required to have ISO 9000 Certification at several levels. To gain certification in this family of quality standards, businesses must undergo a rigorous assessment by outside auditors to determine whether they meet ISO requirements. More and more, the ISO stamp of approval is viewed as a necessity in international business; the ISO certification furnishes customers with an assurance that a set of solid quality standards and processes are in place.

The commitment to total quality operations is at present a way of life in world-class firms. In the United States, the Malcolm Baldridge National Quality Awards were founded to benchmark excellence in quality accomplishments. The following list of award criteria indicates the full extent of the day-to-day commitment that is essential to gaining competitive vantage through a commitment to total quality:

- Top executives integrate quality values into day-to-day management.
- The establishment brings with suppliers to improve the quality of their goods and/or services.

- The establishment trains workers in quality techniques and implements organizations that ensure high-quality products.
- The establishment's products are as good as or improve than those of its competitors.
- The establishment meets customers' necessitates and wants and gets. customer satisfaction ratings equal to or better than those of competitors.
- The establishment's quality system yields cover results such as increased market contribution and lower product cycle times.

Note: The commitment to total quality operations is at present a way of life in international firms. Take the example of Pepsico. It is a living role model in total quality operations; Reader can go their site for more detailed information. http://www.pepsico.com/Purpose/Sustainability/Performance-with-Purpose.aspx

22

Management in Global Environment

Organizations are facing a more and more complicated and quickly changing operational environment. In order to remain competitive and effectual, businesses inevitably need to adapt their strategy, structure, systems, and organizational behaviour. The typical life cycle of organizations, in particular businesses, indicate that those that don't adapt, will not be able to sustain adequate execution to be able to survive in the long run. The power to manage active change is a key challenge faced by leading managers, in particular in Asia. These economies experience noteworthy economic growth and enterprises, as well as governmental organizations, and are under pressure to make managerial, social, and political adaptations.

PROCESS OF GLOBALIZATION

Essentially, Establishment Development (Organizational Development), is a process of applying Behavioural science to an establishment's systems, structure, and processes to encourage organizational effectiveness through change, i.e., to be able to maintain solid organizational performance and prosper. This process may be in response to rapid and important changes in the external operating environment of the establishment, or it may be as a result of an assessment by the establishment that it needs to heighten its organizational performance to be able to attain its objectives. Organizational Development as process has been used successfully in countless organizations in developed countries to self-diagnose organizational shortcomings, to develop treatments and change programs aimed at fundamental organizational renewal, and to promote and ensure high performance. But, is that also the event in developing economies?

Here we will examine the nature of Organizational Development in developing economies, in particular picked out countries in Asia. It also reports on a pilot study undertaken in Vietnam. It is argued that Asia is the new frontier for the Organizational Development vocation, not only to elaborate the application of Organizational Development processes in businesses but also to involve the Organizational Development vocation in shaping the "contemporary" Asian establishment.

Golembiewski argues that one of the restraints faced by Organizational Development practitioners in non-conventional Organizational Development societies outdoor North America and Europe, is the value-laden nature of Organizational Development. Interventions in organizations by Organizational Development practitioners and managers are perceived to be culturally biased, or threatening to Asian employees. He reasons that Organizational Development could adapt its tools, and Western-based behavioural science assumptions, to adopt a more differentiated position suited to inter alia Asia (Golembiowski,1993). Research by Sun (2000) in Chinese state enterprises, and by Lau and Ngo (2001) in multinational enterprises operating in China, Hong Kong and elsewhere in the East Asia region, suggests that Organizational Development can be successfully employed when Western and Eastern perspectives are suitably adapted to environmental (cultural) considerations, and to the situation of the special enterprise. As per Lau and Ngo, organizational reform, in its broad sense is an on-going and much needed phenomenon in China, and provides challenging and unparalleled chances to cross-culturally apply Organizational Development and related change methodologies. Dynamic leadership and change management competences also need to be formulated and implemented.

IMPLICATIONS

In India, Organizational Development has developed from a mostly academic exercise to a process acknowledged as a management tool. The Centre for Establishment Development, for example, is active in consultancy and executive development. Organizational Development is also considered a tool to assist with institution building in non-profit organizations and non-governmental organizations, and to encourage gender equality. India ought to be of particular interest to the Organizational Development vocation for a number of historical and present-day reasons. Indian business society is for the most part English-speaking, they have had a British-founded education, and the business sector is innovative and dynamic. Current economic developments since policy changes in the mid-1990s have enabled India to expand and globalize rapidly, develop a dynamic and good Information Technology sector, and diversify industry successfully into are therefore as pharmaceuticals and manufacturing. With a population of more than one billion and a fast-growing economy, related to a high level of skills and education, India is an area where Organizational Development as a vocation can expand its influence and application. Though much smaller, Singapore is another Asian country where language, education levels, skills availableness, and business culture provide an Organizational Development-friendly surroundings.

There is a long history of business and cultural connections between the Philippines and Western countries. Language and business culture are sufficiently similar, despite more or less different Asian uses of influence and power, which provides a fundamental platform for Organizational Development expansion. Nevertheless, disruptive events, and periodically stagnant economic conditions, linked to peculiar national social and political phenomena, have made it a difficult and complicated functional environment, not only for foreign businesses in but also for domestic enterprises.

Organizational Development as vocation is present as a partner in human resources management consultancies, the Philippine Society for Training and Development, and other private organizations such as the Organizational Change Consultancy International (OCCI).

THE MULTINATIONAL CORPORATION

After World War One, America fell under the shake of "America First" thinking. In 1929, a great financial disaster happened, and America suffered its most defective slump. At first, laissez faire economic methods were adopted, but with the election of Franklin Roosevelt, a British economist's theories were tried. John Maynard Keynes lined up with the idea that government ought to "prime the pump" of the national economy with spending programs. It seemed to work. After World War II, America took the opposite approach and assisted its world neighbours rebuild their economies.

The die was cast for more external involvement. Earlier many years had passed, American companies had invested money in many foreign lands. Revlon, Coca-Cola, GM, most of the oil companies, and even major banks all had big international operations.

If a company desires to venture into the international marketplace, it can use several different methods. In each case, the levels of risk and control move together. The four most common approaches admit the following:

- Exporting. The selling of an establishment's products to a foreign broker or agent is known as exporting. The establishment has almost no control over how products are marketed after the foreign broker or agent purchases them. Because the investment is comparatively small, exporting is a low-risk method of coming in foreign markets. The only real danger here is what the foreign agent might do with the products to hurt the establishment's or product's image.
- Licensure agreement. This approach permits a foreign firm to either manufacture or sell products, or the right to place a brand name or symbols on products. Disney World, for instance, has licensure agreements with many foreign firms. This approach provides more control than an export sale, as a firm can require that certain stipulations be met, yet it is still not the manufacturer in the foreign market.
- Multinational approach. With this approach, a firm is willing to make important commitment to a foreign market. Typically, products or services are modified to meet the foreign market demands, and in many cases, important fixed investments are made in plants and equipment. The most common ways to become a multinational firm are to form joint ventures or universal strategic partnerships, or to launch wholly-owned subsidiaries.
  - Joint ventures take place when a company forms a partnership with a foreign firm to develop new products or to give each other access to local markets. Usually, the roles and responsibilities of each establishment are clearly spelled out in the joint-venture agreement. This approach step-ups both control and risk.
  - Global strategic partnerships are much larger than a simple joint venture. Two firms are bring together and make a long-term commitment, in the form of time and investments, to develop products or services that will prevail world markets. This approach doesn't modify products for a particular market but develops a single product market strategy that can be applied in all markets in hopes of dominating the universal market for that product.
  - Wholly-owned subsidiaries occur when a firm purchases either controlling interest or all of a foreign firm.

Frequently, the subsidiary company is given significant freedom in terms of how to operate in the foreign market, and heavy use of foreign managers and employees is very common. The possessing firm does have the most control, but it also has significant investment risk.

— Vertically integrated wholly-owned subsidiaries exist where a firm owns not only the foreign manufacturer but the foreign distributors and retailers as well. Again, the basic emphasis is on dominating a universal product or service area with a single product market strategy. True universal products are very difficult to develop, and it is even less manageable to dominate all universal markets.

Of these approaching, multinational corporations, defined as organizations operating facilities in one or more countries, are major drives in the movement toward the globalization of businesses. Common characteristics of successful multinational corporations comprise the following:

- Introduction of foreign affiliates
- Universal visions and strategies
- Engagement in manufacturing or in a limited number of industries
- Location in developed countries
- Acceptance of high-skills staffing strategies, cheap labour strategies, or a mixture of both.

THE INTERNATIONAL ENVIRONMENT

International managers face vivid and constant challenges that require training and understanding of the foreign environment. Managing a business in a foreign country needs managers to deal with a large kind of cultural and environmental differences. As a consequence, international managers must continually supervise the political, legal, sociocultural, economic, and technological environments.

The Political Environment

The political environment can further or hinder economic developments and direct investments. This environment is ever-changing. As instances, the political and economic philosophies of a nation's leader may change overnight. The stability of a nation's government, which frequently rests on the support of the individuals, can be very volatile.

Several citizen groups with vested interests can counteract investment operations and opportunities. And local governments may view foreign firms suspiciously.

Political considerations are seldom written down and frequently alter quickly. For instance, to protest Iraq's invasion of Kuwait in 1990, many world governments levied economic sanctions against the import of Iraqi oil. Political considerations affect international business daily as governments enact tariffs (taxes), quotas (annual limits), embargoes (blockages), and other types of limitation in response to political events.

Businesses enlisted in international trade must consider the relative instability of countries such as Iraq, South Africa, and Honduras. Political agitation in countries such as Peru, Haiti, Somalia, and the countries of the former Soviet Union may produce hostile or even dangerous environments for foreign businesses. In Russia, for example, foreign managers frequently need to hire bodyguards; sixteen foreign businesspeople were murdered there in 1993. Civil war, as in Chechnya and Bosnia, may interrupt business activities and place lives in danger. And abrupt change in power can result in a regime that is hostile to foreign investment; some businesses may be fired of a country altogether. Whether they like it or not, companies are frequently involved immediately or circuitously in international politics.

The Legal Environment

The governments has put forth a number of laws that govern the activities of firms engaged in international trade. However, once outside their borders, organizations are likely to find that the laws of the other countries differ from those of their country. Many legal rights taken for granted don't exist in other countries; a firm doing business abroad must understand and adjust the laws of the host country.

For example, in the U.S., the acceptance of corrupts or payoffs is illegal; in other countries, the acceptance of bribes or payoffs may not be illegal-they may be conceived a common business practice. Additionally, some countries have copyright and patent laws that are less strict than those in the U.S., and some countries fail to honour these laws. China, for instance, has lately been threatened with severe trade sanctions because of a history of allowing American goods to be copied or faked there. As a result, businesses engaging in international trade may need to take extra steps to protect their products because local laws may be deficient to protect them.

The Economic Environment

Managers must supervise currency, infrastructure, inflation, interest rates, wages, and taxation. In assessing the economic environment in foreign countries, a business must pay special attention to the following four areas:

- Average income levels of the population. If the average income for the population is very low, no matter how urgently this population needs a product or service, there simply isn't a market for it.
- Tax structures. In some nations, foreign firms pay much higher tax rates than domestic competitors. These tax divergences may be very evident or subtle, as in hidden registration fees.
- Inflation rates. In India, for example, inflation rates have been quite low and relatively stable for many years. In some countries, nevertheless, inflation rates of 30, 40, or even 100 percent per year aren't uncommon. Inflation results in a full general rise in the level of prices, and affects business in many ways. For example, in the mid-1970s, a shortage of crude oil led to many problems because petroleum products supply most of the energy necessitated to create goods and services and to transport goods around the world. As the cost of petroleum products increased, a corresponding gain took place in the cost of goods and services. As a result, interest rates altered dramatically, causing both businesses and consumers to cut down their borrowing. Business profits fell as consumers' purchasing power was eroded by inflation. High interest rates and unemployment reached alarmingly high points.
- Fluctuating exchange rates. The exchange rate, or the value of one country's currency in terms of another country's currency, is influenced primarily by supply and demand for each country's goods and services. The government of a country can, nevertheless, cause this rate of exchange to change dramatically by causing high inflation-by printing too much currency or by changing the value of the currency through devaluation. A foreign investor may sustain large losses if the value of the currency cuts down substantially.

When doing business abroad, business people need to recognize that they cannot assume that other countries offer the same things as are found in industrialized nations. A country's level of development is frequently decided in part by its substructure. The infrastructure is the physical facilities that support a country's economic activities, for instance railroads, highways, ports, utilities and power plants, schools, hospitals, communication systems, and commercial distribution systems. When exercising business in less developed nations, a business may necessitate to compensate for rudimentary distribution and communication systems.

The Sociocultural Environment

Cultural differences, which can be very elusive, are highly important. An establishment that enters the international marketplace on virtually any level must make learning the nation's cultural taboos and proper cultural practices a high priority. If a business fails to understand the cultural methods of doing business, grave misunderstandings and a complete want of trust may occur.

Management conflicts also exist. In China, a proportionate environment is more important than day-to-day productivity. In Morocco, women can assume leadership roles, but they are usually more self-conscious than American women. In Pakistan, women aren't frequently found in management positioning, if they're in the workplace at all. Additionally, the grandness of work in employees' lives varies from nation to nation. For instance, the Japanese feel that work is an important part of their lives. This belief in work, coupled with a strong group orientation, may explain the Japanese willingness to put up with things that workers in other countries would find unendurable.

Similarly, culture may affect what employees find motivating, as well as how they react to rewards and punishments. For instance, Americans tend to emphasize personal growth, accomplishment, and "getting what you deserve" for carrying into action as the most important motivators. However, in Asian cultures, maintaining group solidarity and promoting group needs may be more significant than rewarding individual accomplishments.

Eventually, language differences are particularly important, and international managers must remember that not all words translate clearly into other languages. Many universal companies have had difficulty crossing the language barrier, with results ranging from mild embarrassment to outright failure. For instance, in regards to marketing, seemingly unobjectionable brand names and advertising phrases can take on unintended or hidden meanings when translated into other languages.

Such classic blunders are soon came upon and adjusted; they may result in little more than embarrassments for companies. Managers ought to keep in mind that infinite other, more elusive blunders may go undiscovered and damage product performance in less obvious ways.

The Technological Environment

The technological environment contains the innovations, from robotics to cellular phones, that are rapidly taking place in all types of technology. Earlier a company can expect to sell its product in another country; the technology of the two nations must be compatible.

Companies that join forces with others will be able to speed the pace of research and development while cutting the costs associated with utilizing the latest technology. No matter of the kind of business a company is in, it must choose partners and locations that possess an available work force to deal with the relevant technology. Many companies have preferred China because they provide a willing and capable work force.

FUNCTIONS OF THE INTERNATIONAL MANAGER

Universal competition has drove businesses to change how they manage at home and abroad. The changing rate of change, technological advances, shorter product life cycles, and high-speed communications are all components that contribute to these changes. The new management approach focuses on establishing a new communication system that features a high level of employee participation. Organizational structures must also be flexible enough to change with changing market conditions. Ongoing staff development programs and design-control processes, which are understandable and acceptable, are results from this new approach. Management values are changing, and managers must now have a vision and be able to communicate the vision to everyone in the firm.

Though the international manager executes the same fundamental functions as the domestic manager, he must adjust to more variables and environments. Therefore, each of the five fundamental management functions must change when functioning in a foreign market.

Planning

The first stage of international planning is to decide how to do business globally: whether to export, to enter into licensing agreements or joint ventures, or to operate as a multinational corporation with deftness in a foreign country.

To develop forecasts, aims, and plans for international actions, the manager must monitor environments very closely. Key elements comprise political instability, currency instability, competition from governments, pressures from governments, patent and trademark protection, and intense competition.

International firms ought to be certain that their plans fit the culture of the host country. Normally, firms feel that long-term plans ought to be three to five years in length; but in some cultures, this time period is too short. Many countries must plan with the assistance of governmental agencies. And working through bureaucratic structures, policies, and processes is frequently time-consuming.

Organizing

International businesses must be co-ordinated in order that they can adapt to cultural and environmental differences. No more can organizations just put "carbon copies" or clones of themselves in foreign countries. An international firm must be organized in order that it can be reactive to foreign customers, employees, and suppliers. An entire firm may even be organized as one giant universal company that has several divisions. Above all, the new establishment must establish a very open communication system where problems, ideas, and grievances can quickly be heard and addressed at all levels of management. Without this, employees will not get involved, and their perceptivities and ideas are crucial to the success of the business.

As an establishment passes its operations internationally, it needs to adapt its structure. When the establishment increases its international focus, it carries out the following three phases of structural change:

1. Pre-international stage. Companies with a product or service that incorporates the latest technology, is unique, or is superior may conceive themselves ready for the international arena. The first strategy used to introduce a product to a foreign market is to find a way to export the product. At this phase, the firm adds up an export manager as part of the marketing department and finds foreign partners.
2. International division stage. Pressure may bestride through the enforcement of host country laws, trade restrictions, and competition, placing a company at a cost disadvantage. When a company settles to defend and expand its foreign market position by establishing marketing or production operations in one or more host countries, it demonstrates a separate international division. In turn, foreign operations begin, and a

vice president, reporting directly to the president or CEO, supervises the operations.

3. Global structure stage. A company is prepare to move away from an international division phase when it conforms to the following criteria:
   - The international market is as important to the company as the domestic market.
   - Senior officials in the company have both foreign and domestic experience.
   - International sales constitute 25 to 35 percent of total sales.
   - The technology used in the domestic division has far exceeded that of the international division.

As foreign operations become more important to the bottom line, decision making becomes more centralized at corporate headquarters. An operational product group, geographic approach, or a combination of these approaches ought to be taken on. The firm unifies international activities with universal conclusions at world headquarters.

Staffing

Since obtaining a good staff is so vital to the success of any business, the employing and growth of employees must be done very carefully. Management must be familiar with the country's national labour laws. Next, it must determine how many managers and personnel to hire from the local labour force and whether to reassign home-based personnel.

For example, Indian firms are better off employing local talent and using only a few fundamental expatriates in most cases, because the costs of assigning foreign.-based employees to positions overseas can be quite expensive. Simply, expatriates (individuals who live and work in another country) are expensive suggestions even when things go well.

Adding up all the extras-higher pay, airfare for family members, moving expenses, housing allowances, education benefits for the kids, company car, taxes, and home leave-means that the first year abroad frequently costs the multinational company many times the expatriate's base salary. The total bill for a mean overseas stay of four years can easily top $1 million per expatriate. In any case, managers need to closely analyse how to select and prepare expatriates.

Directing

Cultural differences make the directing function harder for the international manager. Employee attitudes toward work and problem solving differ by country. Language barriers also produce communication difficulties. To minimize problems coming up from cultural differences, organizations are training managers in cross-cultural management. Cross-cultural management trains managers to act with numerous cultures and to value diversity.

Additionally, the style of leadership that is acceptable to employees changes from nation to nation. In nations like France and Germany, informal relations with employees are discouraged. In Sweden and Japan, however, informal relations with employees are strongly encouraged, and a very participative leadership style is used. Incentive systems also vary staggeringly. The type of incentives used in India may not work in Europe, U.S.A or Japan, where static employment and benefits are more significant than bonuses.

Controlling

Geographic distribution and distance, language barriers, and legal restrictions perplex the controlling function. Meetings, reporting, and inspections are normally part of the international control system. Controlling poses special challenges if a company employs in multinational business because of the far-flung scope of operations and the differing influences of diverse environments. Controlling operations is nonetheless a crucial function for multinational managers. In many countries, bonuses, pensions, holidays, and vacation days are legally mandated and considered by many employees as rights. In particular powerful unions exist in many parts of the world, and their requirements restrict managers' freedom to operate.

PERSONAL CHALLENGES FOR GLOBAL MANAGERS

Building an internationally capable manpower whose members know the business and are flexible and open-minded can take years. Multinational organizations can no more rely on just a few managers with multicultural experience or a few experts on a specific country to succeed. In short, all employees must have some minimal level of international expertness and be able to recognize cultural divergences that may affect daily business communications and working relationships.

In general, overseas managers share common traits with their domestic counterparts. Wherever a manager is hired, he or she necessitates the technical knowledge and skills to do the task, and the intelligence and individuals skills to be a successful manager. Choosing managers for expatriate assignments means screening them for traits that predict success in accommodating to what may be dramatically new environments.

Beyond the apparent task-specific qualifications, an establishment necessitates to consider the following qualities and circumstances when selecting expatriates for positions in foreign countries:

- A temperament to communicate, form relationships with others, and try new things
- Effectual cross-cultural communicating and language skills
- Flexibility and open-mindedness about other cultures
- The power to cope with the stress of new situations
- The spouse's career position and personal attributes
- The existence of quality educational facilities for the candidate's children
- Enthusiasm for the foreign duty assignment and a good track record in former foreign and domestic moves

Naturally, the factors that predict a successful deport assignment aren't identical for everyone. These differences-which reflect variations in the expatriate's home culture, his or her company's human resource management practices, and the labour laws specific to the foreign country-must also be factored out into the selection process.

Even if these complexities are borne in mind in the selection process, a person chosen for a foreign assignment may decide not to accept the task offer. The financial package calls for to be reasonably attractive. Additionally, family issues may be a concern. Most candidates, after a position is offered, also want information about how the foreign posting will affect their careers.

If a potential candidate accepts the task offer, he or she ought to be aware of the possible for cultural shock-the confusion and soreness a person experiences when in an unfamiliar culture. Additionally, ethnocentrism, or the tendency to view one's culture as superior to others, ought to be understood and avoided.

It can be reasoned out that Organizational Development, as a vocation and as a discipline, appears to be relatively unknown both in practice and training, in Vietnam. The scope of this discussion is, nevertheless, not representative enough to provide statistically significant information, about the presence of Organizational Development practitioners in firms, or the number of managers and Organizational Development-related professionals (e.g., in HRM) who may have studied Organizational Development or have obtained some Organizational Development training. The preliminary evidence suggests that these may also be limited. There may be some foreign trained Organizational Development staff members attached to multinational companies, but two components suggest that the real number may be rather small. First, local government regulations limit the number of foreign staff members that foreign organizations may employ in its local offices, therefore limiting organizations to key nation managers and critical operations staff, such as engineers or quality control technicians.

Note: Wipro Company is exemplary role model for working in global environment. Started as a small company, now it is an international behemoth with a presence on global scale. Wipro was ranked 4th on the 'Top Companies for Leaders' in India, 5th in Asia Pacific region and 20th globally" in a study conducted by Hewitt Associates in collaboration with Fortune and the RBL Group. For detailed information, reader can visit their site: http://www.wipro.com

Bibliography

A.A. Alchian, "Reliability of Progress Curves in Airframe Production," *Econometrica*, 1963.

A. Taylor, "Detroit Buffs Up," *Fortune,* February, 2004.

A. Tversky and D. Kahneman, "The Framing of Decisions and the Psychology of Choice," *Science,* 1981.

A.A. Cannella and D.C. Hambrick, "Executive Departure and Acquisition Performance," *Strategic Management Journal*, 1993.

A.K. Dixit and B.J. Nalebuff, *Thinking Strategically*, London: W.W. Norton, 1991.

A.M. Brandenburger and B.J. Nalebuff, "The Right Game: Using Game Theory to Shape Strategy," *Harvard Business Review,* July-August 1995.

B. Barney, "Company Resources and Sustained Competitive Advantage," *Journal of Management*, 1991.

B. Bremner and C. Dawson, "Can Anything Stop Toyota?" *Business-Week.* November, 2003.

B. McLean and P. Elkind, *The Smartest Guys in the Room*, New York: Penguin, 2003.

B. Snyder Bulik, "Intel's New Strategy Demands a New Partner," *Advertising Age,* March, 2005.

B. J. Pine, *Mass Customization: The New Frontier in Business Competition*, Boston: Harvard Business School Press, 1993.

B.M. Staw, "The Escalation of Commitment to a Course of Action," *Academy of Management Review,* 1981.

C. Edwards, "Getting Intel Back on the Inside Track," *Business-Week.* November, 2004.

C.H. St. John and J.S. Harrison, "Manufacturing-Based Relatedness, Synergy, and Coordination," *Strategic Management Journal*, 1999.

C.J. Loomis, "AOL Time Warner's New Math," *Fortune,* February, 2002.

C.K. Swank, "The Lean Service Machine," *Harvard Business Review,* October, 2003.

C.W. Hofer and D. Schendel, *Strategy Formulation: Analytical Concepts*, St. Paul, MN: West, 1978.

C.W. L. Hill and R.E. Hoskisson, "Strategy and Structure in the Multi-product Firm," *Academy of Management Review*, 1986.

C.W. L. Hill, "Differentiation versus Low Cost or Differentiation and Low Cost: A Contingency Framework," *Academy of Management* Review, 1988.

C.W.L. Hill, "The Role of Headquarters in the Multidivisional Firm," in *Fundamental Issues in Strategy Research,* ed. R. Rumelt, D.J. Teece, and D. Schendel, Cambridge, MA: Harvard Business School Press, 1994.

D. Bertsimas and S. de Boer, "Dynamic Pricing and Inventory Control for Multiple Products," *Journal of Revenue and Pricing Management,* January, 2005.

D. Kahneman and A. Tversky, "Prospect Theory: An Analysis of Deci-sion under Risk," *Econometrica,* 1979.

D. Welch and K. Kerwin, "Detroit Tries It the Japanese Way," *Business Week,* January, 2004.

D.F. Abell, *Defining the Business: The Starting Point of Strategic Planning*, Englewood Cliffs, NJ: Prentice-Hall, 1980.

D.J. Ravenscraft and F.M. Scherer, *Mergers, Selloffs, and Économic Efficiency*, Washington, DC: Brookings Institution, 1987.

D.J. Teece, "Economies of Scope and the Scope of the Enterprise," *Journal of Economic Behavior and Organization*, 1980.

D.M. Kreps, *Game Theory and Economic Modeling*, Oxford: Oxford University Press, 1990.

Data reported in J. Palmer, "Can Anyone Stop Toyota," *Barrons,* September, 2004.

E.A. Locke, G.P. Latham, and M. Erez, "The Determinants of Goal Commitment," *Academy of Management Review*, 1988.

G. Callioni et al., "Inventory Driven Costs," *Harvard Business Review,* March, 2005.

G. Hamel and C.K. Prahalad, "Strategic Intent," *Harvard Business Review*, May-June 1989.

H. Courtney, J. Kirkland, and P. Viguerie, "Strategy under Uncertainty," *Harvard Business Review*, November-December 1997.

H. Luft, J. Bunker, and A. Enthoven, "Should Operations Be Regionalized?" *New England Journal of Medicine*, 1979.

H. Mintzberg, "Patterns in Strategy Formulation," *Management Science*, 1978.

H. Simon, *Administrative Behavior*, New York: McGraw-Hill, 1957.

H.I. Ansoff, *Corporate Strategy*, New York: McGraw-Hill, 1965.

J. Bowles, "Is American Management Really Committed to Quality?" *Management Review,* April 1992.

J. Greenwald, "September 11th Attacks Show value of Planning for a Crisis," *Business Insurance,* January, 2002.

J. Hallinan, "3M's Next Chief Plans to Fortify Results with Discipline He Learned at GE Unit," *The Wall Street Journal,* December, 2000.

J. Muller, "The Little Car That Could," *Forties,* December, 2003.

J. Schlosser, "Cashing In on the New World of Me," *Fortune,* December, 2004

J.C. Collins and J.I. Porras, "Building Your Company's Vision," *Harvard Business Review,* September-October 1996.

J.H. Gilmore and BJ. Pine II, "The Four Faces of Mass Customization," *Harvard Business Review,* January-February, 1997.

J.P. Walsh, "Top Management Turnover Following Mergers and Acquisitions," *Strategic Management Journal,* 1988.

Jones and Hill, "A Transaction Cost Analysis," *Strategic Management Journa,* 1988.

K.R. Andrews, *The Concept of Corporate Strategy*, Homewood, IL: Dow Jones Irwin, 1971.

M. Hammer, "Deep Change: How Operational Innovation Can Transform Your Company," *Harvard Business Review,* April 2004.

M. Hammer, "Process Management and the Future of Six Sigma," *MIT Sloan Management Review,* Winter 2002.

M. Myagkov and C.R. Plott, "Exchange Economies and Loss Exposure: Experiments in Exploring Prospect Theory," American *Economic Review,* 1997.

M.D. Richards, *Setting Strategic Goals and Objectives*, St. Paul, MN: West, 1986.

M.E. Porter, "What Is Strategy?" *Harvard Business Review,* February, 2000.

M.E. Porter, *Competitive Advantage* (New York: Free Press, 1985); and M.E. Porter, *Competitive Strategy*, New York: Free Press, 1980.

N. Greenwood, *Implementing Flexible Manu-facturing Systems*, New York: Halstead Press, 1986.

P.. Nemetz and L. Fry, "Flexible Manufacturing Organizations: Im-plications for Strategy Formulation," *Academy of Management Review*, 1988.

P.J. Brews and M.R. Hunt, "Learning to Plan and Planning to Learn," *Strategic Management Journal*, 1999.

P.J.H. Schoemaker, "Multiple Scenario Development: Its Conceptual and Behavioral Foundation," *Strategic Management Journa,* 1993.

Q. Hardy, "Google Thinks Small," *Forbes,* November, 2005.

R. Koch, *The 80-20 Principle*, New York, Doubleday, 1996.

R. Reed and R.J. DeFillippi, "Causal Ambiguity, Barriers to Imitation, and Sustainable Competitive Advantage," *Academy of Management Review*, 1990.

R. Roll, "The Hubris Hypotheses of Corporate Takeovers," *Journal of Business,* 1986.

R. Rosmarin, "Your Custom Car Is Ready at Toyota," *Business 2.0,* October, 2004.

R. W. Grant, "Plan-ning in a Turbulent Environment," *Strategic Management Journal*, 2003.

R.E. Hoskisson, M.A. Hitt, and C.W.L. Hill, "Managerial Incentives and Investment in R&D in Large Multiproduct Firms," *Organization Science*, 1993.

R.P. Rumelt, *Strategy, Structure, and Economic Performance*, Cambridge, MA: Harvard Business School Press, 1974.

R.S. Kaplan and D.P. Norton, *The Strategy Focused Organization: How Balanced Scorecard Companies Thrive in the New Business Environment*, Boston: Harvard Business School Press, 2001.

S. Chambers and R. Johnston, "Experience Curves in Services," *International Journal of Operations and Production Management*, 2000.

S. Kotha, "Mass Customization: Implementing the Emerging Paradigm for Competitive Advantage," *Strategic Management Journal*, 1995.

S. Scherreik, "How Efficient Is That Company?" *Business-Week,* December,2003.

S.F. Jablonsky and N.P. Barsky, *The Manager's Guide to Financial Statement Analysis*, New York: Wiley, 2001.

S.P. Seith, "The Impact of Flexible Automation on Business Strategy and Organizational Structure," *Academy of Management Review*, 1992.

T. Copeland, T. Koller, and J. Murrin, *Valuation: Measuring and Mananing the Value of Companies*, New York: Wiley, 2000.

T. Copeland, T. Koller, and J. Murrin, *Valuation: Measuring and Managing the Value of Companies*, New York: Wiley, 1996.

V. R.H. Hayes and W.J. Abernathy, "Managing Our Way to Economic Decline," *Harvard Business Review,* July-August 1980.

V.S. Borland, "Global Technology in the Twenty-First Century," *Textile World,* January 2003.

W.C. Kirn and R. Maugborgne, *Blue Ocean Strategy*, Boston: Harvard Business School Press, 2005.

W.T. Coombs, *Ongoing Crisis Communication: Planning, Managing, and Responding*, Thousand Oaks, CA: Sage Publications, 1999.

Williamson, *Markets and Hierarchies*, New York: Free Press, 1988.

Index